Bridging the Gap between the Abundance of American Higher Education Talent and the Immense Foreign Demand for It

Bridging the Gap between the Abundance of American Higher Education Talent and the Immense Foreign Demand for It

The Great Chasm in Global Education

Richard J. Joseph

OXFORD
UNIVERSITY PRESS

OXFORD
UNIVERSITY PRESS

Great Clarendon Street, Oxford, OX2 6DP,
United Kingdom

Oxford University Press is a department of the University of Oxford.
It furthers the University's objective of excellence in research, scholarship,
and education by publishing worldwide. Oxford is a registered trade mark of
Oxford University Press in the UK and in certain other countries

Published in the United States of America by Oxford University Press
198 Madison Avenue, New York, NY 10016, United States of America

British Library Cataloguing in Publication Data
Data available

Library of Congress Control Number: 2021952598

ISBN 978–0–19–284830–7
DOI: 10.1093/oso/9780192848307.001.0001

Printed and bound by
CPI Group (UK) Ltd, Croydon, CR0 4YY

*To academic freedom, integrity, and the pursuit of the truth
in American higher education*

Preface

This book is much needed and long overdue—so my colleagues tell me. It deals with a topic of broad interest: *the globalization of American higher education.* Many scholars, such as Philip Altbach, Charles Clotfelter, and Simon Marginson, have addressed various aspects of the topic. Few, however, have placed it in a larger U.S. domestic perspective. Yet, in higher education, the international and the domestic are inextricably bound. The one creates a pathway out of the impasses arising in the other.

The book is timely and relevant. American higher education is in crisis. U.S. colleges and universities face flat enrollments, declining net tuition revenues, escalating operating costs, mounting capital expenditures, and narrowing margins. Their operations have been disrupted by the Global Pandemic. Adverse economic and demographic trends do not bode well for their future. Global markets offer a way out of the impasse. Yet, few American colleges and universities have ventured into the international arena. The quintessential question is "*Why?*"

This book deals with the "*Why?*" It also deals with the potential linkage between the financial condition of U.S. colleges and universities and global markets for higher education. Based on empirical and anecdotal evidence, it argues that there is an "abundance" of American higher education talent in the current U.S. domestic market; furthermore, the potential demand for this talent in international markets is immense—hence arises the "gap" between the abundance of American higher education talent and the immense foreign demand for it. Bridging the gap requires fundamental changes in the culture, organization, and governance of traditional U.S. colleges and universities. These institutional features obstruct the pathway leading from the domestic to the international.

The intended audience of the book is a variety of stakeholders, including college and university presidents, trustees, administrators, faculty, staff, and students; officials of government agencies, development banks, multinational corporations, research institutes, and educational foundations; financial supporters of U.S. colleges and universities; even families with college-age children. What they all have in common is an avid interest in the future of American higher education. And they all have a vital stake in strengthening its economic foundation. Admittedly, the book might not appeal to those who are focused less on the realm of finances and more on the realm of ideas. However, to the extent that it stimulates debate among other stakeholders, it is likely to pique their interest.

Although considerable research has gone into the book, it is not a "research paper" in the traditional academic sense. Nor is it a manual on how U.S. colleges and universities can gain a competitive advantage in foreign markets. Rather, it is a structured speculation about a very dramatic and innovative future for American higher education. It is also a pragmatic roadmap for getting there. This approach is appropriate for the book's intended audience. They are likely to be less concerned about developments of the past, and more concerned about possibilities for the future.

The book was written before and during the Global Pandemic and the Russian invasion of Ukraine. In March 2020, its initial findings had to be revised to take into account the impact of the pandemic on the financial condition of U.S. educational institutions. The crisis disrupted the affairs of every American college and university. It also disrupted the historical evolution of the U.S. higher education sector. Yet, even before the crisis, storm clouds loomed over the horizon. In a sense, the Global Pandemic was a catalyst that precipitated a "perfect storm."

The lag time between the occurrence of events and the issuance of public data that reflect their effects has limited the scope of the analysis—not just with respect to the Global Pandemic and the war in Europe, but also with respect to other events that have impacted the U.S. higher education sector. The most credible of public agencies, such as the U.S. Department of Education, UNESCO, the World Bank, and the International Monetary Fund, publish a great deal of their data a few years after the fact. Much can happen during the intervening period, such as the onset of a Global Pandemic, the deepening of a general recession, and the eruption of a major war. Consequently, long-term historical trends that fall short of the present timeframe can be misleading. Letting the imagination take over where the empirical leaves off could give rise to a false sense of knowledge, understanding, and comfort.

This limitation, however, does not preclude the possibility of any analysis at all. Rather, it confines the analysis to empirical data that were released before the present timeframe. And it compels one to engage in a certain degree of projection, estimation, assumption, and speculation, all within reasonable limits.

* * *

Higher education is my passion. It has been my calling for over three decades. As an academic, I am deeply committed to the values of American higher education. I believe that they add market value to the services that U.S. colleges and universities provide internationally. In my opinion, however, elevating business considerations over academic considerations could ultimately corrupt higher education. On the other hand, as a pragmatist I recognize that business-related practices can be instrumental in enhancing the financial viability of U.S. academic institutions.

Despite all the doom and gloom, I am optimistic about the future of American higher education. I believe that international opportunities create a pathway out of the present impasses that U.S. colleges and universities face in the domestic market. As a former dean, provost, chief executive officer, and accreditation reviewer, I have explored many of these opportunities first-hand. I believe that by sharing my knowledge with others, I can help them shape this future.

As I conclude my scholastic odyssey, I would like to thank those who shared their knowledge with me; in particular, Terrence MacTaggart, former Chancellor of the Maine and Minnesota university systems; Peter Smith, Founding President of California State University at Monterrey Bay, former UNESCO official, Congressman, and Lieutenant Governor; Barbara Brittingham, former President of the New England Commission of Higher Education; David Faulkner, Emeritus Professor at Royal Holloway, University of London, and former Fellow of Christ Church College, University of Oxford; Steve Hodges, President of Hult International Business School; Steve Limberg, Professor at The University of Texas at Austin; the late William C. Powers, Jr., former President of The University of Texas at Austin; Ronald Machtley, former Congressman and President of Bryant University; Steven Koltai, entrepreneur, board chair, and former U.S. State Department advisor; Nancy Hensel, former President of The New American Colleges and Universities; and James Chen, China higher education specialist; also, officials at AUTM, who kindly granted me access to their technology transfer database. In addition, I would like to express gratitude to my former colleagues at the University of Texas at Austin, Hult International Business School, and Bryant University who boosted my higher education career. Finally, and most importantly, I would like to thank my partner in life Kathy and daughters Gabriella, Stephanie, and Julia for their unwavering support and assistance. They have truly been an inspiration.

Hopefully, this book will open people's eyes to the enormous opportunities that lay "beyond the horizon;" stimulate further discussion and research on the globalization of U.S. higher education; prompt changes in those features of traditional American colleges and universities that stand in the way of globalization; lead to a more export-oriented U.S. higher education sector; and encourage greater U.S. government and business support for American higher education service providers.

These objectives are subsidiary to much broader aims; namely, strengthening the economic substructure of the U.S. higher education sector, upon which rests its entire ideological superstructure; contributing to the educational enlightenment of other members of the world community; spreading liberal, democratic values around the world; and supporting the critical role that America plays, or should play, globally in knowledge creation, the dissemination of ideas, and the pursuit of the truth.

Richard J. Joseph
Austin, Texas

March 2022

Contents

List of Figures

List of Tables

Introduction: The Great Chasm

This Introduction presents an overview of the book. It addresses the following fundamental questions: "What is the central thesis of the book? What is its purpose? What is its scholarly approach? How does it differ from other scholarly works on U.S. higher education? Why should American colleges and universities strive to bridge the Great Chasm?"

> It is one of the unwritten, and commonly unspoken commonplaces lying at the root of modern academic policy that the various universities are competitors for the traffic of merchantable instruction in much the same fashion as rival establishments in the retail trade compete for custom.[1]
>
> Thorstein Veblen, American social scientist and philosopher

> To keep profit-seeking within reasonable bounds, a university must have a clear sense of the values needed to pursue its goals with a high degree of quality and integrity. When the values become blurred and begin to lose their hold, the urge to make money quickly spreads throughout the institution.[2]
>
> Derek Bok, former President of Harvard University

The context

The American landscape of higher education is changing. Domestic enrollments in U.S. colleges and universities have been relatively flat. The price of a college education has risen at more than twice the inflation rate. Competition in the U.S. market for higher education has intensified. Institutions are chasing after the same pool of student talent.

Many colleges and universities are struggling for survival. They face declining net tuition revenues, escalating operating costs, mounting capital expenditures, and narrowing margins. The vast majority are raising their

---

[1] T. Veblen, *The Higher Learning in America: A Memorandum on the Conduct of Universities by Business Men* (1918), 96–97.

[2] D. Bok, *Universities in the Marketplace: The Commercialization of Higher Education* (2003), 5.

Bridging the Gap between the Abundance of American Higher Education Talent and the Immense Foreign Demand for It.
Richard J. Joseph, Oxford University Press. © Richard J. Joseph (2022). DOI: 10.1093/oso/9780192848307.003.0001

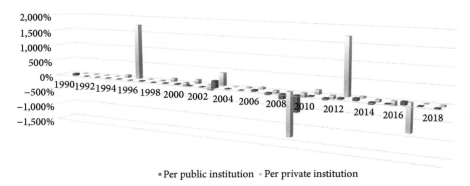

■ Per public institution ■ Per private institution

Fig. 0.1 Annual growth rates in aggregate revenues net of aggregate expenditures per U.S. post-secondary degree-granting institution, 1990–2018.

Source: U.S. Department of Education, Institute of Education Sciences, National Center for Education Statistics. (See Appendix for notes.)

discount rate. Many are slashing their operating costs. Others are discontinuing unprofitable programs.[3] Still others are deferring badly needed upgrades in plant and equipment.

The economic havoc wreaked by the Global Pandemic made matters worse. The sharp rise in unemployment reduced national income and savings, thereby accentuating the downward trend in net tuition revenues. In addition to creating chaos and confusion, the mad dash to deliver courses online further inflated operating costs. The adoption of prophylactic measures to protect the health and safety of students, staff, and faculty contributed to a steep rise in capital expenditures. The loss of revenues from auxiliary services just had to be "written-off."

As Figure 0.1 illustrates, the rate of growth of the U.S. higher education sector has decelerated in recent years. Since 2012, aggregate revenues net of aggregate expenditures per institution have declined. This slowdown raises the specter of economic stagnation. To some extent, it has given rise to an "abundance" of American higher education talent.

On the other side of the world, demand for higher education has never been greater. Despite the economic disruption caused by the Global Pandemic, non-U.S. nationals continue to look to American colleges and universities for quality education. Beyond America's borders, opportunities abound.

---

[3] Other "cost-side" measures include increasing class size, augmenting teaching loads, deferring maintenance of plant and equipment, and substituting part-time faculty or lecturers for full-time faculty and tenured professors. P.G. Altbach, L. Reisberg, and L.E. Rumbley, *Trends in Global Higher Education: Tracking an Academic Revolution* (UNESCO, 2009), 71.

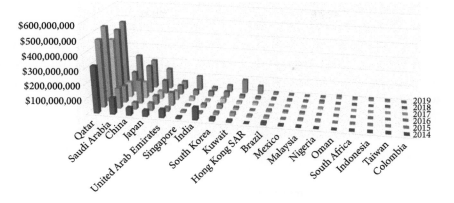

Fig. 0.2 Major emerging markets for U.S. higher education, based on the nominal value of contracts with American colleges and universities, 2014–2019.
Source: U.S. Department of Education, Office of Federal Student Aid, Foreign Gifts and Contracts Report, 2020. (See Appendix for notes.)

Foreign students want professional programs to acquire practical, job-related skills. Foreign colleges and universities seek faculty exchanges, research collaboration, and joint degree programs to raise their institutional profile. Foreign companies want American know-how, technological expertise, and management training to expand their operations. Foreign governments seek U.S. intellectual capital for social advancement and economic development. This demand is particularly robust in the emerging markets of the Arab World, East Asia, and Latin America (see Figure 0.2). The size of these markets exceeds $1.7 billion.[4]

It would seem natural for the global forces of supply and demand to coalesce to bring about an equilibrium for the benefit of all; specifically, the providers of U.S. higher educational services and their potential foreign consumers. Such a result, however, has not been the case for a variety of reasons.

Most traditional U.S. colleges and universities lack the nimbleness required to take advantage of fleeting opportunities that arise in a rapidly changing economic environment. Many are hopelessly mired in a tangle of rules, regulations, bureaucracy, processes, policies, procedures, and politics. For the most part, they are internally focused, supply-side driven,

---

[4] Based on the nominal value of contracts in 2019 between U.S. colleges and universities and parties based in countries and regions other than the United States, Canada, Europe, Australia, and New Zealand. Federal Student Aid, an Office of the U.S. Department of Education, *Foreign Gift and Contract Report* (2020).

unattuned to market fluctuations, and suspicious of anything that smacks of commercialism. Culturally, organizationally, and operationally, they are averse to radical change. Sadly, the end-result has been the perpetuation of the status quo in a sector that is financially "on the edge." Most traditional American colleges and universities are either unable or unwilling to venture into foreign markets, whose participants are willing to pay a premium for their services.

Then, there are political factors. U.S. legislators are committed primarily to the educational advancement of their local constituencies. They are opposed to allocating American taxpayer dollars for the benefit of non-U.S. nationals. U.S. college and university governing boards are conservative and risk averse. They are less inclined to venture into unfamiliar foreign territory, than to pursue limited opportunities in a domestic market that they know and trust. U.S. college presidents are constrained by tight budgets, cautious trustees, vigilant legislators, and faculty critics. They are too distracted by financial crises, campus controversies, and internal politics to explore opportunities abroad. U.S. academics are focused primarily on courses and research for which they have a passion and for which they will be rewarded career-wise. They are disinclined to define learning outcomes in terms of the practical skills that non-U.S. nationals want and need.

The gap between the abundance of U.S. higher education talent and the immense foreign demand for it is *The Great Chasm in Global Education*. It is a chasm of lost opportunities. It is also a space of great economic potential. This book describes the outer limits of the chasm, sheds light on key factors that underlie it, and proposes ways to traverse the gulf so as to realize this potential. Its central thesis is this: to bridge the gap between the abundance of American higher educational talent and the immense foreign demand for it, fundamental reforms in the institutional culture, organizational structure, and governance system of traditional U.S. colleges and universities are needed. Without these reforms, the financial viability of these institutions will be at risk, as will be the economic foundation of the U.S. higher education sector as a whole.

Why bridge the Great Chasm?

The book begins with a fundamental question: "As a general proposition, to improve their overall financial condition, and thus strengthen the economic foundation of the U.S. higher education sector, should

American institutions of higher learning pursue an 'international option'?" This option involves exporting U.S. higher education services abroad. The book argues in the affirmative, for the simple reason that, in light of an intensification of competition in a steadily shrinking domestic market, the alternatives available to American colleges and universities are growing few and far between. While advocating institutional reforms, the book posits that U.S. colleges and universities are to be valued, supported, and strengthened. Founded on the principle of academic freedom, they are repositories of intellectual capital, and thus an important source of America's intangible wealth.

Aside from the forces of supply and demand, a golden opportunity to "consummate a deal," and the self-serving needs of American colleges and universities, there are other reasons why these institutions should pursue an "international option." Among them is an altruistic calling to

- educate and enlighten other members of the international community,
- promote their personal growth and social well-being,
- contribute to the economic development of their societies.

Internationally, American institutions of higher learning are at the forefront of knowledge creation and intellectual advancement. In light of their pre-eminent position, as well as this altruistic calling, they can and *should* play an even greater role in globalizing higher education.[5]

There is yet another reason. It touches on the geopolitical. By fortifying the economic substructure of the U.S. higher education sector, the globalization of U.S. colleges and universities could strengthen America's standing as the world's leader in higher education. Doing so is particularly critical at this historic juncture, in light of a shifting international balance of power, the rise of alternative ideological systems, and extant threats to a liberal world order. Like higher education in other Western societies, American higher education is imbued with the values of a democratic society. Spreading these values around the globe is not just noble, but also vital for the future of this order.

---

[5] G. Hawawini, *The Internationalization of Higher Education and Business Schools* (2016). As Hawawini points out, an institution might also be motivated by other considerations in its drive to internationalize. They include a desire to attract the best students and faculty worldwide, remain academically relevant, and learn from the world. Ibid., 18–22, 25.

But skeptics will understandably ask, "Is this not ideological imperialism and cultural colonialism in disguise?—A surreptitious attempt to impose the American way of thinking on the rest of the world?—Yankee chauvinism and intellectual arrogance in sheep's clothing?"[6] We think not, for the simple reason that the principal beneficiaries of a world order inspired by liberal values are a free people, not any foreign power. Effectively, these values empower the individual in the face of imperialism, colonialism, and oppression. Regardless of where they come from, they support an institutional framework in which free men and women can pursue the truth. Besides, it is to be emphasized, the basic proposition here is to educate and enlighten on the basis of cultural equality, social collaboration, and political parity. These principles go against notions of ideological conquest, cultural domination, and political hegemony.

The book's approach

Bridging the Gap between the Abundance of American Higher Education Talent and the Immense Foreign Demand for It adopts a materialist approach to the challenges facing American colleges and universities in the changing landscape of higher education. Consequently, the principal concepts used in the book are economic, financial, and institutional, not ideological, philosophical, or historical. The primary focus of this scholarly work is the *realm of finances*, which supports the *realm of ideas*. The book posits that only through a strong economic substructure (i.e., the "realm of finances") can the ideological superstructure (i.e., the "realm of ideas") of American higher education flourish. Indeed, a solid substructure makes possible the proliferation of educational, professional, and academic opportunities for students, teachers, scholars, and researchers.[7]

The book argues that if, in this changing landscape, the economic substructure of the U.S. higher education sector is not strengthened, its ideological superstructure, which encompasses teaching, learning, research, scholarship, knowledge creation, and the pursuit of the truth, will lose its vibrancy—not for the elite few of American colleges and universities,

---

[6] See, for example, S. Stein, "Rethinking the Ethics of Internationalization: Five Challenges for Higher Education." *InterActions: UCLA Journal of Education and Information Studies*, vol. 12, no. 2 (2016) (unpaginated).

[7] On the interrelationship between financial capability and the pursuit of mission see B.A. Weisbrod, J.P. Ballou, and E.D. Asch, *Mission and Money, Understanding the University* (2008), 4–5.

but rather for the vast majority (emphasis placed on "vast majority," because the "elite few" are relatively better off than the 4,000-strong mid- to lower-tier institutions, some of which operate at the margin). Bridging the gap between the abundance of American higher education talent and the immense foreign demand for it is one way to fortify the substructure of American higher education, improve the financial condition of the "vast majority" of U.S. colleges and universities, enhance the vibrancy of American teaching, learning, scholarship, and knowledge creation, and promote the dissemination of liberal, democratic values around the world.

Purpose and aims

So, what do we hope to accomplish through this endeavor? Or, to be more straightforward, what is the purpose of the book? It is several-fold:

- to present a global perspective on American higher education;
- to provide insights into adverse trends that pose a risk to the economic foundation of the U.S. higher education sector;
- to propose a viable way to reinforce this foundation; namely, the exportation of U.S. higher education services;
- to convey a sense of the enormous potential of global markets for higher education;
- to identify cultural, organizational, and governance factors that stand in the way of realizing this potential;
- to suggest how these obstacles can be removed;
- to explain how U.S. colleges and universities can preserve their academic integrity while generating the financial resources necessary to sustain their activities in the realm of ideas;
- to highlight ethical issues that occasionally arise in the course of international expansion;
- to explain what needs to be done, and what can be done, to bridge the gap between the abundance of American higher education talent and the immense foreign demand for it.

This multifold purpose is attuned to the interests and concerns of those who have a vital stake in U.S. higher education. They want to know how to enhance the financial viability of American colleges and universities so as to preserve their pre-eminence in the realm of ideas.

Associated with this purpose are three secondary objectives. Their relevance will become clearer as the narrative unfolds.

- First, our aim is not to present a broad survey of U.S. educational institutions, or to explain how they operate across the board or "on the average." Rather, it is to present an ideal-typical construct that can be instrumental in analyzing their essential features and *modus operandi*.[8] This construct has been formulated on the basis of objective facts, first-hand observations, and subjective value judgments. It is intended to serve as a heuristic tool for comparing, to its component parts, the rich reality of American colleges and universities. No doubt, the essential characteristics of the 4,000+ institutions, as well as the manner in which they operate, will vary. Accordingly, we have been careful to qualify our basic propositions. Nonetheless, we believe there is a thread of commonality in the culture, organization, and governance of traditional American academic institutions that permits many generalizations that are built into the construct.
- Second, our aim is not to elevate business over academic considerations. Clearly, the latter are central to the mission and purpose of any institution of higher learning. Business considerations should not detract from or diminish them in any way. By the same token, business considerations are *relevant* to the question of how American colleges and universities can extend their global reach to meet the immense foreign demand for U.S. higher education talent. The distinction is one of significance, not precedence or priority. To be clear: we attach *significance* to business considerations in the pursuit of an institution's mission and strategic goals and believe that they are *relevant* to our central thesis.
- Third, our aim is not to issue a bold new imperative: to wit, that *every* U.S. college or university *should* "go global". Every institution must decide for itself, based on its own peculiar circumstances. Nor is our aim to imply that expanding into foreign markets is the *only* option available to American colleges and universities, or even the *best* option in every situation. Indeed, there are other options, including launching new programs, discontinuing unprofitable ones, expanding auxiliary services, and tapping into new segments of the domestic

---

[8] On this methodology see M. Weber, "'Objectivity' in Social Sciences and Social Policy." In *The Methodology of the Social Sciences*, edited by E.A. Shils and H.A. Finch (1949), 90–112.

market. Rather, our aim is to put forth an *international* option for ameliorating the financial condition of American colleges and universities and to advance it *as a general proposition*. In our view, U.S. academic institutions should pursue this option because, in doing so, they can improve their economic well-being, as well as the social well-being of non-U.S. nationals who seek their services.

As distinguished from other scholarly works

Besides advancing an international option, the book can be distinguished from other scholarly works on American higher education in three respects. First, it envisions the U.S. higher education sector as an "export industry." Accordingly, it argues that if U.S. colleges and universities cannot bring all the world to America for higher education, then they should take American higher education to all the world. Second, it sees the challenges facing U.S. colleges and universities as not just economic, but also institutional. It contends that cultural, organizational, and governance features of traditional American academic institutions often stand in the way of international expansion. Third, it goes beyond the analytical into the practical.

Indeed, the book does more than just *analyze* a longstanding problem plaguing American colleges and universities; i.e., how to maintain their financial viability in the context of adverse demographic and economic trends. Rather, it also puts forth a *constructive solution*; i.e., international expansion with the aim of meeting the immense foreign demand for American higher education talent. While the book offers an empirically based assessment of the current state of the U.S. higher education sector, it also proposes how this state can be altered to produce a better outcome. It contends that this outcome is in the interests of both American institutions of higher learning and non-U.S. nationals who aspire to their services. To be sure, it is a "win-win" proposition for all.

Overview of the book

Here's a preview of our journey:

Chapter 1, "The Value Added by Academic Values," introduces the reader to the "American value proposition." It addresses the fundamental question, "*What is so special about U.S. higher education that makes it so appealing to non-U.S. nationals?"* As the chapter explains, the short answer is educational quality, which is inextricably bound with the core values of the academy. Among these values are academic freedom, quality, and oversight; the pursuit of truth; and the creation of knowledge. The chapter distinguishes these values from those of a business culture. It then sets forth the central value judgment of the book: in the provision of higher education services, academic institutions are to be preferred over business institutions, because they incorporate a system of value that is conducive to educational quality.

Chapter 2, "Beyond Study Abroad: International Higher Education Services," elaborates on what is meant by "higher education services." The term connotes more than just course offerings, degree programs, and student and faculty exchanges. In addition to the foregoing, it encompasses program design and development; higher education advisory; project development, and management; technology transfer; and other services. The chapter describes the nature of these services, the profiles of non-U.S. individuals and entities who typically demand them, the organizational capabilities required to deliver them, and the types of domestic institutions that possess these capabilities. It argues that providing these services is a "natural" for American colleges and universities, because, in doing so, they can leverage off their institutional strengths.

Chapters 3 and 4, "A Higher Education Sector on the Edge: Parts I and II," focus on the American side of the Great Chasm (i.e., the "supply side"). Part I examines the structure of the U.S. higher education sector, as well as the profiles of institutions that make up the sector. It identifies key elements that account for their financial condition, and traces historical trends in revenues, expenditures, enrollments, and closures that reflect this condition. Based on this analysis, the chapter identifies five financial pillars of the U.S. higher education sector: (1) personal disposable income, (2) private donations, (3) student financial aid, (4) investment income, and (5) public funding. These pillars support the economic superstructure of American higher education.

Part II identifies major risks to this substructure. They are linked to the five financial pillars discussed in Part I. The risks heighten in periods of contraction, when escalating costs peak above falling revenues. They diminish in periods of expansion, when the rate of revenue growth exceeds the rate of cost inflation. The chapter then traces various historical trends that portend an erosion of this substructure. Among them are unfavorable demographics, slackening enrollment growth, increased competition, narrowing margins, and declining profitability. Based on this analysis, it reaches an ominous conclusion: given the cyclicality of the U.S. economy, it seems only a matter of time before the risks converge to produce a "perfect storm." That storm may have arrived as a result of the economic havoc wreaked by the Global Pandemic.

Chapters 5 and 6, "Global Markets beyond the Horizon: Parts I and II," purport to give the reader a sense of the enormity of global markets for higher education (i.e., the "demand side"). Part I addresses impediments to the inbound mobility of non-U.S. nationals who seek American higher education. Among them are a tightening of U.S. visa restrictions and rising anti-immigration sentiment in some social circles. The chapter contends that if, as a result of these impediments, U.S. colleges and universities cannot bring all the world to America for higher education, then they should take American higher education to all the world. Indeed, if the scope of inbound student mobility is restricted, then the scope of outbound institutional mobility should be broadened. Lastly, the chapter analyzes, by global region, long-term trends in demographics, gross enrollment ratios, national income, and government expenditures, which shape international demand for higher education services. Based on this analysis, it concludes that the greatest demand is likely to lie in those regions with high income and GDP per capita and high "gross enrollment potential."

Part II focuses on national markets for higher education services in the Arab World, East and Southeast Asia, South Asia, and Latin America. It discusses potential opportunities in these markets, as well as the challenges that U.S. higher education providers are likely to face in entering in them. The chapter then points out that only a handful of U.S. academic institutions have responded to the immense foreign demand for American higher education talent. It argues that notwithstanding their responsiveness, in light of the enormity of international markets for higher education, these institutions can do much more. Lastly, the chapter traces the growth in the number of international branch campuses, the principal destinations for internationally mobile tertiary education students, and potential competitors of U.S. colleges and universities in global higher education export markets.

Chapter 7, "Institutional Barriers to International Expansion," highlights three aspects of traditional American colleges and universities that stand in the way of bridging the Great Chasm: an institutional culture that is averse to commercialization, an organizational structure that is operationally slow, and a system of governance that often leads to indecision, conflict, and paralysis. Relying on a Weberian ideal-typical construct, the chapter explains why these aspects are "obstacles" in the way of international expansion, and what it would take to remove them. The chapter then introduces an "international market-oriented model," designed to facilitate the provision of higher education services abroad. It explains how the model would work, as well as its advantages and disadvantages relative to the "traditional model."

Chapter 8, "How to Bridge the Great Chasm," addresses certain preconditions that must be met before a college or university can "go global." Among them are stakeholder "buy-in," the development of a comprehensive business plan, the formulation of a coherent intellectual property policy, and the assessment of the institutional capability. The chapter then sets forth several collaborative arrangements that can facilitate international expansion. They include forging an alliance with another academic institution, eliciting the support of a foreign government agency or foundation, and partnering with a multinational corporation. The chapter also outlines the advantages and disadvantages of each, and recommends a number of quality controls that can be installed to ensure both academic integrity and educational quality. Finally, the chapter discusses the rudiments of online learning and presents a few ideas on how the e-learning experience can be enhanced.

Chapter 9, "Ethical Dilemmas in International Expansion," highlights a key challenge facing all institutions of higher learning: how to preserve their academic integrity, while generating the financial resources necessary to support their activities in the "realm of ideas." It discusses four ethical dilemmas that occasionally arise in the course of international expansion: the justice of (1) providing international higher education services only to those who can afford them, (2) engaging in foreign practices that contravene U.S. normative standards, (3) providing services in countries whose policies conflict with American liberal values, and (4) compromising academic freedom to remain in good standing with a repressive regime. Lastly, the chapter sets forth the ethical imperative to safeguard academic freedom, and places this imperative in a broad philosophical context.

"Parting Thoughts: Relevance for Other Western Institutions" summarizes the key points made in the book. As these points are specific to American colleges and universities, this section discusses the possibility of extending the central thesis to other Western colleges and universities. It also discusses what assumptions must be made to do so on a sound footing. Based on this discussion, it reaches a "conditional conclusion:" the reasonableness of extending the central thesis to other Western colleges and universities hinges on the degree to which they are similar to their U.S. counterpart in terms of institutional culture, organizational structure, and system of governance.

Our journey will take us to various ports of discovery. Let us begin.

1
The Value Added by Academic Values

The immense foreign demand for American higher education talent is influenced by the cache of U.S. higher education—a "commodity" so alluring that non-U.S. nationals are willing to pay a premium for it. What makes U.S. higher education so attractive is a system of normative values that enhances its marketability. This is the essence of the "American value proposition." The passages that follow elaborate on the American value proposition—what it means, what factors influence it, and how it strengthens foreign demand for U.S. higher education. In addition, the passages discuss what distinguishes an academic culture from a business culture, and why academic institutions should be preferred over business institutions in providing higher education services abroad.

> By compromising basic academic principles, universities tamper with ideals that give meaning to the scholarly community and win respect from the public. These common values are the glue that binds together an institution already fragmented by a host of separate disciplines, research centers, teaching programs, and personal ambitions. They keep the faculty focused on the work of discovery, scholarship, and learning despite the manifold temptations of the outside world. They help maintain high standards of student admissions and faculty appointments. They sustain the belief of scientists and scholars in the worth of what they are. They make academic careers a calling rather than just another way to earn a living.[1]
>
> Derek Bok, former President of Harvard University

> Higher education is one of few areas where this country competes with the rest of the world and wins. The best of American higher education outstrips any in the world. Look where the rest of the world goes for higher education, for graduate degrees. They come here.
>
> Donna Shalala, former U.S. Secretary of Health and Human Services

---

[1] D. Bok, *Universities in the Marketplace: The Commercialization of Higher Education* (2003), 206–207.

Bridging the Gap between the Abundance of American Higher Education Talent and the Immense Foreign Demand for It.
Richard J. Joseph, Oxford University Press. © Richard J. Joseph (2022). DOI: 10.1093/oso/9780192848307.003.0002

The American value proposition

Let's start with the American value proposition. What is so special about U.S. higher education that makes it so appealing to non-U.S. nationals? The short answer is *quality*—a perception influenced by American economic power, political prowess, social vibrancy, and liberal values.[2]

The long answer is *value*—a view shaped by the earnings potential, employment prospects, career paths, and social mobility of U.S. college graduates. Indeed, in the global marketplace for human talent, graduates of U.S. institutions are seen as possessing the credentials necessary to land the best jobs; the knowledge necessary to succeed in a world shaped by Western practices; the skills necessary to analyze, innovate, execute, and solve problems; and the competency required to lead organizations, revitalize communities, shape politics, and build institutions. Consequently, American higher education is highly valued, not just for its power to enlighten, but also for its ability to create wealth, transform societies, and improve personal well-being.[3]

The rankings: shaping global perceptions

Reinforcing these perceptions are the world rankings of colleges and universities. Two such rankings are worth mentioning: the Shanghai Academic Ranking of World Universities, and the Times Higher Education World University Rankings.

---

[2] On American leadership in higher education see S. Marginson and M. van der Wende (Organization for Economic Cooperation and Development), "The New Global Landscape of Nations and Institutions." *Higher Education to 2030, Volume 2, Globalisation* (2009), 17, 33–42.
Perceptions of quality are further enhanced by accreditation. To many non-U.S. nationals, American accreditation represents a "seal of good housekeeping" that signifies high educational standards based on quality assurance. In international markets, it strengthens the American brand by adding value to a degree conferred by a U.S. college or university. Such value translates into higher placement rates, better employment opportunities, elevated salary levels, and greater social mobility. Graduates of *accredited* American colleges and universities generally are expected to find better jobs, hold more responsible positions, add greater value to the enterprise, and earn salaries higher than graduates of non-accredited U.S. colleges and universities.
[3] C.T. Clotfelter, *American Universities in a Global Market* (2010), 3–6; L.B. Palmer and E. Urban, "International Students' Perceptions of the Value of U.S. Higher Education." *Journal of International Students*, vol. 6, no. 1 (2016): 153–174; M. Ohorodnik, "Was It Worth It? International Student Views on the Value of Their U.S. Education." *World Education News and Reviews*, October 8, 2019, https://wenr.wes.org/2019/10/was-it-worth-it-international-student-views-on-the-value-of-their-u-s-education (accessed June 1, 2021); and Institute of International Education, *What International Students Think About U.S. Higher Education; Attitudes and Perceptions of Prospective Students from Around the World* (2015).

The Shanghai Ranking is based on various indicators of "academic or research performance," such as the number of alumni and staff who have won Nobel Prizes or Fields Medals, highly cited researchers, papers published in *Nature* or *Science*, and papers cited in major citation indices. It is also based on the weighted average scores of these indicators divided by the total number of full-time equivalent academic staff.[4] The Times Rankings are based on an assessment of an institution's learning environment; research output, quality, and influence; knowledge transfer capability; and international outlook.[5] Key indicators include the staff-to-student ratio, research-related income, proportion of international students and staff, and number of scholarly citations.

In the 2021 Shanghai Ranking, 16 of the top 20 universities are American. In the 2022 Times Rankings, 12 of the top 20 are American (Table 1.1).

Because these rankings are based on academic criteria (e.g., scholarly research, knowledge creation, the quality of the learning environment), they reflect on core academic values. Because, moreover, they impact the ability of a college or university to attract students, faculty, and staff, they shape perceptions of market value.[6] That the majority of the top 20 academic institutions are American says something about the core values of U.S. higher education. That these institutions are able to generate financial resources by virtue of their academic standing says something about the value attached by others to their system of normative values. Both add weight to the American value proposition.

A preference for academic institutions

In our view, U.S. institutions that are primarily *academic* in character should take the lead in globalizing American higher education. Like other Western colleges and universities, they embody the core values of the academy. Among these values are academic freedom, educational quality, the pursuit of the truth, and the creation of knowledge. Subordinating these

---

[4] Shanghai Academic Ranking of World Universities, Shanghai Ranking Consultancy, August 2020, http://www.shanghairanking.com (accessed June 1, 2021).

[5] Times Higher Education World University Rankings 2020, The Times Higher Education, August 2020, https://www.timeshighereducation.com (accessed June 1, 2021).

[6] V.B. Agarwal and D.R. Winkler, "Foreign Demand for United States Higher Education: A Study of Developing Countries in the Eastern Hemisphere." *Economic Development and Cultural Change*, vol. 33, no. 3 (1985): 623–644; and M.E. McMahon, "Higher Education in a World Market." *Higher Education*, vol. 24 (1992): 465–482.

Table 1.1 Top 20 universities in global rankings

Shanghai Academic Ranking of World Universities 2021			Times Higher Education World University Rankings 2022		
1	🇺🇸	Harvard University	1	🇬🇧	University of Oxford
2	🇺🇸	Stanford University	=2	🇺🇸	California Institute of Technology
3	🇬🇧	University of Cambridge	=2	🇺🇸	Harvard University
4	🇺🇸	Massachusetts Institute of Technology	4	🇺🇸	Stanford University
5	🇺🇸	University of California, Berkeley	=5	🇺🇸	Massachusetts Institute of Technology
6	🇺🇸	Princeton University	=5	🇬🇧	University of Cambridge
7	🇬🇧	University of Oxford	7	🇺🇸	Princeton University
8	🇺🇸	Columbia University	8	🇺🇸	University of California, Berkeley
9	🇺🇸	California Institute of Technology	9	🇺🇸	Yale University
10	🇺🇸	University of Chicago	10	🇺🇸	University of Chicago
11	🇺🇸	Yale University	11	🇺🇸	Columbia University
12	🇺🇸	Cornell University	12	🇬🇧	Imperial College London
13	🇫🇷	Paris-Saclay University	=13	🇺🇸	Johns Hopkins University
14	🇺🇸	University of California, Los Angeles	=13	🇺🇸	University of Pennsylvania
15	🇺🇸	University of Pennsylvania	15	🇨🇭	ETH Zurich
16	🇺🇸	Johns Hopkins University	=16	🇨🇳	Peking University

Continued

Shanghai Academic Ranking of World Universities 2021			Times Higher Education World University Rankings 2022		
17	🇬🇧	University College London	=16	🇨🇳	Tsinghua University
18	🇺🇸	University of California, San Diego	=18	🇨🇦	University of Toronto
19	🇺🇸	University of Washington	=18	🇬🇧	University College London
20	🇺🇸	University of California, San Francisco	20	🇺🇸	University of California, Los Angeles

values to non-academic considerations risks eroding the integrity and quality of U.S. higher education. This, in turn, could weaken the American value proposition.[7]

So, if not *academic*, what could possibly be their essential character? The rise of the for-profit subsector over the past few decades suggests an apt reply. If an educational institution is not academic, it is likely to be *business* in character. By implication, its pursuits are likely to be motivated primarily by commercial considerations. Although the vast majority of such entities are for-profit, a few of them are non-profit. Despite their non-profit status, they conduct their affairs in a distinctly commercial manner.

Some might say that like any other revenue-generating enterprise, a college or university, whether organized for-profit or not-for-profit, is essentially a *business*.[8] Nothing could be further from the truth. Although its operations are *business-like* in many respects, an academic enterprise differs from a commercial enterprise in a fundamental way: its activities

---

[7] As noted by Weisbrod, Ballou, and Asch, "Because a strong reputation often shows that the college or university has been successful in pursuit of its mission, a reputation once developed is a potential revenue good that can be profitably exploited. Somewhat ironically, it is the school's reputation for its unprofitable activities, such as research and many elements of instruction, that often permits it to make profits in other activities . . . Critical to success in higher education . . . is the perception that the school's primary priority and mission is the welfare of the student and the production and dissemination of knowledge and not merely money." B.A. Weisbrod, J.P. Ballou, and E.D. Asch, *Mission and Money, Understanding the University* (2008), 175.

[8] For diverse views on this subject see R.M. Freeland, "Yes, Higher Ed Is a Business—But It's Also a Calling." *The Chronicle of Higher Education*, March 18, 2018; E. Stoller, "The Business of Higher Education." *Inside Higher Ed*, June 5, 2014; and M. Greenberg, "A University Is Not a Business (and Other Fantasies)." *EDUCAUSE Review*, vol. 39, no. 2 (2004): 10–16.

are inspired by a mission.[9] That mission is to educate, enlighten, and contribute to the intellectual advancement of society, as well as the personal well-being of its members. To regard institutions of higher learning as mere businesses is to overlook the critical role that they play in promoting personal growth, social progress, cultural enrichment, and political stability in democratic societies. These intangibles are incapable of measurement from a commercial perspective. They represent intellectual, social, cultural, and political value. In the words of Thorstein Veblen,

> Those items of human intelligence and initiative that go to make up the pursuit of knowledge, and that are embodied in systematic form in its conclusions, do not lend themselves to quantitative statement, and cannot be made to appear on a balance sheet.[10]

Academic versus business culture

There are yet other differences.[11] Typically, a business culture is primarily "results-oriented," with little appreciation or tolerance for protracted process. What matters most is swift decision-making, effective execution, and increasing the "bottom line." By contrast, an academic culture is very much concerned with process—even if it results in major delays. Generally, its adherents have little appreciation or tolerance for autocratic decision-making, the lack of consultation, or hastily derived results. In a business culture, employees are expected to be "team players," who, at the end of the day, tote the party line. In an academic culture, employees are expected to be "critical thinkers" willing to question conventional wisdom and challenge the party line.

Furthermore, in a business culture, the employment relationship is defined primarily by contract. To a large extent, it is guided by legalistic notions of consideration, compensation, and performance. In an academic culture, by contrast, the employment relationship goes beyond the contractual into the collegial. In the latter realm, employees are not just subordinates. They are also *colleagues*.

---

[9] Weisbrod, Ballou, and Asch, *Mission and Money*, 2.

[10] T. Veblen, *The Higher Learning in America: A Memorandum on the Conduct of Universities by Business Men* (1918), 94–95.

[11] For a general discussion of these differences see P. Gibbs, "Marketers and Educationalists—Two Communities Divided by Time?" *International Journal of Educational Management*, vol. 22, no. 3 (2008): 269–278; and L. Goodwin, "The Academic World and the Business World: A Comparison of Occupational Goals." *Sociology of Education*, vol. 42, no. 2 (Spring 1969): 170–187.

What is more, in an academic culture, dissent and disagreement are valued, encouraged, defended, and even protected. In many business environments, these deeds are at best tolerated. At an extreme, they provide grounds for termination. Finally, the primary objectives of a business culture are the generation of profits and the maximization of shareholder value. By contrast, the primary objectives of an academic culture are educational enlightenment and the creation of knowledge.[12]

On a conceptual level, where business values predominate in an educational setting, the student is unwittingly transformed from a "learner" into a "customer," who, relative to the experience, expertise, and judgment of his or her teachers, is always "right"—at least when it comes to service.[13] Faculty are transformed from a "community of scholars" into pliant "service providers," expected to satisfy the customer at virtually any cost.[14] Academic administrators are transformed from shepherding "deans" and wise "provosts" into effective "managers," whose supreme duty is to follow orders, execute decisions, and generate profits. The president is converted from a *primus inter pares* with broad administrative authority[15] into a "chief executive" with dictatorial powers, never to be challenged. Lastly, ideas that define the very persona of the scholar are metamorphosized into "corporate property" subject to appropriation, transfer, licensing, and sale. In an educational milieu imbued with business values, the traditional concepts by which we have come to understand traditional roles, responsibilities, and relationships are distorted, even rendered obsolete. To be sure, the business culture turns the academic world upside down.[16]

---

[12] On the mission of colleges and universities see J.D. Scott, "The Mission of the University: Medieval to Postmodern Transformations." *Journal of Higher Education*, 77–1 (2006), 1–39; A. Flexner, *Universities: American, English, German* (1930); and C. Kerr, *The Uses of the University* (1963). Weisbrod, Ballou, and Asch assert that this mission is threefold: teaching, research, and public service. Weisbrod, Ballou, and Asch, *Mission and Money*, 2.

[13] On the marketization of higher education in general see J. Williams, *Consuming Higher Education: Why Learning Can't Be Bought* (2012); and M. Molesworth, R. Scullion, and E. Nixon, *The Marketisation of Higher Education and the Student as Consumer* (2010).

[14] In a business-like environment shaped by autocratic decision-making, notes Veblen, "the faculty is conceived as a body of employees, hired to render certain services and turn out certain scheduled vendible results." Veblen, *The Higher Learning in America*, 99.

[15] "[B]y tradition the president of the university is the senior member of the faculty, its confidential spokesman in official and corporate concerns, and the 'moderator' of its town meeting like deliberative assemblies. As chairman of its meetings he is, by tradition, presumed to exercise no peculiar control, beyond such guidance as the superior experience of the senior member may be presumed to afford his colleagues. As spokesman for the faculty he is, by tradition, presumed to be a scholar of such erudition, breadth and maturity as may fairly command something of filial respect and affection from his associates in the corporation of learning . . ." Ibid., 208.

[16] These values are not necessarily incompatible. Valuing business execution, for example, does not preclude esteem for academic freedom. Or, valuing scholarship does not obviate the need to improve the "bottom line". In some situations, however, the values do conflict, in which case one set must take precedence over the other, or there should be a compromise.

According to Veblen, any attempt to transform a university into a commercial enterprise goes against its very nature.

> Men dilate on the high necessity of a businesslike organization and control of the university, its equipment, personnel and routine. What is had in mind in this insistence on an efficient system is that these corporations of learning shall set their affairs in order after the pattern of a well-conducted business concern. In this view the university is conceived as a business house dealing in merchantable knowledge, placed under the governing hand of a captain of erudition . . .
>
> Yet when all these sophistications of practical wisdom are duly allowed for, the fact remains that the university is, in usage, precedent, and common-sense preconception, an establishment for the conservation and advancement of the higher learning, devoted to a disinterested pursuit of knowledge . . . [T]he system and order that so govern the work, and that come into view in its procedure and results, are the logical system and order of intellectual enterprise, not the mechanical or statistical systematization that goes into effect in the management of an industrial plant or the financiering of a business corporation.[17]

These observations, of course, are broad generalizations, subject to conditions, qualifications, and exceptions. For example, many academic administrators are just as results-oriented as are business managers. In the most progressive of business environments, dissent and disagreement are not only tolerated, but also encouraged. Many academic institutions expect students to be treated just like customers. Finally, some college presidents can be just as dictatorial as corporate chief executives. Just ask faculty.

Notwithstanding these exceptions and qualifications, there is a modicum of truth in the underlying propositions—the essential elements of this ideal typical construct. To function properly, every enterprise must inculcate its members with a common set of values. It must imbue them with the same normative conceptions of authority, order, roles, responsibilities, and

---

Student admissions is a prime example. Here, business values, such as maximizing tuition revenues, often conflict with academic values, such as ensuring student quality. When they do, one set of values takes precedence over the other or a compromise ensues. At an extreme, if business values take precedence, the institution is likely to admit as many applicants as is possible, to the point where marginal costs equal marginal revenues. Conversely, if academic values take precedence, the institution is likely to admit only those applicants that meet its admissions criteria, and no more. In the vast majority of cases, the outcome is somewhere in between. Typically, the institution will admit as many applicants who meet its admissions criteria as is possible; sometimes more, to generate incremental revenues; sometimes less, to maintain student quality. In such cases, the end-result represents a "blend" of or "trade-off" between academic and business values.

[17] Veblen, *The Higher Learning in America*, 94.

relationships. These conceptions set professional expectations. They influence organizational behavior. They translate into common practices in the workplace, uniform standards for employee performance, and acceptable modes of conduct, communication, and interaction. In the aggregate, they form the ideological basis or "halo" for an institutional order. Max Weber intimates as much when he says,

> Behind the functional purposes, of course, "ideas of culture-values" usually stand. These are ersatz for the earthly or supra-mundane personal master: ideas such as "state," "church," "community," "party," or "enterprise" are thought of as being realized in a community; they provide an ideological halo for the master.[18]

By the same token, an institutional culture is not defined solely by normative values. It is also shaped by subjective attitudes, biases, outlooks, and orientations. In Chapter 7, we will discuss these factors in greater detail. For now, suffice it to say that left uncontrolled, they can stifle innovation, impede organizational change, and obstruct international expansion.

Basic premises

That an institution is primarily academic in character does not preclude it from adopting business practices or embracing commercial values in pursuit of its mission.[19] This point is important, because some business practices and values are essential for international expansion, successful competition, and the effective delivery of higher education services; for example, values that place a premium on expeditious decision-making, effective execution, and cross-functional teamwork. A key challenge that U.S. colleges and universities face in "going global" is figuring out how to

---

[18] M. Weber, "Bureaucracy." In *From Max Weber*, edited by H.H. Gerth and C. Wright Mills (1958), 199.

[19] As William Bowen points out, "Universities do have to become more business-like in relevant respects at the same time that they have to retain their basic commitment to academic values." W.G. Bowen, *Higher Education in the Digital Age* (2013), 28. See also Weisbrod, Ballou, and Asch, *Mission and Money*, 4; J.C. Knapp and D.J. Siegel, eds, *The Business of Higher Education* (2009); and G. Keller, *Academic Strategy: The Management Revolution in American Higher Education* (1983).

Veblen notes, "[B]usiness methods of course have their place in the corporation's fiscal affairs and in the office-work incident to the care of its material equipment ... These things concern the university only in its externals, and they do not properly fall within the scope of academic policy or academic administration." Veblen, *The Higher Learning in America*, 103.

incorporate business-like practices in their institutional chemistry without compromising their academic integrity. We believe that this can be done by preserving shared governance and strengthening academic oversight, while separating academics from management, marketing, finance, and operations. In Chapter 7, we will elaborate on this theme.

Also, in our view, the academic character of an institution is not dependent on a particular mode of organization. Indeed, normative values and organizational structure are distinct and independent variables. This point also is important, because it implies that U.S. colleges and universities can modify their existing organizational structure, or adopt an entirely different one, without necessarily compromising their academic integrity. This assumption underlies our belief that to successfully expand, compete, and operate in foreign markets, traditional academic institutions *can* and *should* restructure, while preserving their core values and academic character.

Summing up

Returning to the central value judgment: in the delivery of international higher educational services, institutions that are primarily *academic* in character should be preferred over those that are primarily *business* in character. They incorporate a system of normative values that are conducive to educational quality, academic integrity, and intellectual advancement. These intangibles are of enormous importance to foreign consumers of U.S. higher education services. They strengthen the American brand, which enhances the perceived market value of these services. This is the essence of the American value proposition.

Let us turn to "higher education services." As you will discover, they go well beyond study abroad.

2

Beyond Study Abroad: International Higher Education Services

This chapter lays the foundation for what follows in the book. Its relevance to the central thesis is two-fold: first, to understand how to bridge the gap between the abundance of American higher education talent and the immense foreign demand for it, one must first grasp the nature of the services that this talent can provide. These passages describe the services. Second, to understand what fundamental reforms in the structure and governance of traditional American colleges and universities are needed, one must first grasp the prototypical structure and governance of these institutions. These passages set forth such a prototype. The chapter begins by explaining what is meant by "international higher education services." It points out that the term goes well beyond study abroad.

> The underlying business-like presumption ... appears to be that learning is a merchantable commodity, to be produced on a piece-rate plan, rated, bought and sold by standard units, measured, counted and reduced to staple equivalence by impersonal, mechanical tests. In all its bearings the work is hereby reduced to a mechanistic, statistical consistency, with numerical standards and units; which conduces to perfunctory and mediocre work throughout, and acts to deter both students and teachers from a free pursuit of knowledge ...[1]
>
> Thorstein Veblen, American social scientist and philosopher

Although the dangers are real, not all ties with industry are suspect, nor should universities refuse every opportunity to earn a financial return from their work. The money campuses can make from patenting scientific discoveries has elicited much valuable effort to put laboratory advances to practical use. The profits earned from executive training programs have led faculties to work harder to serve legitimate needs. Acting prudently, universities can do a

---

[1] T. Veblen, *The Higher Learning in America: A Memorandum on the Conduct of Universities by Business Men* (1918), 190.

Bridging the Gap between the Abundance of American Higher Education Talent and the Immense Foreign Demand for It.
Richard J. Joseph, Oxford University Press. © Richard J. Joseph (2022). DOI: 10.1093/oso/9780192848307.003.0003

lot to share their knowledge with industry, meet the growing demand for continuing education, and even make some money along the way without damaging
themselves in the process.[2]

Derek Bok, former President of Harvard University

International higher education services

For some, "international higher education services" conjures up images of
study abroad. Sponsored by their home college or university, American
students trek to exciting places like London, Paris, or Rome, where they
take art history courses at ivory-tower institutions, explore the scenic coun-
tryside, savor wine and cheese at the neighborhood bistro, and immerse
themselves in the local culture. For others, the term connotes an entirely different set of endeavors: international faculty exchanges, research
projects, joint degree programs, workshops, seminars, and conferences. It
also connotes partnering with ivory-tower institutions in exciting places
like London, Paris, or Rome.[3] In the routinized realm of accounting, the
term connotes something more staid, generic, and quantifiable. "Educational services," in general, refers to "instruction and training . . . provided
by specialized establishments, such as schools, colleges, universities, and
training centers."[4] By implication, "international higher educational services" refers to post-secondary instruction and training beyond the borders
of the United States.

As used here, "international higher education services" is much broader
than all this. In addition to the foregoing, it encompasses

- program design and development,
- higher education advisory services,
- project development and management,
- technology transfer.

Although many of these activities are not central to the mission and purpose of a college or university, they arguably are related to it. And if

---

[2] D. Bok, *Universities in the Marketplace: The Commercialization of Higher Education* (2003), 200.
[3] F. Maringe, "The Meanings of Globalization and Internationalization in HE: Findings from a World
Survey." In *Globalization and Internationalization in Higher Education*, edited by F. Maringe and N.
Foskett (2010), 26.
[4] U.S. Department of Commerce, Bureau of Economic Analysis, "Regional Economic Accounts,"
https://apps.bea.gov/itable/definitions.cfm?did=2113&26reqId=70 (accessed June 1, 2021).

structured and conducted properly, they can actually advance this mission and purpose.

Frequently, the primary beneficiaries of these services are foreign governments, corporations, universities, and students, all who want and value American higher education. Secondary beneficiaries are members of their communities, who derive social, political, and economic benefits from the services. As for the service venue, it might not be exciting at all. Often, it can be found in the heart of an arid desert or tropical rain forest, thousands of miles away from the nearest wine and cheese bistro.

These services are a "natural" for U.S. colleges and universities. In providing them, they can leverage off their institutional strengths. Some services are not predicated on expertise in any particular field or discipline. They can be performed by subject-matter experts in any area of study, from mathematics to the natural sciences to the social sciences to the arts and humanities. For example, a few years ago, a team of history professors at a mid-Atlantic college conducted a quality assurance review of an Indonesian business school.

Other services, such as technology transfer, require specific technical expertise. Large research universities with highly specialized academic staff, such as MIT, Stanford, and Johns Hopkins, have a competitive edge in this market segment, although smaller research institutions, such as Binghamton, Stony Brook, and the University of West Virginia, have made considerable inroads.[5]

Still other services rely on peculiar functional expertise. They can be performed by non-academic staff with extensive experience in administration, operations, finance, technology, or marketing. For example, several years ago, the library staff of a northeastern college advised their Saudi counterpart on the features and content of electronic databases. They also trained the Saudi librarians in methods for researching the databases.

Thus, depending on the nature of the foreign opportunity, and the inherent strengths of the U.S. service provider, the benefits can accrue to a wide array of institutions—from private liberal arts colleges,[6] to public

---

[5] H. Etzkowitz, and D. Göktepe-Hultén, "De-reifying Technology Transfer Metrics to Address the Stages and Phases of TTO Development." In *University Technology Transfer: The Globalization of Academic Innovation*, edited by S.M. Breznitz and H. Etzkowitz (2016), 86–87; and B.A. Weisbrod, J.P. Ballou, and E.D. Asch, *Mission and Money, Understanding the University* (2008), 155.

[6] Especially those that develop career-oriented programs that leverage off their liberal arts curriculum. See W. Zumeta, "State Policy and Private Higher Education: Past, Present, and Future." In *The Finance of Higher Education: Theory, Research, Policy, and Practice*, edited by M.B. Paulsen and J.B. Smart (2001), 393–395; and, in general, D.W. Breneman, *Liberal Arts Colleges: Thriving, Surviving, or Endangered?* (1994).

research universities, to stand-alone business schools, to specialized technical schools.

Let us look at the various service functions.

Program design and development

Many American colleges and universities offer programs in executive and continuing education.[7] Some also offer extension courses for working adults.[8] These institutions can leverage off their existing expertise to design, develop, and deliver new and exciting programs that cater to an international audience. They can create short courses, seminars, and workshops on best American practices in business, teaching, engineering, or healthcare. They can sponsor regional conferences on economic development, women's rights, cybersecurity, or artificial intelligence. They can host networking events or business roundtables that facilitate group participation, interaction, and discussion.

Institutions weak in executive and continuing education can provide other types of services. They can develop international programs on faculty development, staff training, administrative coaching, and student advising. They can organize field trips and study tours that highlight the cultural, historical, or aesthetic aspects of a particular region or country. They can create "how-to" courses on networking, interviewing, time management, and public presentations. They can translate their existing lectures, courses, or degree programs into Mandarin, Arabic, Portuguese, or Spanish for delivery abroad.

Many such programs are open-enrollment. They are "standardized," and thus can be offered to anyone who meets their eligibility requirements. Others are "customized," i.e., tailored to the specific needs of a particular client or clientele. As such, they may not appeal to the interests of a broad and diverse audience. Most courses are non-credit. Participants who meet their requirements are entitled to a certificate, but not a degree. Some, on the other hand, are for-credit. If the credits are transferable, they can be counted toward a baccalaureate or master's degree.

Modes of delivery vary. They range from in-person instruction, to synchronous online learning, to asynchronous online learning, to hybrid

---

[7] For a discussion of executive and continuing education programs see Weisbrod, Ballou, and Asch, *Mission and Money*, 169–170; and Bok, *Universities in the Marketplace*, 82–83, 166–167.

[8] Weisbrod, Ballou, and Asch, *Mission and Money*.

or blended learning. To understand how these modes of delivery work, consider the following examples.

- As part of an American lecture series, an anthropologist based in Los Angeles flies to Lima, where she addresses a group of museum curators on Inca civilization. This mode of delivery is in-person and contemporaneous. Because it requires foreign travel and accommodation, it is usually the most expensive.
- An economist in Baltimore leads an online discussion on international trade, with Chinese government officials based in Beijing. Because the expert conveys content contemporaneously and online, delivery is synchronous. If the origin and destination are far apart from one another, as in the present case, this mode of delivery poses the greatest time zone challenges.
- An engineer in Houston videotapes a lecture on robotics, which is streamed over the Internet to manufacturers in Mumbai. Because content is conveyed remotely and non-contemporaneously, this mode of delivery is asynchronous. Given the lag time between communication and reception, it is perhaps the least interactive. On the other hand, because learners need not wake up in the middle of the night to interact with other participants, it is perhaps the most convenient.
- At the start of a program, an editor in Chicago flies to Cairo, where she discusses women's rights with Egyptian journalists. Upon returning to Chicago, she continues the discussion online via synchronous chat sessions and asynchronous blogs. Because some content is delivered in-person on-site, while other content is delivered remotely via the Internet, this mode of delivery is hybrid or blended. Though effective in terms of learning, it can pose logistical challenges—such as figuring out where and when to deliver content and how to follow up with on-site delivery. It can also be costly.

In terms of scalability, asynchronous programs are at the top of the list. Because the learning experience is not dependent on space or time, they can accommodate a large group of participants in different places and at different times. On the other hand, because interactivity is diminished, these programs, arguably, are less effective in terms of learning.

In-person instruction is the least scalable. In this mode of delivery, the capacity of the expert to convey content at multiple locations is limited by space and time. Broadening the audience to overcome this limitation (e.g., through the use of large lecture halls or short-circuit TVs) could come at the cost of interactivity.

Hybrid or blended learning offers a happy medium. In this mode of delivery, an institution can leverage off the subject matter expertise of a "master instructor" by utilizing junior academic staff (i.e., "facilitators" or "mentors") to assist him or her. Typically, the master instructor delivers core content, while the facilitators or mentors conduct online discussions. As long as the discussion groups are small and online learning is sub-stantially synchronous, interactivity will not be impaired. Real-time dis-cussions can be supplemented with asynchronous blogs, bulletin boards, quizzes, and group projects that can enhance the learning experience (there is more about online learning in Chapter 8).

Higher education advisory services

Referring to an academic institution as a "consultant" is objectionable to some, because it casts the institution in the light of a "business." So, in def-erence to these "conscientious objectors," let us use the more sanitized term "higher education advisor."

The scope of higher education advisory services is broad. It encompasses activities such as strategic planning, enrollment management, curriculum design and development, student services, personal well-being, quality as-surance, and much more. Like program design and development, these services are a "natural" for U.S. colleges and universities. Not only do these institutions possess the requisite knowledge, skills, expertise, and capabil-ity to deliver them, but they also have *academic credibility*, which gives them a competitive edge over professional services firms.

Who would hire an American college or university for professional advice?—Lots of people, including foreign investors, entrepreneurs, cor-porate executives, and government officials, some of whom are looking to launch a new educational venture. Potential clients also include foreign colleges or universities that are looking to add new academic disciplines or expand into new functional areas.

Typically, the experts who deliver the services are faculty, academic administrators, and/or non-academic staff. Occasionally, they are joined by trustees or alumni who are familiar with or have connections with parties in the host country. Sometimes, the service-providing institution assembles a cross-functional team to deliver the service in collaboration with foreign faculty, staff, and/or administrators. In these situations, the approach is usually collegial.

Consider the case of a prominent U.S. university located in the American Southwest. Stakeholders in a Central American college approached its president with a request that the university assist it in the realm of academic affairs. The president gave the nod, and, with her consent, several university professors took on an advisory role. Specifically, they designed and developed courses modeled after their own, recruited, Spanish-speaking instructors to teach the courses, trained the instructors in interactive, team-based, experiential learning, and coached the instructors while they delivered the courses. Ultimately, these services had a profound impact. They improved the quality of academic affairs at the Central American college, helped develop a cadre of foreign faculty versed in best American teaching practices, enhanced the university's brand throughout Latin America, and opened the door to additional engagements in the region.

Project development and management

In the nineteenth century, the boldest pioneers of global education were American missionaries. In the far corners of the world, they founded colleges and universities that transformed societies and helped build nations. Their efforts greatly impacted the social, political, and economic development of their host countries. Many graduates of the institutions they established became heads of state, chief executive officers, central bank governors, and leaders of international agencies.

The present era is no different from the past in terms of opportunity and calling. What *is* different is context. Today, establishing an institution of higher learning requires not just vision, but also capital and expertise. Foreign investors, rich in financial resources, can provide the capital. U.S. colleges and universities, rich in ideas, can provide the expertise. To be successful, they must be willing to combine the expertise with the capital in such a way as to realize a vision of educational advancement.

Establishing an institution of higher learning is no small feat. As a practical matter, it requires a broad understanding of project development and management. What all these projects have in common is a central theme: *higher education.* This theme is consonant with the mission and purpose of every U.S. college and university.

The projects are diverse. They include entrepreneurship centers, research institutes, computer labs, and business incubators and accelerators. They also include colleges and universities, art museums, medical schools, clinics, hospitals, and sports facilities. Core competencies required to deliver the service include

- planning, design, and development;
- recruiting, staffing, and training; and
- managing start-up, operations, and transfer.

These activities are distinguishable from those incidental to other services in that they are *integral* to the project. Thus, they are inseparable from the project and are usually bundled under the same service agreement.

Typically, there are two phases of a higher education project: start-up and operation. In the start-up phase, the project sponsor (often an investor or real-estate developer) contributes fixed assets, such as land, buildings, and equipment to the venture; the project lender (typically a corporation, foundation, or individual investor) supplies financial capital; and the higher education service provider (usually a well-established college or university) contributes intellectual capital and lends its name to the start-up enterprise. In addition, the service provider obtains the necessary licenses, recruits instructors, administrators, and/or staff for the project, and trains them before the commencement of operations.

"Intellectual capital" consists of the service provider's peculiar know-how and expertise, as are embodied in "academic blueprints" for

- governance, organization, and administration;
- courses, curricula, and programs;
- student recruitment, admissions, and financial aid;
- academic, faculty, and student affairs;
- libraries, laboratories, and other academic resources.

By contributing its intellectual capital, the service provider creates the academic infrastructure of the start-up enterprise, without which it cannot evolve into an academic institution.

In the operational phase, the project lender supplies funds for working capital purposes; administrators and staff take up their roles; if instruction is involved, program participants register for courses; and classes begin. Also in the operational phase, the service provider implements the project plan according to the academic blueprints that it designed; advises administrators and staff in best practices; works with subject-matter experts in the delivery of program content; and conducts periodic quality assurance reviews.

Typically, the professional relationships among the project sponsor, project lender, and higher education service provider are defined in a joint venture agreement. Often, under the terms of the agreement, the service provider receives, in addition to a fixed fee, a financial stake in the start-up enterprise. In addition, the service provider obtains representation on its board of directors.

Herein lies the greatest risk to the academic integrity of the project. Underpowering the service provider could adversely affect its ability to provide sound oversight, ensure educational quality, allocate resources for research, scholarship, and faculty development, and create a culture that is primarily academic in character. As an unintended consequence, the academic infrastructure that it so painstakingly built could gradually erode. Frequently, other stakeholders who lack experience in higher education question the "value added" of costly scholarly research. In addition, they are less willing to tolerate dissent, criticism, and grievances expressed in the name of academic freedom. Some are likely to view the start-up project as just another commercial venture, to be shaped in the image and likeness of their other commercial ventures. Consistent with their conception of how a business should be run, their natural inclination is to create an institution that is primarily *business* in character.

These risks can be minimized in a number of ways:

1. By insisting that the higher education service provider is adequately represented on all governing bodies. Limiting the decision-making authority of the service provider understates the enormous value that it adds to the project by contributing its intellectual capital and by lending its academic brand.
2. By appointing to the board, independent directors with extensive higher education experience. Such a move comports with U.S. accreditation standards and sound governance practices.
3. By designating a representative of the service provider as the "chief academic officer" of the start-up institution during the operational phase. This official should be given exclusive authority over academic, faculty, and student affairs.

These requirements should be set forth in the joint venture agreement. All parties to the venture should explicitly sign-off on them (for more about this see Chapter 8).

Technology transfer

Technology transfer is the process by which the results of pure or applied research are commercialized, or brought to market. It involves licensing intellectual property to one or more business entities, and also supporting these entities with research talent and academic resources. Antiviral vaccines, the Google search engine, cancer treatments—all are products of technology transfer.[9] To the extent that it can add value to the economy, technology transfer can also add value to American colleges and universities.[10]

Revenues from technology transfer take many forms, including royalties, license fees, and option payments. If the transferor acquires an ownership stake in a start-up enterprise, they can also take the form of equity. Without adequate financial, marketing, and commercial support, however, an equity interest could decline in value or yield a relatively low rate of return.[11] That is why it is important to supplement the institution's technological capability with strong financial, marketing, and commercial capability.

Often, within the broader organization, technology transfer is facilitated through a technology transfer office (TTO). This office intermediates between the internal units of the organization and external developers and marketers. Specifically, the TTO identifies promising technologies with practical applications, developed by the units. It also identifies business enterprises, outside the organization, that have the interest, inclination, and resources to bring the technologies to market.

A TTO can facilitate technology transfer in a variety of ways:

- In exchange for royalty payments, it can license an invention to a third party that develops it for commercial use.

---

[9] On technology transfer in general see Breznitz and Etzkowitz, eds, *University Technology Transfer*.

[10] Though potentially limited in scope, the financial benefits of technology transfer are nonetheless lucrative for a handful of universities. See Weisbrod, Ballou, and Asch, *Mission and Money*, 156–158.

[11] M. Feldman and P. Clayton, "The American Experience in University Technology Transfer." In *University Technology Transfer: The Globalization of Academic Innovation*, edited by S.M. Breznitz and H. Etzkowitz (2016), 54; and S.M. Breznitz and H. Etzkowitz, "Making Sense of University Technology Commercialization, Diversity and Adaptation." In: *University Technology Transfer*, 464.

- In return for an equity stake, it can transfer the technology to a subsidiary that develops it with the aid of venture capital.
- In return for royalty payments and/or a financial interest, it can transfer the technology to a joint venture that brings it to fruition.

Each alternative has its advantages, disadvantages, and risks. The advantages of licensing include lower developmental costs and lower business risks. Disadvantages include the higher cost of selling a start-up (and often unproven) technology, and possibly also a lower rate of return. The advantages of a spin-off include acquiring the potential for earnings and stock appreciation. Disadvantages include relatively high investment risks and developmental costs. The advantages of a joint venture include cost- and risk-sharing, as well as enhanced operational capability. Disadvantages include reputational risk, the task of managing a business relationship, and possibly also loss of control to the joint venture partner.[12] In selecting a particular alternative, the transferor should weigh the advantages and disadvantages of each, relative to its own peculiar needs and objectives.

In the United States, the Bayh–Dole Act facilitated the enormous expansion of technology transfer since 1980. Enacted in that year, this federal statute allows non-profit organizations, such as colleges and universities, to retain title to the technology they develop with federal funds. To be eligible, the institution must patent the technology, prefer small business owners in licensing, grant the government a license that it can use throughout the world, share royalties with individual inventors, and meet certain other requirements. The Bayh–Dole Act has fueled the tremendous growth of gross license income since 1990. Aggregate income accruing to U.S. universities ballooned from $131 million in 1990 to $1.1 billion in 2000 to over $2 billion in 2020 (Figure 2.1).

Major areas of technology transfer include the biological, biomedical, and computer sciences; engineering; chemistry; and physics. By implication, large research universities with strengths in these areas are likely to have a competitive advantage.

To operate or not?

So, your institution has successfully built a higher education project—perhaps a foreign research institute. Should it now step in to operate the

---

[12] Weisbrod, Ballou, and Asch, *Mission and Money*, 67–68.

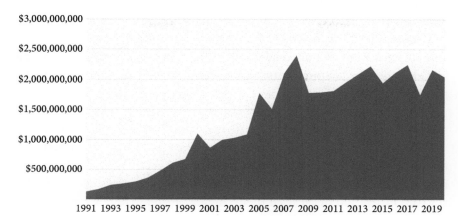

Fig. 2.1 Technology transfer: gross license income received by U.S. universities, 1991–2020.
Source: Association of University Technology Managers. (See Appendix for notes.)

project? The risks of doing so are two-fold: first, if the start-up enterprise struggles, the service provider could get stuck with a hefty bill. Second, if the enterprise fails, the service provider will be perceived as having mismanaged it. Both outcomes could adversely affect the service provider's reputation.

On the other hand, if another party steps in and mismanages the project, its poor performance could also reflect negatively on the service provider, especially if the provider lent its name to the project. The other party might not have the same stake in the start-up enterprise. Or, it might not have lent its name to the venture. Or, its motives might be more "business" than "academic"—which raises a related point: protecting the academic brand.

Protecting the academic brand

A college or university should embark on a joint venture with a business entity with "eyes wide open." It should bear in mind that its joint venture partner will view its academic brand through a commercial lens. The partner might want to exploit the brand solely to generate revenues, without, however, incorporating the normative standards of the academic institution in the institutional make-up of the start-up enterprise. Such a result could ultimately tarnish the brand.

Consider the case of a prominent U.S. liberal arts college. Several years ago, it contracted with a real-estate developer to create a foreign university in the U.S. college's "image and likeness"—which implied, for all practical purposes, that the foreign university would incorporate the standards, policies, and procedures of the U.S. college in its operations and academic affairs. As part of the agreement, the U.S. college promised to lend its brand to the start-up university; also, to supply it with academic blueprints that would pave the way for its U.S. accreditation. The developer, for its part, promised to contribute land, buildings, and equipment to the start-up enterprise; also, to sponsor it for state regulatory and licensing purposes.

Over time, both parties made good on their promises. The developer built the university in a technology park under its control. The U.S. college lent its brand. It supplied the requisite academic blueprints. However, the start-up institution never used them. In fact, it eventually discarded them altogether and adopted what might be pejoratively called "non-academic footprints," patterned after the practices of other foreign universities in the country. Consequently, despite an expectation to the contrary, the policies, procedures, and standards of the U.S. college were never incorporated in the institutional make-up of the start-up university.

The end-result was the creation of a foreign university, inspired by the local practices of non-U.S. entities, which institution never evolved into the "image and likeness" of the U.S. college, despite having been strengthened commercially and financially by its academic brand. Needless to say, the brand suffered.

Such a result can be avoided through a series of measures:

> *First, contract restrictions on how the foreign client or start-up institution can use the brand.* These restrictions should reflect the true nature of the collaborative arrangement. Terms of association that imply that the U.S. college or university "controls" or "is on par with" the start-up institution should be avoided. Such would include any statement or insinuation that the start-up institution is "sponsored by" or "in partnership with" the U.S. college or university. On the other hand, terms of association that connote arm's-length dealing are perfectly acceptable. Thus, it *is* ok to say that the start-up institution is "advised by," "under the guidance of," or "mentored by" the U.S. college or university.

> *Second, regular and continuous audits of how the foreign client and start-up institution actually use the brand.* All marketing material pertaining to the start-up institution should be reviewed periodically by the U.S. college or university. This includes website content, targeted solicitations, public advertisements, logos, tag lines, and

brochures—in print and electronic form, in English and in any foreign language. Furthermore, the U.S. college or university should be given unfettered access to all marketing material. This right of access should be stipulated in the joint venture agreement or in a separate intellectual property agreement.

Third, periodic quality assurance reviews of the start-up institution. The purpose of these reviews is to assess the degree to which (a) the start-up institution's internal affairs meet the service provider's academic standards, (b) its practices comport with the service provider's ethical standards, and (c) its culture reflects the service provider's core values. The reviews should be conducted on-site, in-person, by a team of professionals approved by the service provider. In addition, the start-up institution should be held accountable for addressing any institutional shortcomings or deviations within a reasonable timeframe. It should be required to (a) seek the advice of the U.S. college or university on how to make up for any shortcoming, (b) follow the recommendations of the U.S. college or university concerning how to do so, and (c) allocate sufficient human and financial resources to implement the recommendations.

Fourth, the creation of a mechanism to monitor the progress of implementation. A verbal promise alone will not be sufficient to ensure that the recommendations of the U.S. college or university will be followed; nor will periodic progress reports, which, more often than not, are subjective, uncritical, and self-serving. To ensure that the start-up institution actually makes good on its word, the promise or report should be supplemented with an effective monitoring mechanism. It could take the form of a U.S.-based task force that conducts follow-up visits to the start-up institution. Or it could take the form of an observer-on-the-ground who witnesses activities at the start-up institution first-hand. The observer could be either a representative of the U.S. college or university, or an independent third party acceptable to both the service provider and the foreign sponsor. A representative is preferable, for three reasons: first, he or she will have an interest in preserving the brand of the U.S. college or university. Second, he or she is likely to be in constant contact with its officials and will be in a better position to advise the start-up institution on the service provider's expectations. Third, having experienced the academic life of the U.S. college or university, he or she will have a good idea of what the service provider's "image and likeness" actually means.

Competition and market entry

In overseas markets, the identity of potential competitors of U.S. higher education service providers depends on the market segment specific to the services. In program design and development, competitors are likely to be European business schools with a strong brand, such as IESE, IMD, INSEAD, SDA Bocconi, HEC Paris, and London Business School. In higher education advisory services, they are likely to be private firms, such as Accenture, Bain, EY, Deloitte, McKinsey, and Pricewaterhouse–Coopers. In project development and management, U.K. institutions, such as Heriot-Watt and the University of London, Australian universities, such as Wollongong and Monash, and Indian institutions, such as Indian Institute of Technology and S.P. Jain, are likely to be major players. In technology transfer, they are likely to be European research universities, such as KU Leuven, Imperial College London, University of Cambridge, Federal Institute of Technology in Lausanne, and University of Erlangen–Nuremberg.

The ease of market entry will depend on the type of service to be offered, the functional area to which it relates, and the organizational capability of the service provider. Barriers to entering the market for higher education advisory services are relatively low. Because these services rely primarily on human talent, small private liberal arts colleges can compete effectively with large public research universities. On the other hand, because of the massive investment required, access to the market for technology transfer is somewhat restricted. In this segment, what matters most is research capability in highly technical fields, such as the applied sciences, engineering, and information technology.[13] Although the broad market for program design and development is fairly accessible, the specific segment relating to executive education is less so. Institutions that dominate the U.S. market for executive education, such as Harvard, Stanford, and Duke, are likely to have a competitive edge in corresponding foreign markets. Finally, because of the substantial resources needed to build a higher education project, entry into the market for project development and management is likely to be limited. Colleges and universities with significant financial and planning capability, as well as management bandwidth, will have a competitive edge.

---

[13] For a general discussion see R.L. Geiger, *Knowledge and Money: Research Universities and the Paradox of the Marketplace* (2004).

Organizational structure

Successful market entry depends on the ability of an institution to marshal its resources to take advantage of overseas opportunities. This, in turn, hinges on organizational structure. Ideally, this structure should bring together, in a common enterprise, four major stakeholders: faculty, administrators, staff, and trustees. Each has a distinctive role. Each makes a valuable contribution to the success of the enterprise. Let's look at the prototypical structure of a traditional U.S. college or university.

1. Faculty

The single most valuable intangible asset of any college or university is its faculty.[14] They are the source of its intellectual capital. They are on the front line of teaching, research, and service. Individually, faculty are responsible for supplying content, selecting instructional materials, delivering courses, and assessing academic progress. Collectively, they play a major role in setting educational standards, defining degree requirements, designing programs and curricula, and formulating policies relating to faculty qualifications, rank, promotion, course loads, and research. In the classroom, faculty are masters of their own destiny. Highly individualistic, they need space and freedom to flourish.[15] Try to subordinate them and they will rebel.

2. Administrators

College and university administrators are responsible for managing academic, faculty, and student affairs, which encompass student recruitment, admissions, registration, advising, accreditation, student services, and program coordination. They are also responsible for handling organizational matters, which include human resources, operations, facilities, marketing, and budgeting. Academic administrators, such as the provost, deans, and associate deans, are drawn from the ranks of faculty. Typically, they have had extensive experience in teaching, research, and service, a good

---

[14] See Veblen, *The Higher Learning in America*, 109.

[15] Cf. Veblen, "[T]he exigencies of the higher learning require that the scholars and scientists must be left quite free to follow their own bent in conducting their own work. In the nature of things this work cannot be carried on effectually under coercive rule . . . Tradition and present necessity alike demand that the body of scholars and scientists who make up the university must be vested with full powers of self-direction, without ulterior consideration. A university can remain a corporation of learning, de facto, on no other basis." Veblen, *The Higher Learning in America*, 102–103.

knowledge of academic, faculty, and student affairs, and a profound appreciation for the values of the academy.

3. Non-academic staff

Non-academic staff are "laymen" engaged in functional activities other than teaching and research. They are the librarians, bursars, counselors, recruiters, cooks, and repairmen who support and sustain college and university operations. In the areas of admissions, the registry, student services, financial management, and information technology, they are the driving force behind the organization—cogs in the wheel that make the engine work. Many are dedicated professionals or highly skilled technicians. Some have had successful careers in business, industry, or government. Yet, they are the most undervalued of all internal constituencies. In organizational decision-making, non-academic staff generally take a back seat to faculty, administrators, and trustees. In institutional governance, they play a relatively minor role.

4. Trustees

Trustees and directors (regents in a public university system) are responsible for overseeing the management of the educational enterprise. They approve annual budgets, major strategic initiatives, and new degree programs. They are appointed for a variety of reasons, including substantial financial contributions, important industry connections, unique business expertise, and high professional stature. Some are alumni, motivated by an ardent desire to give back to the *alma mater* that helped them launch their careers. Others are professionals, non-alumni, who are committed to the financial success of the enterprise. Still others are educators, focused on preserving the institution's academic integrity. Each brings to the board a unique perspective on the major challenges facing the institution.

Typically, those with a business background view these challenges from a business perspective. Their adage seems to be, "whatever works in business will also work in academia."[16] Those with an academic background view

---

[16] Veblen was harsh on the likes of these directors, whom he regarded as useless and intrusive: "[I]t should be no difficult matter to show that these governing boards of businessmen commonly are quite useless to the university for any businesslike purpose. Indeed, except for a stubborn prejudice to the contrary, the fact should readily be seen that the boards are of no material use in any connection; their sole effectual function being to interfere with the academic management in matters that are not of the nature of business, and that lie outside their competence and outside the range of their habitual

these challenges from an academic perspective. Their intuition tells them, "whatever works in business will ultimately corrupt academia." At the end of the day, all stakeholders, regardless of perspective, must set aside their differences and find common ground for the sake of institutional stability, functionality, and progress. More often than not, they do so.

Governance

In traditional colleges and universities, institutional decision-making is based on a system of shared governance. This system is predicated on a division of authority among the president, faculty, and board. By convention, the president has executive authority over all institutional affairs. He or she manages the enterprise in close collaboration with the board. The board is responsible for corporate governance. It oversees the strategic, financial, and operational direction of the enterprise. The faculty has an important voice in academic, faculty, and student affairs.[17] Together with the provost, it has authority over courses and curricula; degree requirements; academic policies, procedures, and standards; faculty qualifications, rank, and promotion; teaching, research, and scholarship.

In many institutions, the faculty-at-large or its delegates form a senate or council. The resolutions of this body rise to the level of "recommendations," entitled to great weight and respect by the administration. In higher education, it is often said that through the system of shared governance, the faculty owns the curriculum, the president navigates the ship, and the board sets its course. There is much truth in this adage, especially where stakeholders are both empowered and proactive in the life of the enterprise.[18]

interest . . . [S]ince their complexion has been changed by the substitution of businessmen in the place of ecclesiastics, they have ceased to exercise any function other than a bootless meddling with academic matters which they do not understand. The sole ground of their retention appears to be an unreflecting deferential concession to the usages of corporate organization and control, such as have been found advantageous for the pursuit of private gain by businessmen banded together in the exploitation of joint-stock companies with limited liability." Veblen, *The Higher Learning in America*, 89–90.

[17] Cf. Veblen: "By tradition the faculty is the keeper of the academic interests of the university and makes up a body of loosely-bound noncompetitive co-partners, with no view to strategic team play and no collective ulterior ambition, least of all with a view to engrossing the trade. By tradition, and indeed commonly by explicit proviso, the conduct of the university's academic affairs vests formally in the president, with the advice and consent of the faculty, or of the general body of senior members of the faculty." Veblen, *The Higher Learning in America*, 99.

[18] In higher education, it is not uncommon for the academic staff to be organized into a union. Such an arrangement often sets the interests of faculty, as employees, at odds with those of administrators,

Summary

American higher education talent can be utilized to deliver services that non-U.S. nationals want and value. These services go well beyond study abroad. They include program design and development, higher education advisory services, project development and management, and technology transfer. They are a "natural" for U.S. colleges and universities, because in providing the services, these institutions can leverage off their inherent strengths.

Services, however, are only part of the equation. Another element is domestic markets. Both lie on the American side of the Great Chasm. To some extent, the inability of domestic markets to sustain the current level of services has contributed to an abundance of American higher education talent. Let us explore why.

---

as management. In extreme cases, it transforms the nature of their relationship from collegial to adversarial. For example, in a unionized environment, the provost, who by tradition is supposed to be a faculty advocate, represents management. In the collective bargaining process, one might find him or her sitting at the negotiating table across from fellow academics, demanding concessions from them.

3

A Higher Education Sector on the Edge: Part I

This chapter turns to the American side of the Great Chasm (i.e., the "supply side"). Reflecting the book's materialist approach, it examines the economic substructure of the U.S. higher education sector (the "realm of finances"), from which arises the ideological superstructure of American higher education (the "realm of ideas"). The chapter identifies elements that strengthen this substructure, traces their historical evolution, and describes the profiles of institutions that make up the sector. The description is intended to give the reader an idea of the rich diversity of institutions that constitute the "vast majority" of American colleges and universities. The ranks of these institutions go beyond the elite few.

> Universities share one characteristic with compulsive gamblers and exiled royalty: there is never enough money to satisfy their desires.[1]
>
> Derek Bok, former President of Harvard University

A general malaise

The Global Pandemic shook the U.S. higher education sector by its very foundation. Until the onset of the crisis, the sector had been expanding. Despite occasional setbacks, the financial condition of most U.S. colleges and universities had been stable. In some circles, there was exuberance and optimism. They thought the good days would never end.

Now, almost everywhere, there is pessimism and foreboding. Talk about doom, gloom, and massive disruption. The full extent of the crisis will not be known for years. Yet, it will undoubtedly have a lasting impact on American higher education. The Global Pandemic infected the heart and soul of the U.S. higher education sector, attacking public and private

---

[1] D. Bok, *Universities in the Marketplace: The Commercialization of Higher Education* (2003), 7.

Bridging the Gap between the Abundance of American Higher Education Talent and the Immense Foreign Demand for It.
Richard J. Joseph, Oxford University Press. © Richard J. Joseph (2022). DOI: 10.1093/oso/9780192848307.003.0004

institutions alike, disrupting their operations, calling into question their traditional modes of delivery, and threatening their financial viability.

Even before the crisis, however, storm clouds loomed over the horizon. They reflect social, political, and demographic trends that portend a decline in domestic enrollments and a slackening of economic growth. They also reflect the vagaries of the business cycle that occasionally result in the lowering of revenues below the threshold of escalating costs. As the most clairvoyant knew well, the convergence of these factors could give rise to a "perfect storm" that would shatter the foundation of a sector on the edge. That storm may have arrived as a result of the economic havoc wreaked by the Global Pandemic.

The future of the U.S. higher education sector remains uncertain. It will depend on the *ability* of its participants to weather the storm. It will also depend on their *willingness* to take advantage of new and exciting opportunities. Many such opportunities lie on the other side of the Great Chasm. Taking advantage of them will require new attitudes, practices, and approaches, major organizational reforms, a different *modus operandi*, and a cultural revolution of sorts. No doubt, these changes will take time, effort, and patience to come into being. In the meantime, as American colleges and universities emerge from the crisis, they should start planning ahead. They should position themselves strategically for a new paradigm in higher education.

To convey a sense of the nature and magnitude of the challenges that lie before them, let us proceed as follows: first, we will examine the structure of the U.S. higher education sector. Next, we will focus on its economic foundation, or "substructure." Lastly, we will review the financial condition of institutions within the sector, analyze the sources of revenues and classes of expenditures that account for this condition, and bring to light the financial pillars of American higher education.

The U.S. higher education sector

Structurally, the U.S. higher education sector is fragmented.[2] It consists of a variety of institutions of different control types, and with different en-

---

[2] For an account of the evolution of the U.S. higher education sector see B.A. Weisbrod, J.P. Ballou, and E.D. Asch, *Mission and Money, Understanding the University* (2008), chapter 2.

Number of institutions

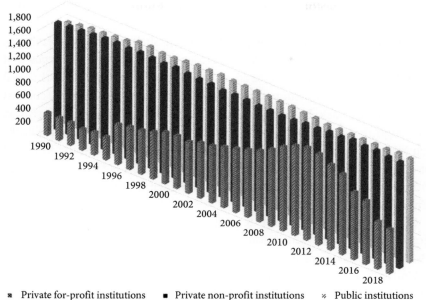

æ Private for-profit institutions   ■ Private non-profit institutions   ⍭ Public institutions

Fig. 3.1 U.S. post-secondary degree-granting institutions, 1990–2019.
Source: U.S. Department of Education, Institute of Education Sciences, National Center for Education Statistics. (See Appendix for notes.)

rollment levels.[3] Approximately 40% are public and 60% are private. Of the latter, about 65% are non-profit and 35% are for-profit (see Figure 3.1). Of the total, about a third confer only associate degrees, while two-thirds confer baccalaureate degrees. Most of the former are two-year junior colleges and special-focus schools. Most of the latter are traditional four-year colleges and universities.

Sector participants include elite private institutions, such as Harvard, Yale, Princeton, MIT, and Stanford; public research universities, such as UCLA, Berkeley, Michigan, and Georgia Tech; and prestigious liberal arts colleges, such as Amherst, Williams, Wellesley, and Swarthmore. They also include specialty schools, such as the Olin College of Engineering, Rhode Island School of Design, The Juilliard School, and Galen College of Nursing; faith-based establishments, such as Nazarene Bible College, St.

---

[3] U.S. Department of Education, Institute for Education Sciences, National Center for Education Statistics (hereinafter referred to as "NCES"), Table 317.10 "Degree-granting postsecondary institutions, by control and level of institution," *Digest of Education Statistics* (annual issues, 1990–2020).

John's Seminary, Hebrew Theological College, and Mid-Atlantic Christian University; and historically black colleges and universities, such as Spelman, Howard, Tuskegee, and Morehouse.

Within their ranks are for-profit entities, such as the University of Phoenix, DeVry, Strayer, and Walden; four-year community colleges that offer baccalaureate degrees, such as Walla Walla, Valencia, Austin, and Snow; and two-year junior colleges that confer associate degrees, such as Harper, Saddleback, Eastern Idaho, and the New Mexico Military Institute. Although the vast majority offer on-site programs, some, such as Southern New Hampshire, Western Governors, and Liberty, are at the forefront of online programs. What they all have in common is this: they all provide post-secondary instruction and training within the boundaries of the United States.

Currently, the number of U.S. post-secondary, degree-granting institutions is about 4,000.[4] This number represents a 32% increase from that for 1975, and a 7% increase from the figure for 1995.

Underlying the increase are divergent subsectoral trends. Although the number of for-profits rose steadily from 1995 to 2012, it has fallen by over 50% since the latter year. This drop is associated with several factors, including poor placement rates, student loan defaults, adverse publicity, and dwindling enrollments. During the same period, the number of private non-profit colleges and universities generally held steady. Today, in absolute terms, they are roughly on par with public colleges and universities.

As for institutional size, the sector can be broken down into three major segments: "small establishments," with enrollments of less than 500 students; "mid-size establishments," with enrollments between 500 and 5,000 students, and "large establishments," with enrollments more than 5,000 students.[5] Private for-profits dominate the first segment; private non-profits, the second; and publics, the third. Foremost among the smaller establishments are junior colleges, the likes of Deep Springs, Miles, and Bay Mills; and special-focus trade, technical, and professional schools, such as the Mayo Clinic College of Medicine and Science, Island Drafting and

---

[4] NCES, Table 317.10, *Digest of Education Statistics* (annual issues, 1990–2020). Including branch campuses, which are counted as separate entities.
[5] NCES, Table 317.40 "Number of degree-granting postsecondary institutions and enrollment in these institutions, by enrollment size, control, and classification of institution," *Digest of Education Statistics* (annual issues, 1990–2020).

Technical Institute, and Gemini School of Visual Arts. Among the mid-size entities are four-year colleges and universities that award baccalaureate and master's degrees, such as Carlton, Rollins, St. Ambroise, and the U.S. Air Force Academy. Leading the pack of large institutions are public research universities with doctoral programs, such as Texas A&M and Ohio State; also, sprawling community colleges, such as Miami Dade, and for-profit institutions that offer online courses, such as Capella. (See Figures 3.2, 3.3, and 3.4.)

The market for U.S. higher education can be broken down into segments, each corresponding to a particular degree, discipline, and geographic area.[6] Thus, there are segments for associate, bachelor's, master's, and doctoral degrees, further subdivided into engineering, economics, fine arts, and other disciplines, and broken down even further into regional, state, and local markets. This pattern is largely shaped by student preferences.

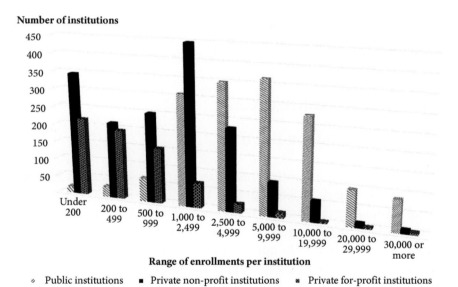

Fig. 3.2 U.S. post-secondary degree-granting institutions, numbers by control and enrollments, fall 2019.

Source: U.S. Department of Education, Institute of Education Sciences, National Center for Education Statistics. (See Appendix for notes.)

[6] R.K. Toutkoushian and M.B. Paulsen, *Economics of Higher Education: Background, Concepts, and Applications* (2016), 286–287.

Aggregate sectoral enrollments

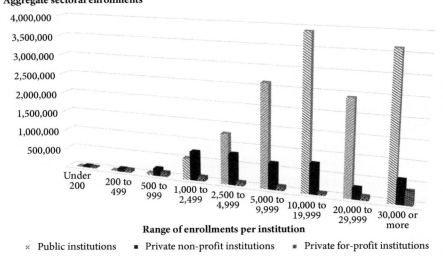

Fig. 3.3 U.S. post-secondary degree-granting institutions, enrollments by control and size, fall 2019.

Source: U.S. Department of Education, Institute of Education Sciences, National Center for Education Statistics. (See Appendix for notes.)

The economic substructure

Overall financial condition

To characterize an academic enterprise as a "business" seems heretical, especially in light of its lofty mission. Yet, at the end of the day, its institutional character is business-like in many respects.[7] For one, it must incur periodic costs to sustain its operations. For another, it must generate sufficient revenues to cover its operating expenses. In addition, it must invest in buildings and equipment to support its core activities. Finally, and most importantly, it must generate a profit—"surplus," if you will—to maintain its financial viability. So, notwithstanding our regard for the primacy of this mission, we must ultimately come to terms with the business-like character of an academic enterprise.

Bear in mind that accounting standards that guide the determination of financial value are different for public and private institutions. For public

---

[7] Weisbrod, Ballou, and Asch, *Mission and Money*, 37–38.

Number of institutions

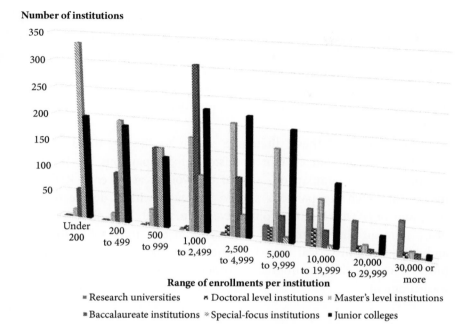

Fig. 3.4 U.S. post-secondary degree-granting institutions, numbers by classification and size, fall 2019.

Source: U.S. Department of Education, Institute of Education Sciences, National Center for Education Statistics. (See Appendix for notes.)

institutions, these standards are set by the Government Accounting Standards Board (GASB); for private institutions, by the Financial Accounting Standards Board (FASB). Rules-related differences make comparisons of contemporaneous *inter*-subsector data difficult (e.g., comparing total expenditures for the public subsector in Fiscal Year (FY) 2020 with total expenditures for the private subsector in FY 2020).

Moreover, within each accounting system, standards change over time. Although they have been fairly constant throughout most of the New Millennium, pre- and post-2003 GASB standards and pre- and post-1995 FASB standards differ substantially. GASB Statement No. 34 (issued in June 1999, to be effective for all public entities after June 2003) changed the manner in which capital assets are reported, as well as the content and format of financial statements.[8] FASB Statement No. 124 (issued in

---

[8] Government Accounting Standards Board, Statement No. 34 "Basic Financial Statements—And Management's Discussion and Analysis—For State and Local Governments," June 1999, https://

November 1995, to be effective for all private entities after December 1995) changed the way in which investments and unrealized gains and losses are reported.[9] Furthermore, account descriptions, particularly for certain classes of expenditures, have varied. These changes make comparisons of historical *intra*-subsector data difficult (e.g., comparing pre-FY 2003 expenditures of the public subsector with post-FY 2003 expenditures of the public subsector).

Because many of these differences relate to timing, these disparities do not mean that current or historical comparisons are impossible, or that such comparisons should be avoided at all cost. Rather, it means that such comparisons should be made with a degree of caution, and only with the foregoing caveats in mind. One should always bear in mind that comparing contemporaneous inter-subsector data and comparing historical intra-subsector data makes sense only for the purpose of deriving an imprecise "order of magnitude," not a precise measurement.

Accounting for financial condition

Revenues

Within the U.S. higher education sector, major sources of revenue are tuition and fees; government appropriations, grants, and contracts; private gifts and grants; and investments (as in the case of endowment funds) (see Table 3.1 for an explanation of revenue terms).[10] Of these sources, tuition and fees is the most substantial. It accounts for a fifth of the total revenues of public institutions and over a third of the total revenues of private non-profit institutions[11] (see Figures 3.5 and 3.6).

---

www.gasb.org/jsp/gasb/document_c/documentpage?cid=1176160029121&accepteddisclaimer=true (accessed June 15, 2021).

[9] Financial Accounting Standards Board, Statement No. 124 "Accounting for Certain Investments Held by Not-for-Profit Organizations," November 1995, https://www.fasb.org/st/index.shtml (accessed June 15, 2021).

[10] For a discussion of these revenue sources see Toutkoushian and Paulsen, *Economics of Higher Education*, 241, 243–245. For a discussion of historical trends to 1995, primary sources of data, and limitations on their use see R.K. Toutkoushian, "Trends in Revenues and Expenditures for Public and Private Higher Education." In *The Finance of Higher Education: Theory, Research, Policy, and Practice*, edited by M.B. Paulsen and J.B. Smart (2001), 16–33.

[11] NCES, Table 333.10 "Revenues of public degree-granting postsecondary institutions, by source of revenue and level of institution" and Table 333.40 "Total revenue of private nonprofit degree-granting postsecondary institutions, by source of funds and level of institution," *Digest of Education Statistics 2020*. As of the date of this writing, more recent revenue data have not been released.

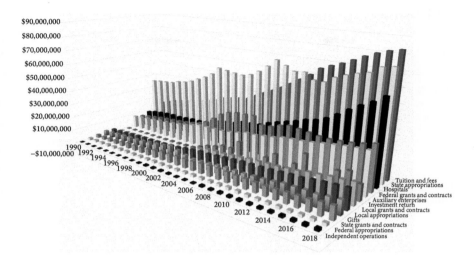

Fig. 3.5 Sources of revenue in thousands of current dollars, U.S. public post-secondary degree-granting institutions, 1990–2018.

Source: U.S. Department of Education, Institute of Education Sciences, National Center for Education Statistics. (See Appendix for notes.)

Table 3.1 Table of terms—revenues

Type of revenue	Total revenues for the essential education activities of the institution
Core revenues: private for-profit institutions	Core revenues for private for-profit institutions reporting under FASB standards include tuition and fees; government appropriations (federal, state, and local); government grants and contracts; private grants and contracts; net investment income; sales and services of educational activities; and other sources. In general, core revenues exclude revenues from auxiliary enterprises (e.g., bookstores, dormitories), hospitals, and independent operations.
Core revenues: private non-profit institutions	Core revenues for private non-profit institutions reporting under FASB standards include tuition and fees; government appropriations (federal, state, and local); government grants and contracts; private gifts, grants, and contracts; investment return; sales and services of educational activities; and other sources.
Core revenues: public institutions	Core revenues for public institutions reporting under GASB standards include tuition and fees; government appropriations (federal, state, and local); government grants and contracts; private gifts, grants, and contracts; investment income; other operating and non-operating sources; and other revenues and additions.

Continued

Table 3.1 *Continued*

Type of revenue	Total revenues for the essential education activities of the institution
Auxiliary enterprise revenues	Revenues generated by or collected from the auxiliary enterprise operations of the institution that exist to furnish a service to students, faculty, or staff, and that charge a fee that is directly related to, although not necessarily equal to, the cost of the service. Auxiliary enterprises are managed as essentially self-supporting activities. Examples are residence halls, food services, student health services, intercollegiate athletics, college unions, college stores, and movie theaters.
Gifts	Revenues received from gifts or contributions as non-exchange transactions. These include bequests, promises to give (pledges), gifts from an affiliated organization or a component unit not blended or consolidated, and income from funds held in irrevocable trusts or distributable at the direction of the trustees of the trusts.
Government appropriations	Revenues received by an institution through acts of a legislative body, except grants and contracts. These funds are for meeting current operating expenses and not for specific projects or programs. The most common example is a state's general appropriation. Appropriations primarily to fund capital assets are classified as capital appropriations.
Grants and contracts	Revenues from governmental agencies and non-governmental parties that are for specific research projects, other types of programs, or general institutional operations (if not government appropriations). Examples are research projects, training programs, student financial assistance, and similar activities for which amounts are received or expenses are reimbursable under the terms of a grant or contract, including amounts to cover both direct and indirect expenses. These include Pell Grants and reimbursement for costs of administering federal financial aid programs.
Investment income	Revenues derived from the institution's investments, including investments of endowment funds. Such income may take the form of interest income, dividend income, rental income, or royalty income and includes both realized and unrealized gains and losses.
Investment return	Income from assets including dividends, interest earnings, royalties, rent, gains (losses), etc.
Sales and services of educational activities	Revenues from the sales of goods or services that are incidental to the conduct of instruction, research, or public service. Examples include film rentals, sales of scientific and literary publications, testing services, university presses, dairy products, machine shop products, data processing services, cosmetology services, and sales of handcrafts prepared in classes.

Source: U.S. Department of Education, Institute for Education Services, National Center for Education Statistics, IPEDS 2020–2021 Data Collection System, Glossary, https://surveys.nces.ed.gov/ipeds/public/glossary.

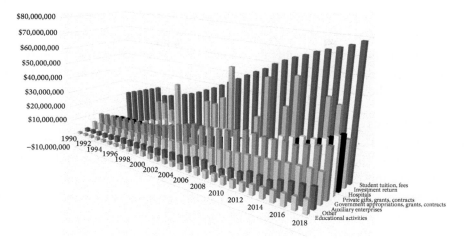

Fig. 3.6 Sources of revenue in thousands of current dollars, U.S. private non-profit post-secondary degree-granting institutions, 1990–2018.

Source: U.S. Department of Education, Institute of Education Sciences, National Center for Education Statistics. (See Appendix for notes.)

The share of each source in the total revenue mix has changed noticeably over time.[12] Since the early-1990s, both public and private entities have grown more dependent on tuition and fee revenues.[13] Public institutions have grown less dependent on state funding, while private institutions have grown less dependent on government funding in general.[14]

Contributing to changes in the compositional mix are several factors, including fluctuations in the economy, the vagaries of financial markets, demographic trends, and institutional efforts to diversify sources of revenue.[15] Also at play are competing pressures on state budgets, a growing reluctance on the part of legislators to fund higher education expenditures *carte blanche*, and their preference for providing financial aid directly to

[12] See Toutkoushian and Paulsen, *Economics of Higher Education*, 239, 245; and Toutkoushian, "Trends in Revenues and Expenditures," *The Finance of Higher Education*, 22.

[13] For public entities, the share of tuition and fees in their total revenue mix increased from about 16% in 2003 to nearly 20% in 2018. For private non-profit entities, the corresponding share increased from 29% to 32%. NCES, Tables 333.10 and 333.40, *Digest of Education Statistics 2020*.

[14] For public institutions, the share of state grants, contracts, and appropriations in their total revenue mix declined from about 28% in 2003 to roughly 21% in 2018. For private institutions, the share of government gifts, grants, and contracts in their total revenue mix fell from nearly 15% in 2003 to about 12% in 2018. NCES, Tables 333.10 and 333.40, *Digest of Education Statistics 2020*.

[15] See R.K. Toutkoushian and M.B. Paulsen, *Economics of Higher Education*, 231–274; Weisbrod, Ballou, and Asch, *Mission and Money*, 16; and Toutkoushian, "Trends in Revenues and Expenditures," *The Finance of Higher Education*, 22–25

students.[16] The scaling back of government funding, coupled with a rise in the level of tuition rates, reflects the growing privatization of American higher education. Neoliberals rationalize this trend in terms of equity: because private citizens benefit more from higher education than does the state, they should bear a greater part of the burden.[17]

Expenditures

The principal categories of expenditure and expense include instruction, institutional support, and research. "Instruction" encompasses faculty compensation. "Institutional support" includes the salaries of administrative, financial, and operational staff. "Research" encompasses the scholarly endeavors of both individuals and the institution as a whole (see Table 3.2 for an explanation of expense terms). Of these expenditures, instruction is

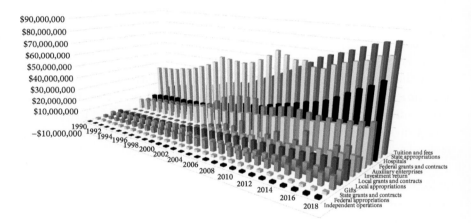

Fig. 3.7 Classes of expenditure in thousands of current dollars, U.S. public post-secondary degree-granting institutions, 1990–2018.

Source: U.S. Department of Education, Institute of Education Sciences, National Center for Education Statistics. (See Appendix for notes.)

[16] W. Zumeta, "State Policy and Private Higher Education: Past, Present, and Future." In The Finance of Higher Education: Theory, Research, Policy, and Practice, edited by M.B. Paulsen and J.B. Smart (2001), 380–383.

[17] E.P. St. John and M.B. Paulsen, "The Finance of Higher Education: Implications for Theory, Research, Policy, and Practice," In *The Finance of Higher Education: Theory, Research, Policy, and Practice*, edited by M.B. Paulsen and J.B. Smart (2001), 348; and Toutkoushian and Paulsen, *Economics of Higher Education*, 199–230.

Table 3.2 Table of terms—expenses

Type of expense	Total expenses for the essential education activities of the institution
Core expenses: private for-profit and non-profit institutions	Core expenses for FASB (primarily private non-profit and for-profit) institutions include expenses on instruction, research, public service, academic support, student services, institutional support, net grant aid to students, and other expenses. For both FASB and GASB institutions, core expenses exclude expenses for auxiliary enterprises (e.g., bookstores, dormitories), hospitals, and independent operations.
Core expenses: public institutions	Core expenses for public institutions reporting under GASB standards include expenses for instruction, research, public service, academic support, student services, institutional support, scholarships and fellowships, and other operating and non-operating expenses.
Academic support	A functional expense category that includes expenses of activities and services that support the institution's primary missions of instruction, research, and public service. It includes the retention, preservation, and display of educational materials (e.g., libraries, museums, and galleries); organized activities that provide support services to the academic functions of the institution (e.g., a demonstration school associated with a college of education, or veterinary and dental clinics if their primary purpose is to support the instructional program); media such as audiovisual services; academic administration (including academic deans but not department chairpersons); and formally organized and separately budgeted academic personnel development and course and curriculum development expenses.
Auxiliary enterprises	Expenses for essentially self-supporting operations of the institution that exist to furnish a service to students, faculty, or staff, and that charge a fee that is directly related to, although not necessarily equal to, the cost of the service. Examples are residence halls, food services, student health services, intercollegiate athletics (only if essentially self-supporting), college unions, college stores, faculty and staff parking, and faculty housing.
Hospital services	Expenses associated with a hospital operated by the postsecondary institution (but not as a component unit) and reported as a part of the institution. This classification includes nursing expenses, other professional services, general services, administrative services, and fiscal services.
Institutional support	A functional expense category that includes expenses for the day-to-day operational support of the institution. This encompasses expenses for general administrative services, central executive-level activities concerned with management and long-range planning, legal and fiscal operations, space management, employee personnel and records, logistical services such as purchasing and printing, and public relations and development.

Continued

Table 3.2 *Continued*

Type of expense	Total expenses for the essential education activities of the institution
Instruction	A functional expense category that includes expenses of the colleges, schools, departments, and other instructional divisions of the institution and expenses for departmental research and public service that are not separately budgeted. This encompasses general academic instruction, occupational and vocational instruction, community education, preparatory and adult basic education, and regular, special, and extension sessions. It also includes expenses for both credit and non-credit activities. It excludes expenses for academic administration where the primary function is administration (e.g., academic deans).
Public service	A functional expense category that includes expenses for activities established primarily to provide non-instructional services beneficial to individuals and groups external to the institution. Examples are conferences, institutes, general advisory services, reference bureaus, and similar services provided to particular sectors of the community. This function includes expenses for community services, cooperative extension services, and public broadcasting services.
Research	A functional expense category that includes expenses for activities specifically organized to produce research outcomes and commissioned by an agency either external to the institution or separately budgeted by an organizational unit within the institution. The category includes institutes and research centers and individual and project research. This function does not include non-research sponsored programs (e.g., training programs).
Scholarships and fellowships	That portion of scholarships and fellowships granted that exceeds the amount applied to institutional charges such as tuition and fees or room and board. The amount reported as expense excludes allowances and discounts. The FASB survey uses the term "net grants in aid to students" rather than "scholarships and fellowships."
Student services	A functional expense category that includes expenses for admissions, registrar activities, and activities whose primary purpose is to contribute to students' emotional and physical well-being and to their intellectual, cultural, and social development outside the context of the formal instructional program. Examples include student activities, cultural events, student newspapers, intramural athletics, student organizations, supplemental instruction outside the normal administration, and student records. Intercollegiate athletics and student health services may also be included except when operated as self-supporting auxiliary enterprises.

Source: U.S. Department of Education, Institute for Education Services, National Center for Education Statistics, IPEDS 2020–2021 Data Collection System, Glossary, https://surveys.nces.ed.gov/ipeds/public/glossary.

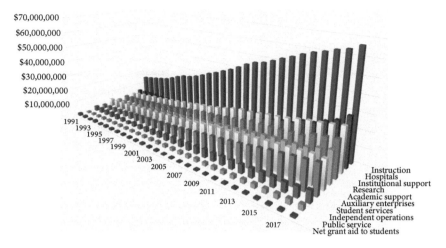

Fig. 3.8 Classes of expenditure in thousands of current dollars, U.S. private post-secondary degree-granting institutions, 1990–2018.

Source: U.S. Department of Education, Institute of Education Sciences, National Center for Education Statistics. (See Appendix for notes.)

the most substantial. For both public and private institutions, it accounts for about a third of total operating expenses[18] (see Figures 3.7 and 3.8).

Unlike the mix of revenues, the relative percentage of costs in the total expenditure mix has changed little over time. For example, between 2003 and 2020, for both public and private non-profit entities, the percentage of research costs in the total expenditure mix held steady at about 10%.[19] Institutional support stood at about 13% for the private non-profits and nearly 10% for the publics. A notable exception is hospital service expenses, which, for both public and private non-profit institutions, rose significantly.[20] The increase reflects a multitude of factors, including the growing importance of higher education research in the U.S. healthcare system, the responsiveness of American universities to surging national demand, and the upward spiral of hospital operating costs. (For a description of basic account categories, see Table 3.3.)

"Cost creep"

Several developments are driving up the operating costs of American colleges and universities. First, economic forces are putting upward pressure

---

[18] NCES, Table 334.10. "Total expenditures of public degree-granting postsecondary institutions, by purpose and level of institution" and Table 334.30 "Total expenditures of private nonprofit degree-granting postsecondary institutions, by purpose and level of institution," *Digest of Education Statistics 2020.* As of the date of this writing, more recent expenditure data have not been released.

[19] Ibid.

[20] Ibid.

Table 3.3 Table of terms—basic account categories

Account title	Description
Capital assets	Tangible or intangible assets that are capitalized under an institution's capitalization policy; some of these assets are subject to depreciation and some are not. These assets consist of land and land improvements, buildings and building improvements, machinery, equipment, infrastructure, and all other assets that are used in operations and that have initial useful lives extending beyond one year. Capital assets also include collections of works of art and historical treasure and library collections; however, under certain conditions, such collections may not be capitalized. They also include property acquired under capital leases and intangible assets such as patents, copyrights, trademarks, goodwill, and software. Excluded are assets that are part of endowment funds or other capital fund investments in real estate.
Operating	Operating revenues and expenses result from providing goods and services. Operating transactions are incurred in the course of the operating activities of the institution.
Non-operating	Non-operating activities are those outside the activities that are part of the operating activities of the institution.

Source: U.S. Department of Education, Institute for Education Services, National Center for Education Statistics, IPEDS 2020–2021 Data Collection System, Glossary, https://surveys.nces.ed.gov/ipeds/public/glossary.

on factor input markets. The result has been a steady increase in the salaries of highly specialized personnel, as well as escalating instructional, research, and administrative expenses. Second, colleges and universities are placing greater emphasis on student support, social amenities, living conditions, and personal well-being. New residence halls, food courts, student unions, healthcare centers, and sports facilities are pushing up the cost of student and auxiliary services. Third, competition for student talent has intensified. The result has been the ballooning of amounts for scholarships, fellowships, and other forms of financial aid. Fourth, U.S. colleges and universities are increasingly having to cope with government regulations. The rules deal with everything from athletics, to financial aid, to campus safety, to human resources, immigration, sexual misconduct, and taxation.[21] Their proliferation is driving up the cost of compliance and reporting.

---

[21] For a list of regulatory compliance requirements see Higher Education Compliance Alliance, "Compliance Matrix," https://www.higheredcompliance.org/compliance-matrix (accessed June 1, 2021).

Then, there are internal dynamics. As many scholars have pointed out[22], the system of incentives in many U.S. colleges and universities adds to inflationary pressures. In some instances, it encourages "empire building." The system tends to reward research and scholarship more than, if not at the expense of, teaching and advising. In addition, it discourages cost-saving innovations, particularly in the realm of instructional technologies.[23]

Economies of scale are difficult to achieve in a labor-intensive industry with a multitude of academic disciplines and faculty specializations.[24] While some institutions have achieved scale by leveraging off their academic talent (e.g., through the use of online platforms, large lecture halls, and lower-paid adjuncts), those that rely heavily on small classes, in-person delivery, and highly-paid tenured faculty have not.

Throughout academia, there is a general disinclination to restructure. As a consequence, costs continue to mount, while output per student has hardly budged. William Baumol refers to this phenomenon as the "cost disease."[25] Derek Bok attributes it to the very nature of an academic institution. "The need for money," he tells us,

> is a chronic condition of American universities, a condition inherent in the very nature of an institution forever competing for the best students and faculty. Such talented, ambitious people are constantly asking for more programs, more books, more equipment, more of everything required to satisfy their desire to pursue new interests and opportunities.[26]

Domestic trends

Long-term trends are important, because they reflect the historical evolution of the U.S. higher education sector. Four trends are noteworthy: aggregate net surplus, cyclicality, institutional closures, and enrollments.

---

[22] See, in general, D.W. Breneman, *Liberal Arts Colleges: Thriving, Surviving, or Endangered?* (1994); W.F. Massy, "A New Look at the Academic Department." *Pew Policy Perspectives*, June 2, 1990; W.F. Massy and A. Wilger, "Productivity in Postsecondary Education: A New Approach." *Educational Evaluation and Policy Analysis*, vol. 14 (1992), 361–376; and R. Zemsky, "The Lattice and the Ratchet: Toward More Efficient Higher Education Systems." Presentation at the Annual Conference of the Education Commission of the States, Seattle, WA, July 13, 1990.

[23] Zumeta, "State Policy and Private Higher Education," *Finance of Higher Education*, 390–391.

[24] For a discussion of the labor-intensive nature of U.S. higher education in general see H.R. Bowen, *The Costs of Higher Education: How Much Do Colleges and Universities Spend Per Student and How Much Should They Spend?* (1980).

[25] In theory, the rising costs per unit of output are associated with a rate of salary growth in a labor-intensive sector that is higher than the rate of productivity growth. W.J. Baumol and W.G. Bowen, *Performing Arts, the Economic Dilemma: A Study of Problems Common to Theater, Opera, Music, and Dance* (1966).

[26] Bok, *Universities in the Marketplace*, 10.

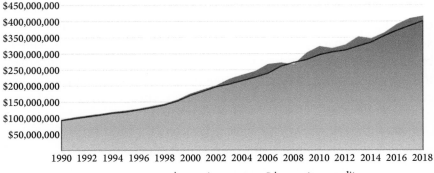

Fig. 3.9 Aggregate revenues and aggregate expenditures in thousands of current dollars, U.S. public post-secondary degree-granting institutions, 1990–2018.
Source: U.S. Department of Education, Institute of Education Sciences, National Center for Education Statistics. (See Appendix for notes.)

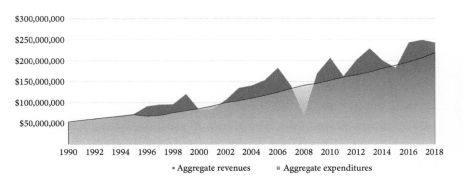

Fig. 3.10 Aggregate revenues and aggregate expenditures in thousands of current dollars, U.S. private non-profit post-secondary degree-granting institutions, 1990–2018.
Source: U.S. Department of Education, Institute of Education Sciences, National Center for Education Statistics. (See Appendix for notes.)

Aggregate net surplus

Since the start of the New Millennium, aggregate revenues net of aggregate expenditures ("aggregate net surplus") for institutions within the U.S.

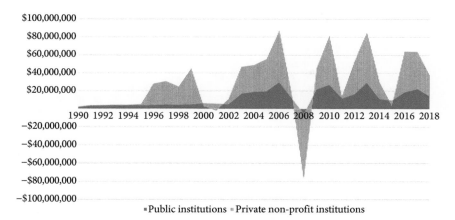

Fig. 3.11 Aggregate revenues net of aggregate expenditures in thousands of current dollars, U.S. post-secondary degree-granting institutions, 1990–2018. *Source*: U.S. Department of Education, Institute of Education Sciences, National Center for Education Statistics. (See Appendix for notes.)

higher education sector, a rough gauge of overall profitability, has fluctuated.[27] For public colleges and universities, aggregate net surplus initially rose from $17 billion in 2003 to nearly $30 billion in 2006, then fell to about –$6 billion in 2008, climbed to $29 billion in 2013, then dropped to about $15 billion in 2018 (and $8 billion in 2019)[28] (see Figure 3.11). On a per institution basis, aggregate net surplus zigzagged from about $9.8 million in 2003 to $17.6 million to -$3.4 million to nearly $18 million to slightly more than $9 million (and $5 million, respectively), over the same intervals (see Fig. 3.12).[29] For private non-profit institutions, the net amount increased from $30 billion in 2003 to $58 billion in 2006, then fell to –$72 billion in 2008, rose to $56 billion in 2013, then dropped to about $23 billion in 2018 (and $14 billion in 2019).[30] On a per institution basis, it went from $18 million in 2003 to $35.3 million to –$44.4 million to $33.6 million to nearly $14 million (and $8.5 million, respectively) over the same intervals.[31]

---

[27] See Toutkoushian and Paulsen, *Economics of Higher Education*, 249.
[28] NCES, Tables 333.10 and 334.10, *Digest of Education Statistics* (annual issues, 2010–2021).
[29] NCES, Tables 333.10, 334.10, and 317.10, *Digest of Education Statistics* (annual issues, 2010–2021).
[30] NCES, Tables 333.40 and 334.30, *Digest of Education Statistics* (annual issues, 2010–2021).
[31] NCES, Tables 333.40, 334.30, and 317.10, *Digest of Education Statistics* (annual issues, 2010–2021).

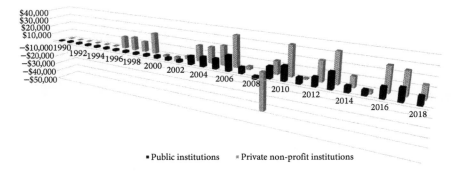

Fig. 3.12 Aggregate revenues net of aggregate expenditures in thousands of current dollars per institution, U.S. post-secondary degree-granting institutions, 1990–2018.

Source: U.S. Department of Education, Institute of Education Sciences, National Center for Education Statistics. (See Appendix for notes.)

Cyclicality

As the latter trend suggests, the overall financial condition of institutions within the sector tracks broad movements in the economy (as can be inferred from the peaks and troughs evident in Figures 3.11 and 3.12). In periods of expansion, the sector as a whole flourishes. Revenues are high enough to cover escalating operating expenses. At the start of the business cycle, credit expands, resulting in lower borrowing costs for most colleges and universities. Conversely, in periods of contraction, the sector as a whole struggles. Mounting operating expenses, more fixed than variable, peak above falling revenues. Hefty borrowing costs diminish earnings and cut into profit margins.

The latter developments occurred in the Great Recession of 2008.[32] In this turbulent period, most colleges and universities saw a significant decline in revenues. The decline stemmed from a precipitous drop in tuition and fee receipts, private gifts and grants, and investment income. While total revenues fell, total expenditures rose. For private institutions, total revenues plunged by nearly 24%, while total revenues increased by

---

[32] Toutkoushian and Paulsen, *Economics of Higher Education*, 377–379. On the decline in full-time enrollments during the Great Recession in general see B. Long, "The Financial Crisis and College Enrollment: How Have Students and Their Families Responded?" In *How the Financial Crisis and Great Recession Affected Higher Education*, edited by J. Brown and C. Hoxby (2015), 209–233.

7%.[33] For public institutions, total revenues slid by only 2%, while total expenditures grew by 5%.[34]

Due to long-term contracts and commitments, many colleges and universities were unable to cut costs fast enough or deep enough to maintain healthy profit margins. Most resorted to tuition increases, to the extent possible in a shrinking, highly competitive market. Others were able to procure government grants and private loans to stay afloat. For the unfortunate few, however, such measures proved ineffective. Some institutions were acquired by cash-rich investors. Others simply fell by the wayside.

Institutional closures

Long-term trends in institutional closures are telling. They shed light on the overall financial condition of the sector, its vulnerability to fluctuations in the economy, structural changes in underlying subsectors, and the financial impact of government regulations.[35] Tracking the business cycle, the number of closures increased in four periods of contraction: 1973–1975, 1990–1992, 2007–2008, and 2020–2021[36] (see Figure 3.13). They coincide with a drop in personal income, softening consumer demand, and a decline in student enrollments. Massive closures also occurred in two periods of expansion: 1995–1996 and 2012–2015. Less cyclical in nature, they coincide with structural changes in specific subsectors, influenced by macroeconomic and social factors.

The mid-1990s saw massive closures of two-year colleges. These institutions lost ground to four-year colleges as a result of a rise in personal income, which made a bachelor's degree more affordable for students of modest means.[37] A wave of closures also occurred during the business upswing of the 2010s. Regulatory restrictions on for-profit entities made

---

[33] NCES, Table 333.40, *Digest of Education Statistics* (annual issues, 2010–2020).

[34] NCES, Tables 333.10 and 334.10, *Digest of Education Statistics* (annual issues, 2010–2020).

[35] For a discussion of the risks underlying institutional closures in general see R. Zemsky, S. Shaman, and S.C. Baldridge, *The College Stress Test* (2020).

[36] NCES, Table 317.50 "Degree-granting postsecondary institutions that have closed their doors, by control and level of institution," *Digest of Education Statistics*, (annual issues, 2018–2020).

[37] From 1993 to 1998, total fall enrollments in two-year higher education institutions fell from 5,722,390 to 5,489,314, while those in four-year higher education institutions rose from 8,764,969 to 9,017,653. NCES, Table 303.25 "Total fall enrollment in degree-granting institutions, by control and level of institution," *Digest of Education Statistics 2020*. As Grawe points out, in the 1990s two-year colleges increasingly served as an entry point to a four-year degree. Grawe, *Demographics and the Demand for Higher Education* (2018), 58–60.

many ineligible for student loan financing.[38] Adverse publicity linked to poor placement rates and student loan defaults drastically eroded their enrollment base.

Enrollments

As can be inferred, the financial health of American colleges and universities is inextricably linked to aggregate enrollments. They steadily increased from nearly 11 million in 1975 to over 15 million in 2000.[39] Peaking at more than 21 million in 2010, they have since declined (see Figure 3.14). Reflecting the ebb and flow of consumer demand, enrollments have fluctuated dramatically for the privates, primarily because of their high tuition dependency and sensitivity to the vagaries of the market.[40] The swings are even more volatile for the for-profits, because of their extreme vulnerability to negative consumer sentiment and stringent government regulation.

For the U.S. higher education sector as a whole, average fall enrollments per institution have risen steadily since 1990, despite a tapering off in recent years (see Figure 3.15). For the public subsector, they grew from 6,900 in

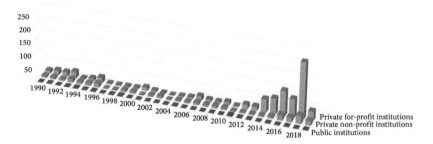

Fig. 3.13 Closures of U.S. post-secondary degree-granting institutions, 1990–2019.

Source: U.S. Department of Education, Institute of Education Sciences, National Center for Education Statistics. (See Appendix for notes.)

---

[38] U.S. Department of Education, "Department of Education Establishes New Student Aid Rules to Protect Borrowers and Taxpayers," October 8, 2010, https://www.ed.gov/news/press-releases/department-education-establishes-new-student-aid-rules-protect-borrowers-and-taxpayers (accessed June 1, 2021).

[39] NCES, Table 303.10 "Total fall enrollment in degree-granting postsecondary institutions, by attendance status, sex of student, and control of institution" and Table 105.30 "Enrollment in elementary, secondary, and degree-granting postsecondary institutions, by level and control of institution," *Digest of Education Statistics* (annual issues, 2018–2020).

[40] Weisbrod, Ballou, and Asch, *Mission and Money*, 31.

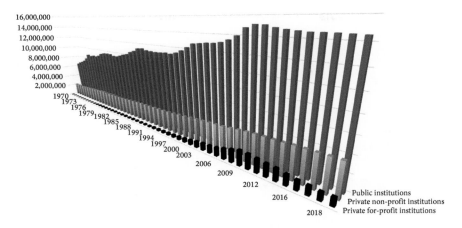

Fig. 3.14 Total fall enrollments, U.S. post-secondary degree-granting institutions, 1970–2019.

Source: U.S. Department of Education, Institute of Education Sciences, National Center for Education Statistics. (See Appendix for notes.)

1990 to almost 9,000 in 2019.[41] For the private non-profit subsector, they climbed from 1,670 to about 2,500.[42] For private for-profits, they increased from 620 to about 1,400.

Financial pillars of American higher education

The financial well-being of institutions in the U.S. higher education sector is associated with several economic, demographic, and financial factors. The most important is personal disposable income.

Personal disposable income

To date, the level of U.S. personal disposable income per capita has always exceeded the level of U.S. tuition, fees, and room and board per student[43]

---

[41] NCES, Tables 317.10 and 307.10 "Full-time-equivalent fall enrollment in degree-granting post-secondary institutions, by control and level of institution, *Digest of Education Statistics 2020*.

[42] NCES, Tables 317.10 and 307.10, *Digest of Education Statistics 2020*.

[43] NCES, Table 330.10 "Average undergraduate tuition and fees and room and board rates charged for full-time students in degree-granting postsecondary institutions, by level and control of institution: selected years," *Digest of Education Statistics* (annual issues, 1980–2020); and Federal Reserve Bank of St. Louis, Economic Research Division, "Disposable personal income: per capita: in current dollars," *Federal Reserve Economic Data*, A229RC0, https://fred.stlouisfed.org (accessed June 1, 2021).

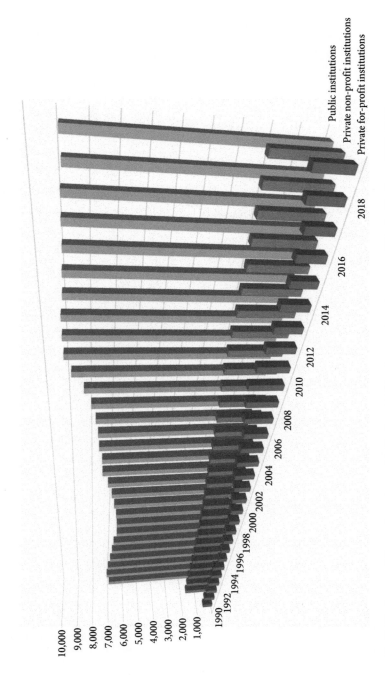

Fig. 3.15 Average fall enrollments per institution, U.S. post-secondary degree-granting institutions, 1990–2019.

Source: U.S. Department of Education, Institute of Education Sciences, National Center for Education Statistics. (See Appendix for notes.)

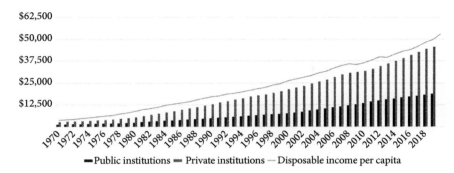

$62,500

$50,000

$37,500

$25,000

$12,500

1970 1972 1974 1976 1978 1980 1982 1984 1986 1988 1990 1992 1994 1996 1998 2000 2002 2004 2006 2008 2010 2012 2014 2016 2018

■ Public institutions ■ Private institutions — Disposable income per capita

Fig. 3.16 Cost of a U.S. college education relative to U.S. disposable income per capita, 1970–2019.

Sources: cost data: U.S. Department of Education, Institute of Education Sciences, National Center for Education Statistics; income data: Federal Reserve Bank of St. Louis, Federal Reserve Economic Data. (See Appendix for notes.)

(see Figure 3.16). Thus, in principle, a student or his/her family should be able to defray the cost of a college education in whole or in part through "surplus" earnings (although the income "cushion" is greater for a public college education than for a private college education). The student or his/her family is likely to be able to cover whatever remains unfunded, out of personal savings; public or private grants, loans, scholarships, fellowships; and/or other forms of financial aid.[44] Of course, such a possibility is predicated on good credit, exceptional merit, and/or ability-to-pay.

Since 1990, on the average, the cost of a college education per student absorbed 43% of U.S. disposable income per capita[45] (see Figure 3.17 for an illustration of long-term trends). For a private college education, the figure is 78%; for a public college education, 32%. Moreover, since 1970, the rate of cost inflation has exceeded the rate of income growth, to the point where today, the average cost of a U.S. college education is likely to absorb more than half of an individual's "surplus earnings." The ratio of public college costs per student to personal disposable income per capita rose from 29%

---

[44] Of course, the outcome would be substantially different for earners who support more than one student.

[45] NCES, Table 330.10, *Digest of Education Statistics* (annual issues, 1980–2020); and Federal Reserve Bank of St. Louis, "Disposable personal income: per capita: in current dollars," *Federal Reserve Economic Data*. For a discussion of college costs per student as a percentage of personal income per capita see J. McGee, *Breakpoint: The Changing Marketplace for Higher Education* (2015), 47–48; and S. Baum, "College Education: Who Can Afford It?" In *The Finance of Higher Education: Theory, Research, Policy, and Practice*, edited by M.B. Paulsen and J.B. Smart (2001), 40–43.

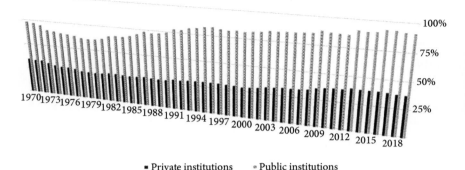

Fig. 3.17 Cost of a U.S. college education as a percentage of U.S. disposable income per capita, 1970–2019.

Sources: cost data: U.S. Department of Education, Institute of Education Sciences, National Center for Education Statistics; income data: Federal Reserve Bank of St. Louis, Federal Reserve Economic Data. (See Appendix for notes.)

in 1975 to 30% in 1995 to 39% in 2015. It stands at 38% today.[46] The ratio of private college costs per student swelled from 64% to 82% to 91% during the same period. It stands at 92% today.[47]

The inescapable conclusion is this: the cost of a traditional U.S. residential college education weighs heavily on students and families of modest means. Sadly, a college education has grown beyond the reach of many low-income Americans.

Private donations

Rising personal disposable income has also made possible a significant increase in private donations.[48] For private colleges and universities, aggregate private gifts, grants, and contracts climbed from $4.5 billion in 1990 to nearly $16 billion in 2000 to around $22 billion in 2010. For public colleges and universities, it rose from roughly $3.5 billion to nearly $9 billion to about $6 billion over the same intervals[49] (see Figure 3.18). Reliance on

---

[46] NCES, Table 330.10, *Digest of Education Statistics* (annual issues, 1980–2020); and Federal Reserve Bank of St. Louis, "Disposable personal income: per capita: in current dollars," *Federal Reserve Economic Data*.

[47] NCES, Table 330.10, *Digest of Education Statistics* (annual issues, 1980–2020); and Federal Reserve Bank of St. Louis, "Disposable personal income: per capita: in current dollars," *Federal Reserve Economic Data*.

[48] On private funding of U.S. higher education in general see Toutkoushian and Paulsen, *Economics of Higher Education*, 247–248; and Weisbrod, Ballou, and Asch, *Mission and Money*, chapter 6.

[49] NCES, Tables 333.10 and 333.50 "Total revenue of private non-profit degree-granting postsecondary institutions, by source of funds and classification of institution," *Digest of Education Statistics* (annual issues, 1998–2020).

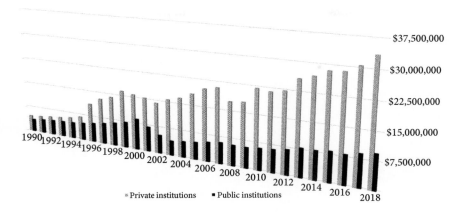

Fig. 3.18 Private gifts in thousands of current dollars to U.S. post-secondary degree-granting institutions, 1990–2018.
Source: U.S. Department of Education, Institute of Education Sciences, National Center for Education Statistics. (See Appendix for notes.)

gifts, grants, and contracts is greater for private non-profit institutions than for public institutions. The latter generally have access to government capital appropriations, while the former must seek out private gifts and grants to finance their capital expenditures.[50]

Student financial aid

In a sense, student financial aid is an indirect subsidy to American colleges and universities, because it increases the financial resources at the disposal of those who "consume" their services. Historically, this subsidy has been large enough to support skyrocketing tuition rates. It has sustained a level of revenues sufficient to cover mounting operating costs.

Student aid and non-federal loans, 1970–2019
As a result of a series of legislative measures enacted since 1965, the volume of student financial aid has grown by leaps and bounds[51] (see Figure 3.19).

---

[50] NCES, Tables 333.10 and 333.50, *Digest of Education Statistics* (annual issues, 1998–2020).
[51] Among the most important of these measures are the Higher Education Act of 1965 (HEA), which provided for federal financial assistance to students; the 1972 Amendments to the HEA, which established the Pell Grant Program; and the Middle Income Student Assistance Act of 1978, which loosened student aid eligibility requirements. W. Zumeta, "State Policy and Private Higher Education, *Finance of Higher Education*, 379–283; M.S. McPherson and M.O. Schapiro, *Keeping Colleges Affordable, Government and Educational Opportunity* (1991), 25–43; F. Keppel, "The Higher Education Acts Contrasted, 1965–86: Has Federal Policy Come of Age?" *Harvard Educational Review*, vol. 57, no. 1 (1987): 49–67; M. Mumper, "The Transformation of Federal Aid to College Students: Dynamics of Growth and Retrenchment." *Journal of Education Finance*, vol. 16 (1991): 315–331; and J.C. Hearn, "The Paradox of

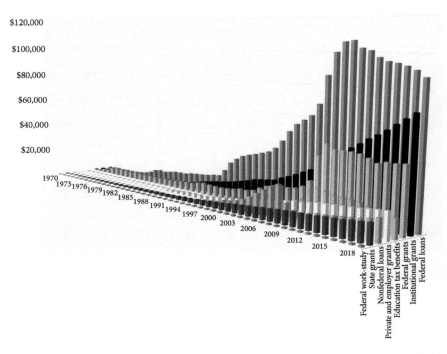

Fig. 3.19 Student aid and nonfederal loans in millions of current dollars, 1970–2019. *Source*: College Board, Trends in Student Aid 2020. (See Appendix for notes.)

It soared from a modest $3.7 billion in FY 1970 to a massive $45.6 billion in FY 1990 to an astounding $258 billion in FY 2019.[52] Most of this aid has been in the form of federal loans and grants, which today account for over half the total. In FY 1970, the nominal value of federal loans and grants stood at $2.5 billion. By FY 2019, it had ballooned to over $130 billion.[53] So vital is student financial aid for the economic well-being of the U.S. higher education sector that without it, scores of institutions would go bust. Witness, for example, the massive fallout that occurred in the 2010s as a result of government regulations that deprived many for-profits of revenues from student financial aid.[54]

Growth in Financial Aid for College Students, 1965–1990." In *Higher Education Handbook of Theory and Research: Volume IX*, edited by J.C. Smart (Bronx, Springer, 1993), 109–116.

[52] The College Board, Table 2 "Student Aid and Nonfederal Loans in Current Dollars (in Millions), 1970–71 to 2018–19," *Trends in Student Financial Aid 2021*.

[53] The College Board, "Student Aid and Nonfederal Loans," *Trends in Student Financial Aid 2021*.

[54] While the proliferation of financial aid has improved access to higher education in general, as a result of a recent shift in emphasis from need-based grants to student loans, it has worked to the detriment of individuals from low income families. J.C. Hearn, "Access to Post-Secondary Education:

Investment income

For institutions with sizeable endowments, investment income is a major source of revenue. It is often seen as a supplemental source that can be tapped in the event of a cash crunch. Yet, notwithstanding this conventional view, many U.S. colleges and universities rely on a steady stream of interests, dividends, rents, and royalties to support their current operations.

Fluctuations in the level of investment income track broad movements in equity, debt, and real-estate markets. Peaks occurred in the late-1990s and early-2010s, while troughs occurred in the recessions of 2001 and 2008. For both public and private institutions, investment returns exceeded annual movements in the Dow Jones Industrial Average in two brief periods: 2000–2002 and 2018. In other times, they either fell short of or matched broader movements in the stock market[55] (see Figure 3.20). These trends

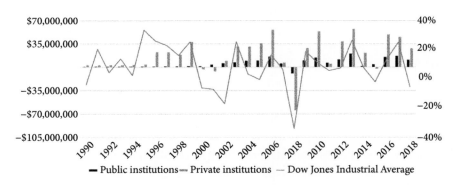

Fig. 3.20 Investment income in thousands of current dollars, U.S. post-secondary degree-granting institutions relative to annual movements in the Dow Jones Industrial Average, 1990–2018.

Source: income data: U.S. Department of Education, Institute of Education Sciences, National Center for Education Statistics; market data: Macrotrends. (See Appendix for notes.)

Financing Equity in an Evolving Context." In *The Finance of Higher Education: Theory, Research, Policy, and Practice*, edited by M.B. Paulsen and J.C. Smart (2001), 443–445. See also S. Slaughter and L.L. Leslie, *Academic Capitalism: Politics, Policies, and the Entrepreneurial University* (1997). As an unintended result, individuals from middle-class families have become the primary beneficiaries of student financial assistance. S. Baum, "College Education: Who Can Afford It?" *Finance of Higher Education*, 43–46.
[55] Underperforming the market could be attributable to trading restrictions associated with institutional investment policy. Also, there is a distinction between investment returns, which are calculated on the basis of principal, and investment income, which is an absolute amount. Such income can be generated from investments in stocks, bonds, real estate, and other assets.

speak to the adeptness of college and university portfolio managers, whose investment activities are constrained by policy.

Government funding

The principal forms of government funding are appropriations, grants, and contracts.[56] Typically, legislative bodies *appropriate* funds, often for general administrative purposes. Government agencies make *grants* for specific projects or programs. Public agencies award *contracts*, for consideration. Often, these forms of funding are earmarked for specific types of expenditures, and are labeled accordingly For example, *operating grants* and *contracts* are earmarked for current operating expenses. *Capital appropriations* are earmarked for acquiring, constructing, or improving capital assets.

For public colleges and universities, government funding is the single most important source of short- and long-term finance. These institutions rely heavily on state appropriations to finance their capital expenditures. They depend on federal grants and contracts to cover a portion of their operating costs.[57] For private non-profit colleges and universities, government funding is a major source of revenue, but not to the extent that it is for the publics (see Figure 3.21). For private colleges and universities, federal appropriations, gifts, and contracts rank third as a source of revenue, following tuition and private donations.[58]

As with student financial aid, the spectacular growth of government funding since the early-1990s has fueled the enormous expansion of the U.S. higher education sector.[59] For both public and private non-profit entities, federal appropriations, grants, and contracts skyrocketed from roughly $25 billion in 1995 to nearly $55 billion in 2005 to $73 billion in 2015.[60] Total state and local funding soared from over $50 billion to $85 billion to about $108 billion during the same intervals.[61]

---

[56] On the various forms of government funding see Toutkoushian and Paulsen, *Economics of Higher Education*, 246–247.

[57] NCES, Table 333.10, *Digest of Education Statistics* (annual issues, 1998–2020).

[58] NCES, Table 333.50, *Digest of Education Statistics* (annual issues, 1998–2020).

[59] See Zumeta, "State Policy and Private Higher Education," *Finance of Higher Education*, 379–396.

[60] NCES, Tables 333.10 and 333.50, *Digest of Education Statistics* (annual issues, 1998–2020).

[61] NCES, Tables 333.10 and 333.50, *Digest of Education Statistics* (annual issues, 1998–2020).

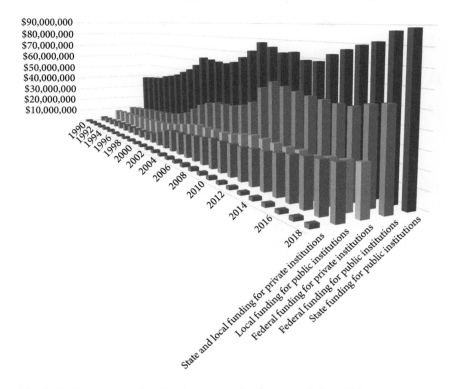

Fig. 3.21 Government funding in thousands of current dollars, U.S.
post-secondary degree-granting institutions, 1990–2018.

Source: U.S. Department of Education, Institute of Education Sciences, National Center for
Education Statistics. (See Appendix for notes.)

Summary

These five elements—personal disposable income, private donations, student financial aid, investment income, and government funding—are the financial pillars of the U.S. higher education sector. Together with less significant sources, they fortify the economic substructure of American higher education, from which arises its ideological superstructure. Because of this fundamental relationship—indeed, because the realm of finances supports the realm of ideas—these elements also constitute risk factors. Let us examine the risks in greater detail.

4

A Higher Education Sector on the Edge: Part II

This chapter addresses major risks to the economic foundation of the U.S. higher education sector. They include a drop in the aggregate levels of personal disposable income, student financial aid, private donations, investment income, and public funding. As noted earlier, these sources constitute the financial pillars of American higher education. The chapter also discusses adverse trends that are symptomatic of a general *malaise* in the sector. Among them are flat enrollments, intensifying competition, slackening economic growth, deteriorating financial ratios, and declining financial surplus. The discussion is relevant to the central question, "What has contributed to the abundance of American higher education talent since the start of the New Millennium?"

> A ship in harbour is safe, but that is not what ships are built for.[1]
>
> John A. Shedd, American author and professor

> Anything can be achieved in small, deliberate steps. But there are times you need the courage to take a great leap; you can't cross a chasm in two small jumps.[2]
>
> David Lloyd George, former Prime Minister of the United Kingdom

Risk factors

Bearing in mind the financial pillars of the U.S. higher education sector, let us look at factors that risk their solidity. The most critical is income.[3]

---

[1] J.S. Shedd, *Salt from My Attic* (1928).
[2] D.L. George, *War Memoirs of David Lloyd George: 1914–1915* (1933), 740.
[3] For a discussion of the risks associated with new student enrollments, net cash price, student retention, and major external funding see R. Zemsky, S. Shaman, and S.C. Baldridge, *The College Stress Test* (2020).

Bridging the Gap between the Abundance of American Higher Education Talent and the Immense Foreign Demand for It.
Richard J. Joseph, Oxford University Press. © Richard J. Joseph (2022). DOI: 10.1093/oso/9780192848307.003.0005

Income

It is axiomatic that if personal disposable income per capita falls below the average cost of a college education, student demand will soften, enrollments will decline, and tuition revenues will fall. Likewise, if the average cost of a college education peaks above a certain income threshold, similar consequences are likely to ensue. No doubt, individuals with substantial savings or access to financial aid will be able to cover the incremental cost. Those with inadequate resources might have to postpone their college education or forego it altogether.

Some income risks are specific to higher education subsectors. A substantial increase in personal disposable income per capita could make a baccalaureate degree more affordable, thus cannibalizing enrollments at two-year community colleges. A substantial decrease could tilt student preferences in favor of less expensive offerings, such as short courses, certificate programs, or online degree programs, thereby reducing enrollments at residential degree colleges.

These risks heighten in periods of recession, when aggregate personal income takes a nosedive; also, in periods of expansion, when the rate of cost inflation exceeds the rate of income growth. Institutions most at risk are private colleges and universities; those that offer only residential degree programs; and those that confer only associate or baccalaureate degrees.

Student financing

As has been pointed out, the expansion of student financial aid has strengthened demand for U.S. higher education, thereby sustaining a high level of tuition revenues. It follows, logically, that a reduction in this aid could weaken student demand, thereby lowering this level below escalating operating costs. The reduction could occur as a result of more stringent Title IV eligibility requirements, a possibility linked to student attrition and placement rates, post-graduation starting salaries, and student loan defaults. It could also occur as a result of more onerous credit terms or a general contraction of student loans and grants. The latter contingencies are linked to the overall state of the economy, fiscal and monetary policies, budget constraints, student credit histories, post-graduation earnings potential,[4] and politics.

---

[4] This potential, in turn, depends on numerous factors, including the reputation of the degree-granting institution, the practical skills imparted by its programs, the type of degree conferred, its perceived value in the marketplace, its relevance to well-paying jobs, the availability of these jobs, competition in labor markets, the state of the economy, and industry growth.

Although all colleges and universities incur a degree of risk, the most vulnerable are those with weak brands, low retention rates, poor placement rates, and programs with unclear career paths or none at all. Foremost among the latter are many for-profit entities.

Private funding

For most colleges and universities, a significant decline in private donations could stall or block badly needed capital expenditures. It could also diminish the funds needed to support current operations. Like tuition revenues, the total amount of private gifts and grants is linked to aggregate personal income, which in turn depends on the overall state of the economy. When personal income declines, educational institutions get a double whammy: first, a drop in tuition revenues, and second, a reduction in private donations. Because private non-profits rely on private gifts and grants to a greater extent than do either public or for-profit institutions, they are the most at risk.[5]

Investment income

Market, liquidity, credit, and inflation risks are incidental to investing. A slight fall in the price of stock, a rise in the rate of interest, or a weakening of the U.S. dollar could result in a bloodbath of portfolio losses. So could a scarcity of buyers willing to buy or sellers willing to sell at the asking price. A downgrade in credit-rating could diminish the value of bond holdings. So could a rate of inflation that exceeds the rate of interest.

As an investment strategy, diversification can minimize these risks. Yet, several factors impair the ability of academic institutions to broadly diversify: first, policy restrictions on certain types of investments, such as derivatives, commodities, and cryptocurrencies; second, prohibitions on certain types of transactions, such as short-selling, buying on margin, and wash sales; and third, internal pressures to divest of investments in companies whose policies or practices are "unacceptable." Having less room in the broader market to maneuver, institutions the most at risk are colleges

---

[5] Also linked to the level of private funding are tax breaks that encourage charitable contributions. Restricting or eliminating these breaks could put a damper on philanthropic activity, thereby accentuating the risks incurred by donation-dependent colleges and universities.

and universities with sizeable endowments, restrictive investment policies, and/or politically proactive constituencies.

Public funding

The risk relating to public funding is both political and financial. It is linked to the size of government budgets, which in turn depends on the volume of tax revenues. It is also linked to the willingness of public officials to subsidize colleges and universities, under what conditions, and to what extent. Here are a few thoughts.

Public officials who control sizeable purse strings of American higher education are increasingly calling into question the effectiveness of U.S. colleges and universities in preparing students for the workplace, the size of their cost base, the necessity of their expenditures, the degree of their operational efficiency, and the affordability of their price. Faced with public outcry over the rising cost of a college education, they are pressing academic institutions to hold the line on pricing and spending. They are also encouraging them to develop alternative, more affordable modes of delivery. They are less willing than before to sign off on the ambitious agendas of college and university presidents. To be sure, their generosity comes with strings attached, including tuition controls, student success rates, productivity metrics, and organizational reforms.[6]

The potential consequences of these measures are a mixed bag. On the one hand, they could improve institutional effectiveness by making administrators more accountable for the learning outcomes of their programs, the financial results of their operations, and the career success of their graduates. On the other hand, they could stifle institutional autonomy and thwart independent judgment, both essential for academic integrity. In addition, by opening the door to political meddling in the classroom, they could undermine the role of faculty in academic oversight. The end-result could be a substantial increase in student numbers, at the expense of educational quality.

---

[6] See W.F. Lasher and D.L. Greene, "College and University Budgeting: What Do We Know? What Do We Need to Know?" In *The Finance of Higher Education: Theory, Research, Policy, and Practice*, edited by M.B. Paulsen and J.B. Smart (2001), 518–519, 539–540; M. Mumper, "State Efforts to Keep Public Colleges Affordable in the Face of Fiscal Stress," *The Finance of Higher Education*, 331–342; and, in general, J.C. Burke and A.M. Serban, *Current Status and Future Prospects of Performance Funding and Performance Budgeting for Public Higher Education: The Second Survey* (1998).

Then, there are other ramifications. Legislative pressures to admit more students could adversely affect faculty-student ratios, course rigor, classroom dynamics, and the overall level of learning. Conditioning public funding on high exam scores, course grades, or graduation rates could unwittingly lower standards for academic assessment. Politically motivated attempts to dictate what should or should not be taught in the classroom could strike a serious blow at academic freedom. Scaling back public funding could drive tuition rates higher and accelerate the move to privatization.

Leaders of American higher education walk a tight rope. If they refuse, under any circumstances, to compromise the institution's core values, they risk confronting public officials who control a multitude of purse strings. If they refuse, under any circumstances, to confront these officials, they risk compromising the institution's core values. In the first instance, the end-result is likely to be an erosion of the institution's financial foundation, and in the second instance, an erosion of its ethical foundation. Institutions the most at risk are public colleges and universities, and also private colleges and universities that have major government contracts.

An impending storm

Despite the long-term expansion of the U.S. higher education sector, storm clouds have loomed over the horizon for years. They reflect adverse demographic, market, and economic trends that heighten some, if not all, of the foregoing risks. Let's examine them.

Demographic trends

Past

Inextricably linked to the level of U.S. college enrollments are demographics.[7] Three themes emerge from an analysis of past demographic trends: first, reflecting an aging population, the U.S. college age population (ages 18 to 24), as a percentage of the total U.S. population, significantly

---

[7] On the impact of demographics on U.S. college and university enrollments in general see N. Grawe, *Demographics and the Demand for Higher Education* (2018).

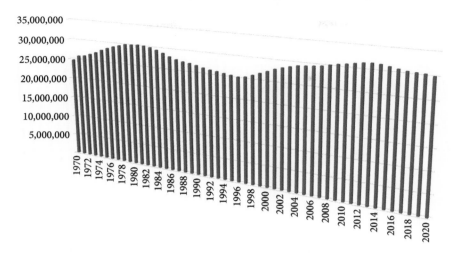

Fig. 4.1 U.S. college age population in thousands, 1970–2020.

Source: U.S. Department of Education, Institute of Education Sciences, National Center for Education Statistics. (See Appendix for notes.)

decreased[8] (see Figure 4.1). It fell from 12% in 1970 to 10% in 1995 to 9% in 2020. In absolute terms, U.S. college-age numbers fluctuated. They initially climbed from 24.7 million in 1970 to 30.2 million in 1981; then retreated to 25.3 million in 1996; peaked at 31.5 million in 2013; then leveled off at 30 million in 2020.[9]

Second, notwithstanding these fluctuations, the college participation rate surged[10] (see Figures 4.2 and 4.3). The upsurge was strong enough to support the steady growth of U.S. college enrollments for decades. The rate rose from 26% in 1970 to 34% in 1995 to 40% in 2020.[11] The numbers climbed from 7.4 million to 12.2 million to 16.7 million over the same intervals.[12] The participation rate for four-year colleges was significantly higher than that for two-year colleges. It also accelerated at a faster pace.

[8] U.S. Department of Education, Institute for Education Sciences, National Center for Education Statistics, (hereinafter referred to as "NCES"), Table 101.10 "Estimates of resident population, by age group," *Digest of Education Statistics* (annual issues, 1990–2020).

[9] As Grawe points out, the overall numbers are a function of the domestic fertility rate. Grawe, *Demographics*, 6, 12–14.

[10] NCES, Table 302.60 "Percentage of 18- to 24-year-olds enrolled in college, by level of institution and sex and race/ethnicity of student," *Digest of Education Statistics* (annual issues, 1980–2020). See also Grawe, *Demographics*,114; and J. McGee, *Breakpoint: The Changing Marketplace for Higher Education* (2015), 24.

[11] NCES, Table 302.60, *Digest of Education Statistics* (annual issues, 1980-2020).

[12] NCES, Table 303.70 "Total undergraduate fall enrollment in degree-granting postsecondary institutions, by attendance status, sex of student, and control and level of institution," *Digest of Education Statistics* (annual issues, 1980-2020).

Fig. 4.2 Percentage of U.S. college-age population enrolled in college, 1970–2020.

Source: U.S. Department of Education, Institute of Education Sciences, National Center for Education Statistics. (See Appendix for notes.)

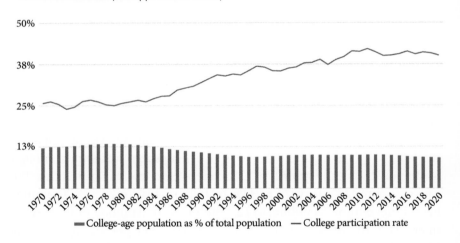

Fig. 4.3 U.S. college-age population as a percentage of total U.S. population relative to college participation rate, 1970–2020.

Source: U.S. Department of Education, Institute of Education Sciences, National Center for Education Statistics. (See Appendix for notes.)

For four-year institutions, the rate soared from 17% in 1973 to over 31% in 2020. For two-year institutions, it swelled from 7% to 10% during the same timeframe.[13] These divergent trends support the conclusion that ballooning enrollments at four-year colleges has come at the expense of weakening enrollments at two-year colleges.

---

[13] NCES, Table 302.60," *Digest of Education Statistics* (annual issues, 1980–2020).

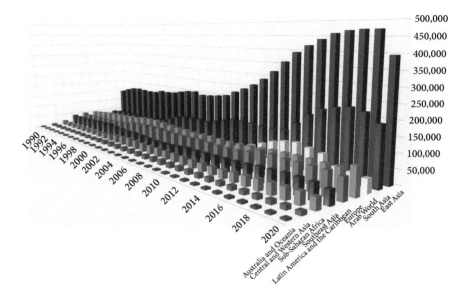

Fig. 4.4 Foreign students enrolled in U.S. colleges and universities by global region, 1990–2020.

Source: U.S. Department of Education, Institute of Education Sciences, National Center for Education Statistics; and Institute of International Education, Open Doors. (See Appendix for notes.)

Third, propelling the upward thrust in U.S. college enrollments has been a rise in the number of non-U.S. (i.e., "foreign") matriculants of college age (see Figure 4.4), as well as the number of U.S. matriculants beyond college age.

As a percentage of total U.S. college enrollments, the number of non-U.S. matriculants ("international students") grew from 1.7% in 1970 to 3.2% in 1995 to 5.5% in 2019.[14] The U.S. gross enrollment ratio, calculated on the basis of *all* age groups (i.e., both college-age and non-college-age students) enrolled in tertiary education, climbed from 47% to 79% to 88% during the same intervals[15] (see Figure 4.5). These trends suggest that over the

---

[14] Institute of International Education, Table 1 "International Student and U.S. Higher Education Enrollment," *Open Doors 2020*. See also McGee, *Breakpoint*, 33.

[15] UNESCO Institute for Statistics, "Gross enrolment ratio, tertiary, both sexes (%)," and "School enrollment, tertiary (% gross), http://data.uis.unesco.org (accessed November 1, 2021); see also the World Bank, DataBank, https://data.worldbank.org/indicator/se.ter.enrr. "Gross enrollment ratio" is the ratio of total enrollment, regardless of age, to the population of the age group that officially corresponds to the level of education at issue. Here, the applicable level is "tertiary education," which encompasses all post-secondary education, including both public and private universities, colleges, technical training institutes, and vocational schools at the undergraduate and post-graduate levels. UNESCO Institute for Statistics, "Glossary," http://uis.unesco.org/en/glossary (accessed June 1, 2021).

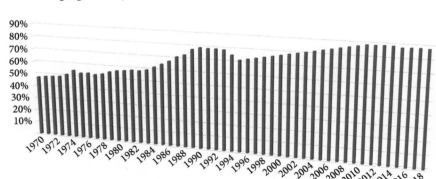

Fig. 4.5 U.S. tertiary education gross enrollment ratios, 1970–2018.
Source: The World Bank. (See Appendix for notes.)

past half century, any slack in enrollment capacity resulting from a drop in U.S. college-age numbers was taken up by the admission of both international students and American adult learners (i.e., U.S. citizens over age 24). To some extent, their rising enrollment numbers cushioned the modest decline in U.S. college age enrollments.

Future

As many analysts have pointed out,[16] demographic projections do not bode well for the future of the U.S. higher education sector. They portend a growing U.S. college age population to the mid-2020s, followed by a leveling off, then a gradual decline.[17] Because the college participation rate will not rise fast enough to offset this decline, the result is likely to be a steady drop in U.S. college enrollments well into the third decade of the New Millennium (see Figure 4.6).

The decrease will be steeper for the privates than for the publics. Although private college enrollments surged by 36% between 2002 and 2016, they are projected to be flat between 2016 and 2027, then dip thereafter.[18] Public college enrollments increased by 14% between 2002 and 2016.

---

[16] In general, see Grawe, *Demographics*; McGee, *Breakpoint*; W.J. Hussar and T.M. Bailey, *Projections of Education Statistics to 2028* (NCES, May 2020); and P. Bransberger, C. Falkenstern, and P. Lane, *Knocking at the College Door*, 10th ed (Boulder, Western Interstate Commission for Higher Education, 2020) (hereinafter referred to as "WICHE").

[17] NCES, Table 303.10 "Total fall enrollment in degree-granting postsecondary institutions, by attendance status, sex of student, and control of institution," *Digest of Education Statistics 2020*.

[18] NCES, Table 303.30 "Total fall enrollment in degree-granting postsecondary institutions, by level and control of institution, attendance status, and sex of student," *Digest of Education Statistics 2020*.

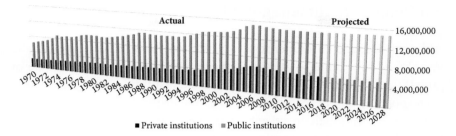

Fig. 4.6 Fall enrollments in U.S. post-secondary degree-granting institutions, actual and projected, 1970–2029.

Source: U.S. Department of Education. Institute of Education Sciences, National Center for Education Statistics. (See Appendix for notes.)

They are projected to rise slightly between 2016 and 2027, then gradually taper off.[19]

According to forecasts, a key factor contributing to the expected decline will be a sharp drop in the number of U.S. high-school graduates in the late-2020s.[20] This figure is largely a function of domestic birth rates, which fell sharply in the aftermath of the Great Recession[21] and during the Global Pandemic.[22] Cross-border migration trends—in particular, an increase in the number of college-age children of Hispanic immigrants—could partially offset the decline in non-Hispanic white enrollments.[23] Weighing against a full offset are a lower college attainment rate among Hispanics,[24] lower per capita income, and an increasingly restrictive U.S. immigration policy.

Adverse demographic trends coupled with the escalating cost of a college education and personal income constraints will translate into declining tuition revenues for the vast majority of American colleges and universities. Particularly hard hit will be tuition-dependent institutions with a large cost base; most notably, private colleges with limited access to public and private funding.[25]

---

[19] NCES, Table 303.30, *Digest of Education Statistics 2020*.

[20] Grawe, *Demographics*, 45–46; and WICHE, *Knocking*, 11.

[21] Grawe, *Demographics*, 6; and WICHE, *Knocking*, 11.

[22] B.E. Hamilton, J.A. Martin, M.P.H. Osterman, and M.J.K. Osterman, "Births: Provisional Data for 2019," *NVSS Vital Statistics Rapid Release* (U.S. Department of Health and Human Services, Centers for Disease Control and Prevention, National Center for Health Statistics, National Vital Statistics System, May 2020), https://www.cdc.gov/nchs/data/vsrr/vsrr-8-508.pdf (accessed June 1, 2021).

[23] See Grawe, *Demographics*, 7–9, 51–54.

[24] Grawe, *Demographics*, 24, 51, 56.

[25] In particular, private four-year colleges that rely heavily on enrollments of non-Hispanic white students. A higher participation rate among Hispanics is likely to benefit two-year community colleges to a greater extent than four-year colleges. Grawe, *Demographics*, 60.

Slackening enrollment growth

Although average enrollments per institution have inched up over the years, they have done so at a snail's pace. Since 1990, the annual rate of growth in fall college enrollments per public institution averaged 1%; the corresponding figure for private non-profit institutions was 1.4%[26] (see Figure 4.7). Although in recent years the rate of for-profit enrollment growth has skyrocketed, the surge is largely a function of fewer institutions, which reduces the number plugged into the denominator of the growth ratio.

Even more disturbing, since 2010 the average rate of growth of enrollments per institution has decelerated markedly. For the publics, it slowed to a trifling 0.04%. For the private non-profits, it was a paltry 0.77%.[27] This trend suggests that, on the whole, American colleges and universities have not succeeded at significantly broadening their enrollment base; furthermore, that lowering the net price by raising the discount rate has not resulted in significantly greater volume. The slowdown adds urgency to the need to find alternative sources of revenue. It also raises the specter of a sector on the verge of stagnation.

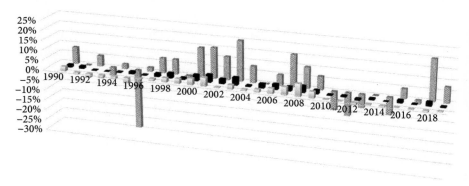

▪Public institutions ▪Private non-profit institutions ▪Private for-profit institutions

Fig. 4.7 Annual growth rates in average fall enrollments per U.S. post-secondary degree-granting institution, 1990–2019.

Source: U.S. Department of Education, Institute of Education Sciences, National Center for Education Statistics. (See Appendix for notes.)

[26] NCES, Table 307.10 "Full-time-equivalent fall enrollment in degree-granting postsecondary institutions, by control and level of institution," *Digest of Education Statistics 2020.*

[27] NCES, Table 307.10, *Digest of Education Statistics 2020.*

Increased competition

Until the onset of the Global Pandemic, U.S. colleges and universities maintained a steady stream of enrollments. They did so, however, at a hefty cost. The rising tide of institutional grants bears testimony to this cost[28] (see Figures 4.8 and 4.9). These grants typically take the form of scholarships, tuition waivers, and housing discounts. Although some are funded by state legislatures, most are offset against the institution's gross revenues in the form of tuition discounts.

The spectacular growth in the volume of institutional grants reflects an intensification of competition in what are essentially mature, slow-growth markets. This competition is largely a function of crowded markets,[29] and also the high bar that colleges and universities set in recruiting students. Because many of them set the same high bar in the same markets, they are effectively chasing after the same pool of student talent. To attract the best and the brightest, and to maintain a steady stream of enrollments, many

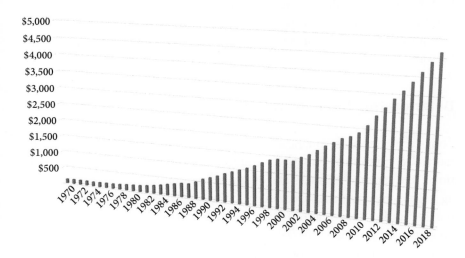

Fig. 4.8 Average institutional grants per full-time equivalent student, 1970–2019.
Source: U.S. Department of Education, Institute of Education Sciences, National Center for Education Statistics; and College Board, Trends in Student Aid. (See Appendix for notes.)

---

[28] R.K. Toutkoushian and M.B. Paulsen, *Economics of Higher Education: Background, Concepts, and Applications* (2016), 297; and D.W. Breneman, J.L. Doti, and L. Lapovsky, "Financing Private Colleges and Universities: The Role of Tuition Discounting." In *The Finance of Higher Education: Theory, Research, Policy, and Practice*, edited by M.B. Paulsen and J.B. Smart (2001), 471–472.
[29] B.A. Weisbrod, J.P. Ballou, and E.D. Asch, *Mission and Money, Understanding the University* (2008), 43–46.

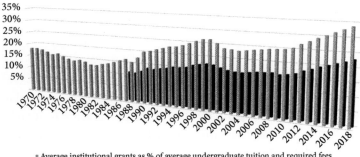

Average institutional grants as % of average undergraduate tuition and required fees
Average institutional grants as % of average graduate tuition and required fees

Fig. 4.9 Average institutional grants as a percentage of average higher education costs, 1970–2018.

Sources: U.S. Department of Education, Institute of Education Sciences, National Center for Education Statistics; and College Board, Trends in Student Aid. (See Appendix for notes.)

haplessly raise their discount rate in what is essentially a mad "race to the bottom." Because colleges and universities ultimately absorb this cost, institutional grants take a heavy toll on their profit margins. Indeed, to the extent that tuition discounts reduce gross revenues, they go straight to the bottom-line.

Deteriorating financial ratios

Long-term trends in financial ratios indicate a deterioration in the financial condition of American colleges and universities. One such ratio is the average annual rate of growth of aggregate revenues net of aggregate expenditures (previously defined as "aggregate net surplus") per institution (see Figure 0.1 in the Introduction). Deduced from aggregate sectoral data, this ratio sheds light on average *profitability per institution*, based on an order of magnitude. The overall trend is dismal. Since 1990, the average annual rate of growth of aggregate net surplus per institution has been negative: for the public subsector, a troubling −7%; for the private subsector, an alarming −40%.[30] The slowdown

[30] Since 2010, the rate has decelerated even more for private institutions: a whopping 86%. NCES, Table 333.10 "Revenues of public degree-granting postsecondary institutions, by source of revenue and level of institution," Table 333.40 "Total revenue of private non-profit degree-granting postsecondary institutions, by source of funds and level of institution," Table 334.10 "Total expenditures of public degree-granting postsecondary institutions, by purpose and level of institution," and Table 334.30 "Total expenditures of private non-profit degree-granting postsecondary institutions, by purpose and level of institution," *Digest of Education Statistics* (annual issues, 1990–2020).

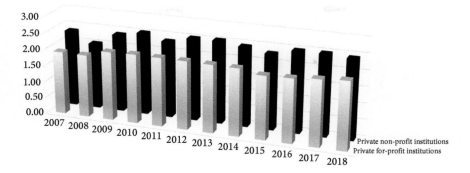

Fig. 4.10 Average financial responsibility composite scores of U.S. private post-secondary degree-granting institutions, 2007–2018.
Source: U.S. Department of Education, Office of Federal Student Aid. (See Appendix for notes.)

suggests declining profitability in a highly competitive, shrinking domestic market.

An even better gauge of financial condition is the financial responsibility composite score (see Figure 4.10). Published by the U.S. Department of Education, Office of Student Financial Aid, these scores measure the financial well-being of private institutions eligible for Title IV funding.[31] In principle, the higher the score, the greater the financial well-being. For private non-profits as a whole, the average financial responsibility composite score fell from 2.52 in FY 2010 to 2.44 in FY 2018.[32] For private for-profits, it dropped from 2.12 to 2.07. The decrease is a cause for concern for many private institutions. It reveals the extent to which their financial condition has deteriorated since 2010.

Declining net surplus per employee

Another indicator of financial condition is average aggregate net surplus per employee. Also deduced from aggregate sectoral data, this ratio is a rough gauge of *profitability per employee,* based on an order of magnitude. In calculating aggregate net surplus, we focused on post-1995 data for the private subsector and post-2002 data for the public subsector. We used 1996 and 2003 as starting points, because major FASB and GASB accounting changes took effect in those years.

Refer to Figures 4.11 and 4.12. They reveal that since 2006, average aggregate net surplus per employee has been on the wane, with occasional

---

[31] See U.S. Department of Education, Office of Student Aid, "Financial Responsibility Composite Scores," https://studentaid.gov/data-center/school/composite-scores (accessed June 1, 2021).
[32] Ibid. See also R. Zemsky, S. Shaman, and S.C. Baldridge, *The College Stress Test* (2020).

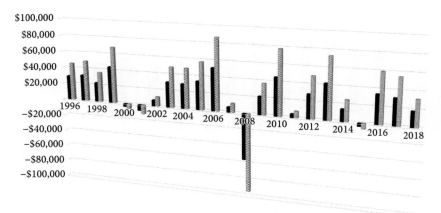

Aggregate revenues net of aggregate expenditures per employee

Aggregate revenues net of aggregate expenditures per non-faculty employee

Fig. 4.11 Aggregate revenues net of aggregate expenditures per employee, U.S. private post-secondary degree-granting institutions, 1996–2018.

Source: U.S. Department of Education, Institute of Education Sciences, National Center for Education Statistics. (See Appendix for notes.)

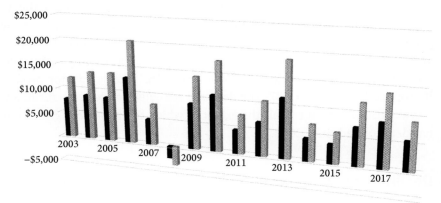

Aggregate revenues net of aggregate expenditures per employee

Aggregate revenues net of aggregate expenditures per non-faculty employee

Fig. 4.12 Aggregate revenues net of aggregate expenditures per employee, U.S. public post-secondary degree-granting institutions, 2003–2018.

Source: U.S. Department of Education, Institute of Education Sciences, National Center for Education Statistics. (See Appendix for notes.)

upward "hiccups." The pattern is the same for both public and private institutions, and whether the calculation is based on *all* employees or just *non-faculty* employees. The downward trend points to declining profitability per employee. Depending on the relative value of capital inputs, it could also spell declining *productivity per employee*. What this means, for all practical purposes, is that on the average, the level of net surplus generated by every employee in the U.S. higher education sector has been falling since 2006, and furthermore, that the financial returns generated by every employee could be diminishing.[33] Lower employee profitability (and possibly also productivity) supports the notion of an "abundance" of American higher education talent in a "sector on the edge."

Present abundance, future oversupply?

Taken altogether, adverse demographic trends, slackening enrollment growth, increased competition, deteriorating financial ratios, and declining aggregate net surplus per employee are symptomatic of a general *malaise* in the American higher education sector. They indicate softening demand in crowded, mature, and shrinking domestic markets. They also suggest that the U.S. higher education sector could be transitioning from a state of "equilibrium" to a state of "oversupply." As used here, "oversupply" does not mean surplus intellectual capital, for clearly, its abundance can only enhance the learning experience, invigorate society with new ideas, promote innovation and economic growth, and enrich American culture. Rather, here the term connotes surplus personnel, programs, assets, and capacity, which, in light of softening demand in a crowded domestic market, are contributing to declining profitability, and possibly also diminishing returns.

So what does this mean for the future? Based on past experience and given the cyclicality of the industry, one possibility is this: if there is ever going to be massive disruption, it is likely to occur in a major recession. At that critical juncture, some, if not all, of the risk factors could converge to become a stark reality. Specifically, personal disposable income could shrink, student demand could weaken, operating costs could surge above operating revenues, tuition discounts could devour whatever remains of any profit margin, private sources of capital could dry up, and legislators could balk at requests for badly needed funding. No institution would be

---

[33] Whether such returns are in fact diminishing would depend on the relative level of capital inputs.

spared of its devastating effects, although the principal casualties would be mid- to lower-tier private colleges and universities.

A "perfect storm"

In early-2020, this author predicted,

> Given the cyclicality of the U.S. economy, it seems like only a matter of time before the higher education sector contracts. At that critical juncture, the convergence of risk factors could stir up a whirlwind of devastating forces. It could give rise to a "perfect storm."[34]

That storm may have arrived as a result of the Global Pandemic. The crisis marks a turning point in the history of American higher education. Its devastating effects rival those of the Great Recession. Here's what can be gleaned from currently available data:

- In the fall of 2020, undergraduate enrollments across the United States fell dramatically.[35] Total student enrollments declined by 4%, and first-time student enrollments by 16%. Hardest hit were America's community colleges. Their overall enrollments fell by more than 9%, while their first-time enrollments plummeted by 23%. At public colleges and universities, total enrollments declined by one percentage point, while freshmen enrollments tanked by nearly 14%. At private non-profit institutions, the corresponding figures were −2% and −12%, respectively. The only subsector that seems to have been spared of massive devastation was the for-profit subsector. As college students swarmed in droves to take online courses, for-profit enrollments surged[36] (see Figure 4.13).

---

[34] In March 2020, the initial manuscript of this book had to be revised to reflect the devastating effects of the Global Pandemic.

[35] Based on data provided in National Clearinghouse Center, Table 1: "Estimated National Enrollment by Institutional Sector: 2018–2020, and Table 2: "Estimated First-Time Postsecondary Student Enrollment by Institutional Sector: 2018–2020," *Term Enrollment Estimates Fall 2020* (2021).

[36] As did enrollments in private non-profit institutions with a strong presence in the online education market. See P. Hill, "The Colleges that Prospered during the Pandemic," *The Chronicle of Higher Education*, July 28, 2021.

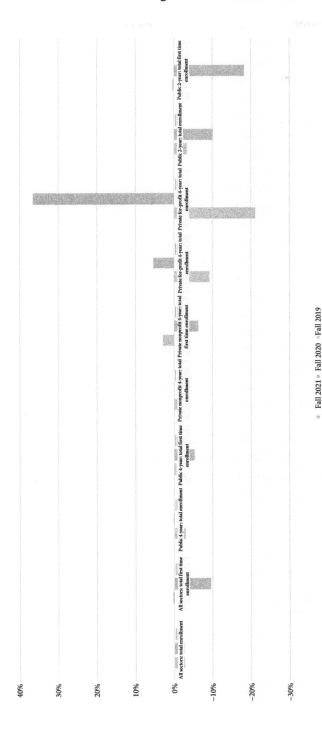

Fig. 4.13 Percentange in estimated annual enrollments from previous year, U.S. post-secondary degree-granting institutions, fall 2019 to fall 2021.

Source: National Student Clearinghouse Research Center. (See Appendix for notes.)

- Non-profit enrollments declined for several reasons.[37] Some students decided to defer their college education out of health and safety concerns. Others abandoned their plans for post-secondary education as a result of a steep drop in personal income, stemming from a sharp rise in unemployment. The faint of heart could not fathom the thought of experiencing college online. And non-U.S. students faced a barracade of travel bans that prevented them from pursuing their studies in the United States.

- Accompanying the drop in enrollments was a significant decline in tuition revenues. According to Moody's Investor Service, the decline was 3% for private non-profits and 1% for publics.[38] For the whole of 2021, aggregate revenues fell by about $85 billion. Yet, despite the drop in enrollments, most colleges and universities "held the line" on tuition rates.[39] Raising the rate to make up for the revenue shortfall, they feared, could backfire by depressing enrollment numbers even further. So, out of desperation, they did what most colleges and universities usually do in normal times: they raised their discount rate. About 60% of private colleges raised it by over 50%. Almost 30% raised it by more than 60%.[40] Predictably, the result was a sharp decline in net income and a narrowing of profit margins. For the first time in recent history, *net* tuition revenue was negative.[41]

- When it rains, it pours. Due to an eleventh-hour shift to online delivery, fewer students resided on campus. Fewer residents translated into lower revenues from room, board, parking, and student services. To make matters worse, the cancellation of football games, theatrical performances, cultural exhibits, and social gatherings slashed revenues from auxiliary services.[42] It also led to lengthy furloughs and massive lay-offs of non-academic staff.

---

[37] National Clearinghouse Center, Tables 1 and 2, *Term Enrollment Estimates*. See also Moody's Investor Service, "Outlook for US Higher Education Sector Remains Negative in 2021 as Pandemic Effects Curtail Revenue," December 8, 2020, https://www.moodys.com/research/moodys-outlook-for-us-higher-education-sector-remains-negative-in—pbm_1255981 (accessed June 1, 2021).

[38] Moody's, "Outlook for US Higher Education Sector," December 8, 2020.

[39] P.N. Friga, "How Much Has Covid Cost Colleges? $183 billion." *The Chronicle of Higher Education*, February 5, 2021.

[40] Friga, "How Much Has Covid Cost Colleges?" *The Chronicle of Higher Education*; also, L. Gardner, "Moody's Forecasts Widespread Drop in Tuition Revenue. Here's Why That Matters," *The Chronicle of Higher Education*, October 29, 2020.

[41] Friga, "How Much Has Covid Cost Colleges?" and Gardner, "Moody's Forecasts Widespread Drop," *The Chronicle of Higher Education*.

[42] National Association of Independent Colleges and Universities, "Survey: The Financial Impact of Covid 19 on Private Nonprofit Colleges," http://naicu.imediainc.com/naicu/media/pdf/covid-19/covid-survey-summary-release.pdf (accessed June 15, 2021).

- The torrential downpour produced a flash flood of extraordinary expenses. For health and safety reasons, U.S. colleges and universities poured huge sums of money into Covid-19 testing, face masks, protective equipment, and classroom partitions. To facilitate the transition from in-person to online delivery, they invested heavily in digital technology, instructional design, online program management, and staff training. In the first half of 2021, total Covid-related expenditures soared to $24 billion, not taking into account contingent liabilities, such as refunds demanded by students for services never rendered. In late-2020, Moody's predicted a 5–10% decline in operating revenues for 60% of all public universities and 75% of all private universities.[43]
- Overwhelmed with a barrage of Covid-related expenditures, state legislatures hardly lifted a finger at the onset of the pandemic to bail out local colleges and universities. On the other hand, the federal government stepped in with a financial stimulus package, but only belatedly.[44]

As we emerge from the crisis, it is still too early to assess the full extent of the damage. What is clear, however, is that by attacking the financial health of American colleges and universities, the Global Pandemic shook the U.S. higher education sector by its very foundation.

Summary

In the past, the captains of American higher education have steered their vessels through narrow straits and turbulent waters. The chaos wreaked by the Global Pandemic will make their voyage infinitely more difficult. It will give rise to challenges fundamentally different from those of the past. Meeting them will require not just skilled navigators, but also wider seas—a metaphor for "broader markets."

Despite all the talk about doom and gloom, there is a ray of hope. It emanates from over the horizon, beyond the boundaries of the United States. Like the beacon of a lighthouse, it can guide the ship captains to broader, calmer, and more bountiful seas. To succeed in their historic journey, they should follow the beacon and sail beyond the horizon. The enormity of what lies ahead is astounding.

---

[43] Moody's Investors Service, "2021 Outlook Negative as Pandemic Weakens Key Revenue Streams," December 8, 2020, https://www.moodys.com/researchdocumentcontentpage.aspx?docid=pbm_1251126 (accessed June 15, 2021).

[44] Friga, "How Much Has Covid Cost Colleges?" *The Chronicle of Higher Education.*

5

Global Markets beyond the Horizon: Part I

This chapter turns to the international side of the Great Chasm (i.e., the "demand side"). Herein arises the immense foreign demand for American higher education talent. This demand has been strengthened by the expansion of the world economy in the New Millennium. It has been shaped by the pressing need, in emerging markets, to forge an educated workforce, train professionals, and build institutions that can contribute to the economic, social, and political well-being of the nation.

The first part of the chapter lays the groundwork for the passages that follow. It elaborates on these ideas: As a result of tighter U.S. visa restrictions and rising anti-immigrant sentiment, the door to a massive influx of foreign students in the United States has been all but shut. This limitation adds weight to the proposition that if all the world cannot come to America for higher education, then why not take American higher education to all the world?

The second part of the chapter purports to convey a sense of the enormity of international markets for higher education. It points out that by tapping these markets, U.S. colleges and universities can enhance their financial viability. Simultaneously, they can serve the educational needs of non-U.S. nationals, solidify the economic substructure of U.S. higher education, and strengthen the critical role that America plays, or should play, globally in the realm of ideas.

> If you are planning for a year, sow rice; if you are planning for a decade, plant trees; if you are planning for a lifetime, educate people.
>
> Chinese proverb

Bridging the Gap between the Abundance of American Higher Education Talent and the Immense Foreign Demand for It.
Richard J. Joseph, Oxford University Press. © Richard J. Joseph (2022). DOI: 10.1093/oso/9780192848307.003.0006

Education is the most powerful weapon you can use to change the world . . .
The power of education extends beyond the development of skills we need for
economic success. It can contribute to nation-building and reconciliation.[1]

Nelson Mandela, former President of South Africa

Bringing all the world to America

For decades, the United States has been the preferred destination for
higher education services. Rather than deliver these services abroad, most
U.S. colleges and universities have delivered them in the United States.
Enhanced by the aura of the American value proposition, they have attracted thousands of East Asian, Middle Eastern, Latin American, South
Asian, and African nationals to their home shores. There, they have provided short courses, degree programs, management training sessions,
faculty symposia, conferences, seminars, and academic advice. While the
principal beneficiaries of these services reside abroad, the locus of delivery
has been the United States (see Figure 5.1).

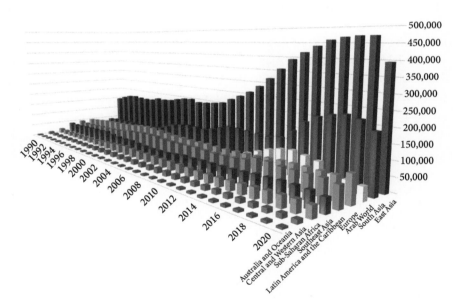

Fig. 5.1 Foreign students enrolled in U.S. higher education institutions by global
region, 1990–2020.
Source: U.S. Department of Education, Institute of Education Sciences, National Center for
Education Statistics. (See Appendix for notes.)

---

[1] Nelson Mandela, as quoted in V. Strauss, "Nelson Mandela on the power of education," *Washington Post*, December 5, 2013.

The magnetic pull of American higher education talent is evidenced by the large number of international students enrolled in U.S. colleges and universities. This number climbed from 408,000 in 1990, to roughly 548,000 in 2000, to 723,000 in 2010, to nearly a million today.[2] As a percentage of total enrollments, it grew from 3–4% at the start of the New Millennium to 5–6% in the mid-2010s.[3] The greatest influx of students came from East and South Asia, followed by the Arab World, Europe, and Latin America. Their willingness to travel to the United States for study attests to the irresistible force of the American value proposition.

The door closing

Recent social and political developments, however, have put a damper on the influx. Large segments of the American population have turned decidedly anti-immigrant. Gallup polls indicate that the vast majority of Americans oppose increasing the level of immigration to the United States.[4] This sentiment, along with national security concerns and the residual effects of the Global Pandemic, has resulted in a tightening of U.S. visa restrictions and a slowing of inbound student mobility.[5] It has also eroded America's standing as the preferred destination for higher education. Many families in the Islamic World, East Asia, and Latin America now question the wisdom of sending their children to the United States for study.[6] Increasingly, they are turning to seemingly safer and more welcoming destinations, such as Canada, Australia, Malaysia, Argentina, and Turkey.

---

[2] U.S. Department of Education, Institute for Education Sciences, National Center for Education Statistics (hereinafter referred to as "NCES"), Table 310.20 "Foreign students enrolled in institutions of higher education in the United States, by continent, region, and selected countries of origin," *Digest of Education Statistics* (annual issues, 1990-2020).

[3] NCES, Tables 310.20 and 303.10 "Total fall enrollment in degree-granting postsecondary institutions, by attendance status, sex of student, and control of institution; and Table 105.30 "Enrollment in elementary, secondary, and degree-granting postsecondary institutions, by level and control of institution," *Digest of Education Statistics* (annual issues, 1990–2020).

[4] For the results of recent Gallup polls on U.S. immigration see https://news.gallup.com/poll/1660/immigration.aspx (accessed July 15, 2021).

[5] The Biden Administration recently reaffirmed America's commitment to international education. Whether this reaffirmation will lead to a significant easing of visa restrictions and a massive influx of international students into the United States has yet to be seen. See U.S. Department of State, EducationUSA, Joint Statement of Principles in Support of International Education (July 2021), https://educationusa.state.gov/us-higher-education-professionals/us-government-resources-and-guidance/joint-statement (accessed August 1, 2021).

[6] See K. Fischer and S. Aslanian, "Fading Beacon," *The Chronicle of Higher Education*, August 2, 2021.

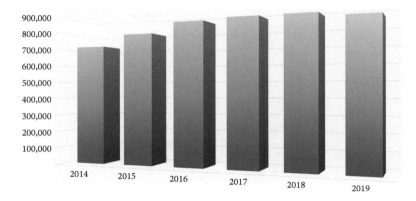

Fig. 5.2 Total internationally mobile tertiary education students enrolled in institutions in the United States, 2014–2019.
Source: UNESCO Institute for Statistics. (See Appendix for notes.)

Indicative of the deceleration, the number of internationally mobile tertiary education (IMTE) students who pursued their studies in the United States inched up by only 1% between 2017 and 2019[7] (see Figure 5.2). This contrasts with a robust 19% increase for the period 2014–2017. The slowdown was greater for IMTE students from the Arab World compared with those from other parts of the world. Trump Administration policy might have played a role in dampening the influx from Muslim-majority countries.

Also reflecting the deceleration is a sharp decline in the number of F-1 visas issued since 2015. This type of visa is given to non-U.S. nationals who attend full-time degree or academic programs at accredited American schools, colleges, or universities.[8] Depending on the terms of sponsorship, it can be valid for two to five years.

From 2003 to 2015, the number of F-1 student visas rose steadily. (Refer to Figure 5.3.) It peaked in the latter year, fell sharply in the latter part of the decade, then tanked in 2020 as a result of travel restrictions relating to

[7] UNESCO Institute for Statistics, "Inbound internationally mobile students by region of origin," and "Inbound internationally mobile students by country of origin," http://data.uis.unesco.org (accessed July 1, 2021).

[8] U.S. Department of Education, Bureau of Educational and Cultural Affairs, BridgeUSA, https://j1visa.state.gov/basics/other-u-s-visas (accessed June 1, 2021); and U.S. Department of Homeland Security, U.S. Citizenship and Immigration Services, "Students and employment," https://www.uscis.gov/working-in-the-united-states/students-and-exchange-visitors/students-and-employment (accessed June 1, 2021).

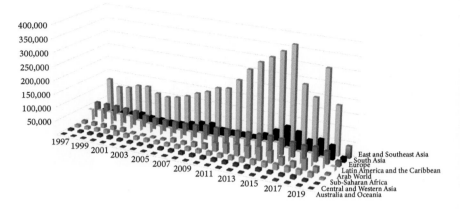

Fig. 5.3 U.S. F-1 student visas issued to residents of various global regions, 1997–2020.
Source: U.S. Department of State, Bureau of Consular Affairs. (See Appendix for notes.)

the Global Pandemic. From 2015 to 2020, the number of F-1 student visas, as a percentage of total U.S. visas, fell by 3%. The overall decline portends a lower level of international student enrollments in the next 2 to 5 years.

In terms of diversity, the composition of F-1 visa holders has noticeably changed.[9] In 2010, the percentage of visa holders from East and Southeast Asia stood at 54%. By 2020, it had declined to about 39%. The percentage of holders from South Asia stood at 8%. It had risen to 16%. Europe's share increased from 13% to nearly 18%; Latin America's, from 10% to almost 14%; that of Sub-Saharan Africa, from about 4% to 5%. The shares of the Arab World and Central and Western Asia fell from 8% to slightly less than 6%, and from 3% to 2%, respectively. Australia/Oceania's share held steady at about 1%. Accounting for these changes are several factors, including growing Chinese and Arab preference for destinations other than the United States, strained U.S. relations with Central Asian countries such as Iran, pandemic-related restrictions aimed at specific countries and regions, and a growing concern, in some U.S. circles, that a massive influx of students from the Middle and Far East could pose a risk to national security.

[9] Based on data presented in U.S. Department of State, Bureau of Consular Affairs, Table XVI(B) "Nonimmigrant Visas Issued by Classification," and in Table XIX "Nonimmigrant Visas Issued by Issuing Office," *Nonimmigrant Visa Statistics* (annual reports, 2013–2020), https://travel.state.gov/content/travel/en/legal/visa-law0/visa-statistics/nonimmigrant-visa-statistics.html (accessed June 15, 2021).

Aside from U.S. visa restrictions, social and cultural factors weigh against a massive influx. While most college and university officials profess to ethnic, cultural, and national diversity, some privately express the belief that opening their doors to a floodgate of international students will drastically change the cultural complexion of their campuses. They also voice concern that a large group of foreign students will not be able to integrate successfully into traditional college life.

Several years ago, senior officials at a private American college weighed a proposal to create an English-as-a-foreign language (EFL) program for Chinese students. The average annual enrollment at the college was 2,800 students. The maximum capacity of the EFL program would have been 20 students per year. To be admitted to the program, the foreign students would have had to meet all of the college's graduate admissions requirements, except the one pertaining to English language proficiency. It was contemplated that the EFL program would elevate the students' linguistic skills to the minimum level of proficiency; also, that after successfully completing the EFL program, the foreign students would be admitted to one of the college's master's programs. Thus, effectively, the EFL program would create a pipeline leading from the huge pool of student talent in China to the U.S. college's undersubscribed master's programs.

Despite sagging graduate enrollments and a gaping budget deficit, the officials categorically rejected the proposal. They expressed concern that the foreign students would not be able to assimilate socially. They also expressed concern that the EFL program would create a "Chinese ghetto" on campus. However biased and perhaps unfounded, such beliefs are not uncommon at some traditional institutions. They act as a brake on increasing international student enrollments at U.S. colleges and universities on a grand scale.

If all the world cannot come to America . . .

So, if, as a result of regulatory barriers, anti-immigration sentiment, and cultural biases, all the world cannot come to America for higher education, then why not take American higher education to all the world? Indeed, if inbound student mobility is restricted, why not increase the outbound mobility of American academic institutions?—Why not *export* U.S. higher education services to the rest of the world? Foreign demand for U.S. higher education services is immense, as global social, economic, and demographic trends indicate.

More on methodology

Before turning to these trends, let us explain our methodology.

- In the analysis that follows, we focused primarily on the emerging markets of East and Southeast Asia, the Arab World, South Asia, Latin America and the Caribbean, Central and Western Asia, and Sub-Saharan Africa. Less attention was given to higher education markets in North America, Europe, and Australia for three reasons: first, these markets are relatively mature. Thus, their growth rates are somewhat slower than those of major emerging markets. Second, they are saturated with potential competitors, many of whom are comparable in quality to U.S. colleges and universities. Third, their college participation rates are relatively high, implying that to make significant inroads into these markets, U.S. colleges and universities would have to offer generous financial incentives. Doing so could adversely impact their bottom line, thus defeating a major purpose of international expansion.
- The scope of our analysis is limited by the availability of empirical data with the following characteristics:
  - reliability: derived from the same authoritative source(s);
  - breadth: broad in terms of geographical coverage;
  - uniformity: based on the same methodology, empirical assumptions, and geo-schemes;
  - completeness: reported at regular intervals throughout the reporting period.

  We found such data at the following sources:
  - International Monetary Fund (IMF), World Economic Outlook Database;
  - United Nations Educational Scientific and Cultural Organization (UNESCO), Institute for Statistics;
  - United Nations, Department of Economic and Social Affairs, Population Division, World Population Prospects;

- U.S. Department of Education, Institute for Education Sciences, National Center for Education Statistics Integrated Postsecondary Education Data System (IPEDS);
- The World Bank DataBank.

• Within these sources, datasets are fairly complete. However, significant gaps exist in some of them, particularly with respect to data for countries in Sub-Saharan Africa, Central and Western Asia, those that comprised the former Yugoslavia and Soviet Union, and the two Germanys between 1970 and 1977. To fill these gaps so as to paint a more coherent picture of long-term trends, we made the following adjustments:

o For the sake of uniformity, as well as comparability with other graphical illustrations in this book, we reconfigured geographic units to comport with the United Nations geo-scheme[10], with the following exception: "Arab World" was created as a separate category to reflect the cultural cohesiveness of this expansive region. Subsumed under this category is a listing of the member states of the Arab League. To avoid double-counting, these states were excluded from the countries listed under the headings "Sub-Saharan Africa" and "Central and Western Asia."

o For each year in a particular reporting period, regional averages were calculated by totaling available country-specific data, then dividing the total by the number of countries that reported substantially all (i.e., more than 50%) of these data. In determining this number, those countries for which data were scant or of nominal value were eliminated from the calculation so as not to skew the regional averages downward. For countries with data more complete and of greater value, statistical gaps were filled by taking the difference between the figures preceding and following the gap, then accruing the difference over the intervening period. Where a gap occurred at the beginning or at the end of a reporting period, the initial or final figure was drawn from other reliable sources (e.g., government databases), or estimated with reference to data for countries with similar economies, cultures, histories, and/or polities (e.g., Estonia relative to Latvia, North Macedonia relative to Greece, South Sudan relative to Sudan).

---

[10] See United Nations, Department of Economic and Social Affairs, Statistics Division, "Methodology, Geographic Regions," https://unstats.un.org/unsd/methodology/m49 (accessed June 1, 2021).

- In the case of per capita values, national and regional averages were weighted to reflect differences in national and regional populations.

The result is a series of estimates, imprecise, yet useful in conveying an *order of magnitude* between and among global regions. This order can be gleaned from the graphical illustrations in this chapter, which are based on a combination of statistical data and extrapolated values for the majority of countries within a particular region. (For an elaboration of this methodology see the notes to illustrations in Chapter 5, which are presented in the Appendix.)

International trends

Long-term trends are telling because they convey a sense of global demand for higher education services. Particularly noteworthy are the following trends: the increase in (1) world population numbers, (2) college-age population numbers, (3) tertiary education enrollments, (4) gross enrollment ratios, (5) GDP per capita, and (6) net national income per capita. They tell a story.

As the world's population expands, so do the ranks of those who seek higher education. As the world economy grows, so do the financial resources at the disposal of prospective consumers. Those who aspire to higher education, have the financial means to pay for it, and are ready and willing to do so are the driving force behind *actual* demand. Those who aspire to higher education, have the financial means to pay for it, but are not ready or willing to do so are a major force behind *potential* demand. Complicating this picture are a variety of personal, social, cultural, and economic factors, which are discussed later in the chapter.

Population growth

General population
Population growth gives rise to a proliferation of wants and needs. With such growth, a greater number of individuals want to acquire the skills necessary for productive careers. A greater number of businesses want to train their managers and staff in best practices. A greater number of schools want to develop their faculty. A greater number of governments want to lay a solid foundation for the social and economic advancement of their

citizens.[11] With population growth, the nations of the world want more educational projects, more technology transfer, more degree and non-degree programs, and more academic advisory services. These wants and needs, fortified by financial resources, shape the immense foreign demand for American higher education talent.

In 2020, the world's population stood at 7.8 billion. This represents a 110% increase from the corresponding figure for 1970. Accounting for the total are the following shares: East and Southeast Asia, 30.1%; South Asia, 24.9%; Sub-Saharan Africa, 13.8%; Europe, 9.6%; Latin America and the Caribbean, 8.5%; the Arab World, 5.6%; North America, 4.7%; Central and Western Asia, 2.4%; Australia and Oceania, 0.5%. In addition, the United States accounts for 4.2% of the total. (See Figure 5.4.)

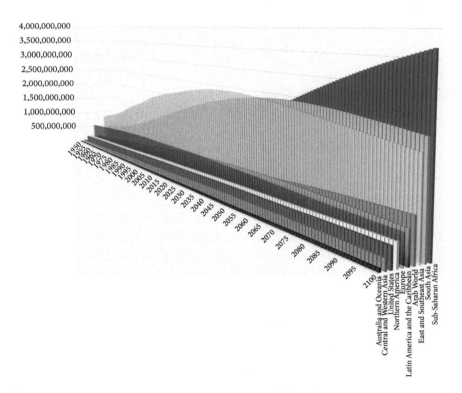

Fig. 5.4 World population in thousands by global region, historical and projected, 1950–2100.

Source: United Nations, Department of Social and Economic Affairs. (See Appendix for notes.)

[11] The discussion that follows is based on data found in United Nations, Department of Economic and Social Affairs, Population Division, *World Population Prospects 2020*.

Since 1970, regional population growth has surged. For Sub-Saharan Africa, the growth rate was 289%; the Arab World, 255%; South Asia, 161%; Latin America and the Caribbean, 128%; Central and Western Asia, 121%; Australia and Oceania, 114%; East and Southeast Asia, 83%; North America, 60%; and Europe, 14%. During the same period, the U.S. population grew by a modest 58%. Accounting for regional and national variations are differences in fertility rates, infant mortality rates, living conditions, and stages of economic development. Also accounting for the variations are diverse migration patterns. Globally, people moved from less to more prosperous regions. Within regions, they moved from middle- to high-income countries.[12]

Although East and Southeast Asia is the world's most populous region, as a result of declining fertility rates, its pace of growth has slowed noticeably in recent years. In 2006, Sub-Saharan Africa overtook Europe as the third most populous region. In 2007, the Arab World surpassed North America to become the sixth most populous region. According to U.N. projections, the population of India will surpass that of China by middle of the 21st Century. Toward the end of the century, the population of Sub-Saharan Africa will overtake that of every other region.[13]

College-age population

Along with the growth in the general population has been an increase in college-age numbers (see Figure 5.5). Since the start of the New Millennium, the rate of increase was 72% for Sub-Saharan Africa; 30% for the Arab World; 29% for Australia and Oceania; 25% for South Asia; 13% for North America; 10% for Latin America and the Caribbean; and 6% for Central and Western Asia. The numbers decreased in only two regions: Europe (−24%) and East and Southeast Asia (−7%).

On the other hand, the college-age population[14] as a percentage of total population has markedly declined over the past half century (see Figure 5.6). From a level of 10.8% in 1950, the ratio peaked at 11.4% in 1985, fell to 10.3% in 2000, then dropped to 9.2% in 2020. The downward

---

[12] United Nations Department of Economic and Social Affairs, Population Division, File ST/ESA/SER.A/452, *International Migration 2020 Highlights*, https://www.un.org/development/desa/pd/sites/www.un.org.development.desa.pd/files/undesa_pd_2020_international_migration_highlights.pdf. On the impact of international migration on demand for higher education see J. Spring, *Globalization of Education*, 2nd ed. (2015), 190–208.
[13] United Nations, *International Migration 2020 Highlights*.
[14] Defined as the five-year age group starting from the official secondary school graduation age. UNESCO Institute for Statistics, "Glossary," http://uis.unesco.org/en/glossary (accessed June 1, 2021). By implication, "college-age population" is the age group encompassing18- to 23-year-olds.

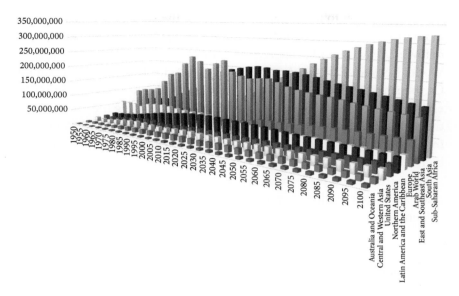

Fig. 5.5 World college-age population in thousands by global region, historical and projected, 1950–2100.

Source: United Nations, Department of Social and Economic Affairs. (See Appendix for notes.)

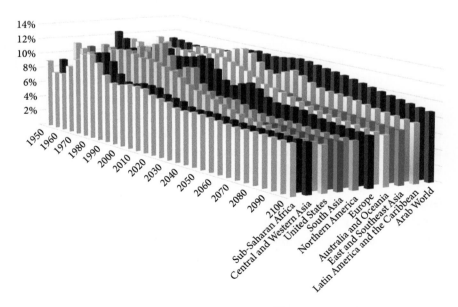

Fig. 5.6 World college-age population as a percentage of total population by global region, historical and projected, 1950–2100.

Source: United Nations, Department of Social and Economic Affairs. (See Appendix for notes.)

trend is common to all global regions. Since the start of the New Millennium, the college-age population as a percentage of total population fell as follows: 2.2% each for Europe, Central and Western Asia, 1.9% for the Arab World, 1.8% for East and Southeast Asia, 1.4% for Latin America and the Caribbean, 0.7% for South Asia, 0.5% for Australia and Oceania, and 0.4% each for Sub-Saharan Africa and North America. During the same period, the corresponding ratio for the United States decreased by 0.3%. Contributing to the decline in all parts of the world are better living conditions and higher life expectancy.[15]

Notwithstanding the percentage decline, the growth in numbers indicates significant market potential. This potential is largely unrealized, as is evidenced by statistics on tertiary education enrollments.

Tertiary education enrollments

Gross enrollment numbers

Beyond the more advanced regions of the world, nations with the highest tertiary education enrollments lie in East and Southeast Asia, South Asia, and Latin America and the Caribbean (see Figure 5.7). Nations with the lowest lie in Sub-Saharan Africa, Central and Western Asia, and the Arab World. Reflecting a major shift in enrollment trends, Europe was overtaken by East and Southeast Asia in 2005 and by South Asia in 2012. North America was overtaken by Latin America and the Caribbean in 2008. In recent years, enrollments in Europe and North America have been on the decline, while those in East and Southeast Asia, South Asia, and Latin America and the Caribbean have been on the rise. These divergent trends suggest faltering demand for higher education in the more advanced nations of the world and surging demand in major emerging markets.

Gross enrollment ratios

A better gauge of market potential is "gross enrollment ratio." It expresses the relationship between total enrollments at a particular education level

[15] United Nations, Population Division, Department of Economic and Social Affairs, File MORT/7-1 "Life expectancy at birth (both sexes combined) by region, sub-region and country, 1950–2100 (years), Estimates, 1950–2020," POP/DB/WPP/Rev.2019/MORT/F07-1, *World Population Prospects 2019* (2019), https://population.un.org/wpp (accessed June 1, 2021); and United Nations, Population Division, Department of Economic and Social Affairs, World Population Prospects 2019, File MORT/7-1, "Life expectancy at birth (both sexes combined) by region, sub-region and country, 1950–2100 (years), Estimates, 1950–2020," POP/DB/WPP/Rev.2019/MORT/F07-1.

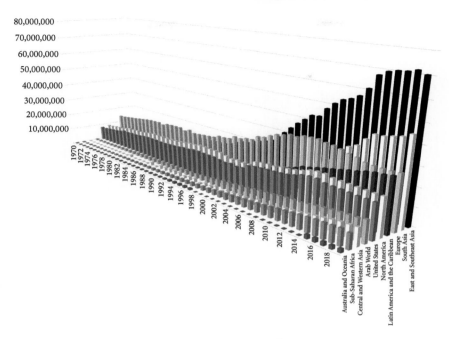

Fig. 5.7 Enrollment in higher education by global region, 1970–2019.
Source: UNESCO Institute for Statistics. (See Appendix for notes.)

and the total population of the official age group that corresponds to this level. For higher education, often referred to as "tertiary education," the gross enrollment ratio is the relationship between total enrollments at public and private universities, colleges, technical training institutes, and vocational schools and the total population of 18- to 24-year-olds that corresponds to this level.[16] If every 18- to 24-year-old were enrolled in tertiary education programs, the gross enrollment ratio would be *at least* 100%. The ratio could exceed 100% if members of other age groups (e.g., 25- to 30-year-olds) were also enrolled in these programs.

Figure 5.8 illustrates, by order of magnitude, long-term trends in gross enrollment ratios for countries in various global regions. The highest ratios are for countries in North America, followed by those for the nations of Europe. Lagging behind are countries in Latin America and the Caribbean,

---

[16] As used by the World Bank, "higher education" refers to all post-secondary education, including public and private universities, colleges, technical training institutes, and vocational schools. The World Bank, "Higher Education," https://www.worldbank.org/en/topic/tertiaryeducation#what_why (accessed June 1, 2021). For a discussion of tertiary enrollments in the various global regions in general see R.B. Freeman, "What Does Global Expansion of Higher Education Mean for the United States?" In *American Universities in a Global Market*, edited by C.T. Clotfelter (2010), 374–376.

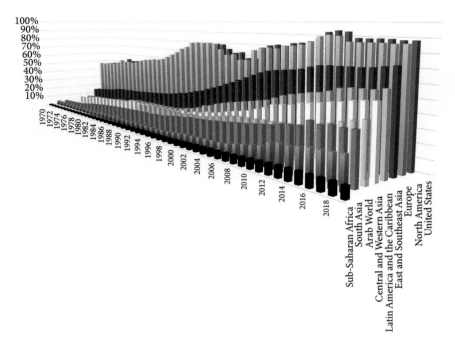

Fig. 5.8 Tertiary education gross enrollment ratios by global region, 1970–2019.
Source: UNESCO Institute for Statistics. (See Appendix for notes.)

East and Southeast Asia, Central and Western Asia, and the Arab World. Trailing far behind are nations in South Asia and Sub-Saharan Africa. This hierarchy points to a "great divide" in the massification of higher education. A larger proportion of the populations of the Global North and West are enrolled in higher education compared to those of the Global South and East.

Gross enrollment potential

A crude gauge of the "capacity" for incremental enrollments is "gross enrollment potential." Based on the reciprocal value of the gross enrollment ratio, it is calculated by subtracting the gross enrollment ratio (for a particular country or region) from a whole digit, or one hundred percentage points. In principle, the larger the difference, the greater the potential; conversely, the smaller the difference, the less the potential. To illustrate, if the gross enrollment ratio for a particular country or region were 45%, the gross enrollment potential would be 55% (i.e., 100% – 45%). This reciprocal value signifies that if an additional 55% of the applicable age group[17] were enrolled in programs at the applicable educational level, the result would be a 100% participation rate, or universal enrollment for that age group. Of course, aspiring to such a standard would be extremely idealistic, if not overly ambitious. Nonetheless, as a rough measure of capacity, the concept is useful.

Comparing gross enrollment potential to a global norm provides an even better gauge of capacity. Understanding why requires a little imagination. If policymakers in a less-developed country aspired to increase the proportion of their population enrolled in tertiary education programs, they might base their target percentage on a global standard. One such standard is the "world norm." It is calculated by taking the average of regional values, weighted by regional population numbers.[18]

Figure 5.9 presents a graphical illustration of regional gross enrollment potentials relative to the world norm. It indicates, by order of magnitude, that countries in Sub-Saharan Africa, South Asia, and the Arab World

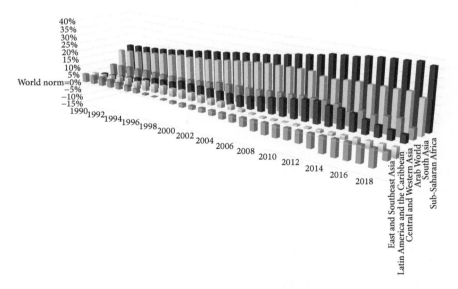

Fig. 5.9 Tertiary education gross enrollment potential by global region relative to world norm, 1990–2019.

Source: UNESCO Institute for Statistics. (See Appendix for notes.)

---

[17] In theory, the additional 55% could be taken up by enrollments of members of other age groups.
[18] UNESCO Institute for Statistics, "Gross enrolment ratio, tertiary, both sexes (%)," http://data.uis.unesco.org/index.aspx?queryid=142; and "School enrollment, tertiary (% gross)" (accessed June 1, 2021).

have the greatest gross enrollment potential, because their capacity for incremental enrollments exceeds the world norm.

Countries with less gross enrollment potential lie in Central and Western Asia, East and Southeast Asia, and Latin America and the Caribbean. Their capacity for incremental enrollments falls short of the world norm. On the other hand, this capacity exceeds the norm defined by the gross enrollment ratios of the more advanced nations of Europe and North America.

The broad implication is this: if nations in Sub-Saharan Africa, South Asia, and the Arab World aspire to the world norm and have sufficient financial resources to realize their aspirations, their demand for tertiary education programs will be substantial. If nations in Central and Western Asia, East and Southeast Asia, and Latin America and the Caribbean aspire to the world norm and have sufficient financial resources, their demand will be great, though somewhat lower. If these countries aspire to the North American or European norm and have sufficient financial resources to realize their aspirations, their demand will be significant, but based on a different standard.

Realizing the potential

As the previous discussion implies, market demand can be actual or potential. Potential demand is based primarily on aspirations. Actual demand is based on aspirations, given potency through adequate financial means. It follows, logically, that realizing potential demand could be limited by financial resources. Other factors could also be at play.

Some individuals with adequate financial means might not *want* to pursue a particular course of study. Or, they might not meet its admissions requirements. Some might not be able to afford the cost of a particular tertiary education program. Or, they might not have access to financial aid on reasonable terms. Still others might face exorbitant opportunity costs if they leave their jobs or abandon their families. Or, they might not be able to find a program suitable for their career interests.

Then there are macro-level constraints. In some parts of the world, countries lack the infrastructure, facilities, faculty, and equipment needed to accommodate incremental enrollments.[19] Social factors could also pose obstacles. Gender, religion, ethnicity, and caste could impede broad access to tertiary education programs.[20] So could language and distance from major urban centers. As a result, incremental enrollments could remain

---

[19] See P.G. Altbach, L. Reisberg, and L.E. Rumbley, *Trends in Global Higher Education: Tracking an Academic Revolution* (UNESCO, 2009), 38–39; and, in general, D. Bloom, D. Canning, and K. Chan, *Higher Education and Economic Development in Africa* (World Bank, 2005).

[20] Altbach, Reisberg, and Rumbley, *Trends in Global Higher Education*, 39.

just a possibility. Realizing this possibility requires not just "capacity" but also human, material, and financial resources, as well as a propitious social, economic, and cultural climate.

National wealth and income

GDP per capita

A crude indicator of financial means is GDP per capita.[21] Though not synonymous with national wealth, it is closely associated with it.

Beyond North America, Europe, and Australia, regions with the highest GDP per capita (historical and projected) are East and Southeast Asia, and the Arab World (see Figure 5.10). Following these regions, by order of

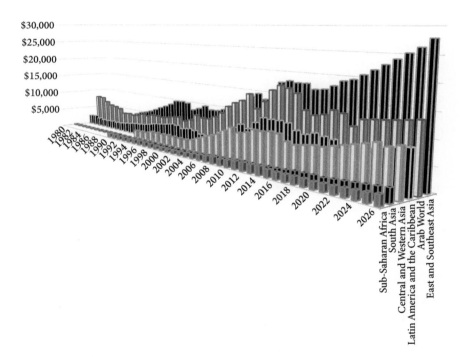

Fig. 5.10 GDP per capita in current U.S. dollars by global region, historical and projected, 1980–2026.

Source: International Monetary Fund. (See Appendix for notes.)

[21] "GDP per capita is gross domestic product divided by midyear population. GDP is the sum of gross value added by all resident producers in the economy plus any product taxes and minus any subsidies not included in the value of the products. It is calculated without making deductions for depreciation of fabricated assets or for depletion and degradation of natural resources." The World Bank, DataBank, Metadata Glossary, https://databank.worldbank.org/metadataglossary/all/series?search=gdp%20per%20capita (accessed July 15, 2021).

magnitude, are Latin America and the Caribbean, and Central and Western Asia. Lagging far behind are South Asia and Sub-Saharan Africa. This order suggests that in the emerging markets of the world, nations in East and Southeast Asia and the Arab World are likely to have the greatest financial means to pay for higher education services. By implication, they are in the best position to influence market demand.

Net national income per capita

Another gauge of financial means is net national income (NNI) per capita.[22] NNI is gross national product, plus wages, salaries, and property income from abroad, minus fixed asset depreciation. This quantity divided by total average population produces NNI per capita. NNI differs from GDP in that it measures income generated by the residents of a country, whether earned at home or abroad. By contrast, GDP measures income generated from production activities within the country, whether earned by residents or non-residents.[23]

Beyond North America, Europe, and Australia, the regions with highest historical NNI per capita are East and Southeast Asia, and Latin America and the Caribbean (see Figure 5.11). Next by order of magnitude are Central and Western Asia, and the Arab World. Lowest in the hierarchy are South Asia and Sub-Saharan Africa. This order suggests that beyond the most advanced regions of the world, nations in East and Southeast Asia, and Latin America and the Caribbean are in the strongest position to influence market demand. Those in the weakest position lie in South Asia and Sub-Saharan Africa.

What is striking about the data underlying the figures is that they suggest that even individuals with significant "financial means" might not be able to afford a four-year residential U.S. college education. For the 2019–2020 academic year, the average cost of college tuition, fees, and room and board for full-time students at all U.S. institutions was about $35,000.[24] This is more than six times 2019 NNI per capita each for Central

---

[22] Typically, one would look to disposable income per capita in determining ability to pay for higher education. However, because reliable and uniform data on disposable income are not available for many countries, a good proxy is NNI per capita.

[23] "Adjusted net national income is GNI minus consumption of fixed capital and natural resources depletion." The World Bank, DataBank, Metadata Glossary, https://databank.worldbank.org/metadataglossary/all/series?search=net%20national%20income%20per%20capita (accessed July 15, 2021).

[24] NCES, Table 330.10 "Average undergraduate tuition and fees and room and board rates charged for full-time students in degree-granting postsecondary institutions, by level and control of institution," *Digest of Education Statistics 2020.*

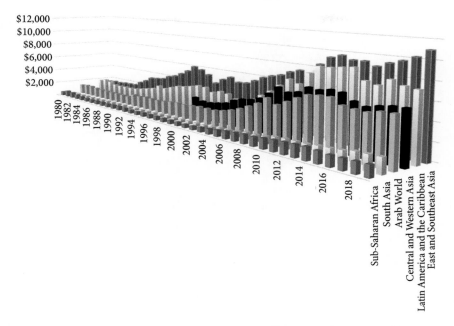

Fig. 5.11 Net national income per capita in current U.S. dollars by global region, 1980–2019.

Source: The World Bank. (See Appendix for notes.)

and Western Asia, and the Arab World; more than four and a half times the estimate for Latin America and the Caribbean; and over three times that for East and Southeast Asia.

Government expenditures on education

Where personal financial means are inadequate, governments can play a pivotal role in shaping market demand. Many control large budgets that can be used to subsidize higher education and/or augment the financial means of those who seek it.

Figure 5.12 presents a graphical illustration of government educational expenditures as a percentage of GDP. It indicates that beyond Europe, North America, and Australia, countries that spend the highest percentage of their GDP on education lie in Latin America and the Caribbean, the Arab World, and Sub-Saharan Africa. Countries that spend the lowest lie in East and Southeast Asia, and South Asia. To some extent, this order of magnitude reflects diverse national priorities and different conceptions of

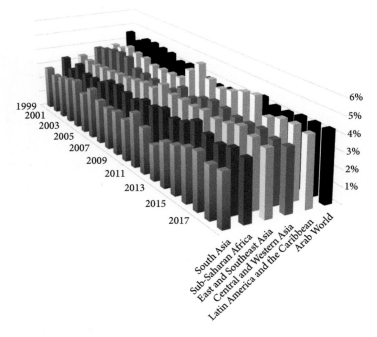

Fig. 5.12 Government expenditure on education as a percentage of GDP by global region, 1999–2018.
Source: The World Bank. (See Appendix for notes.)

the role of government in funding education. In many parts of the world, particularly East and Southeast Asia, governments play a relatively minor role, and education is more privatized.[25]

The epicenter of potential demand

So wherein lies the greatest potential demand for higher education services? Conceived in graphical terms, the epicenter of this demand lies somewhere near the intersection of high gross enrollment potential and high GDP/NNI per capita. At that point on the x- and y-axes, nations with the greatest capacity for incremental enrollments will also have the greatest financial resources. Of the emerging markets of the world, most nations that fit these parameters lie in East and Southeast Asia, Latin America

---

[25] Altbach, Reisberg, and Rumbley, *Trends in Global Higher Education*, 12–14, 69, 79–87. The current trend in Latin America and the Caribbean is also toward privatization.

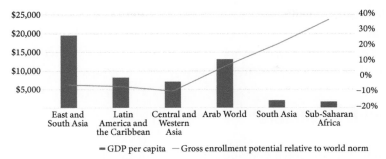

Fig. 5.13 Gross enrollment potential relative to world norm and GDP per capita by global region, 2019.

Sources: gross enrollment data: UNESCO Institute for Statistics; GDP data: The World Bank. (See Appendix for notes.)

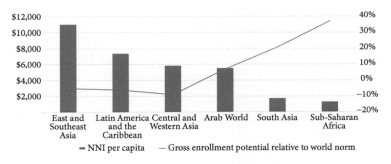

Fig. 5.14 Gross enrollment potential relative to world norm and NNI per capita by global region, 2019.

Sources: gross enrollment data: UNESCO Institute for Statistics; NNI data: The World Bank. (See Appendix for notes.)

and the Caribbean, Central and Western Asia, and the Arab World (see Figures 5.13 and 5.14). Broad segments of their population, primarily the middle classes, have sufficient financial means to realize their aspirations. Thus, they are in a good position to influence market demand.

Sadly, this state of affairs will leave the nations of Sub-Saharan Africa and South Asia far behind the pack. Despite their huge capacity for incremental enrollments, they lack the financial resources necessary to significantly influence market demand. Accentuating this shortfall will be the expected surge in their population numbers in the latter part of the twenty-first century. Without an overriding surge in their per capita wealth and income numbers, the gap between their potential and actual demand will widen.

No doubt, there will always be pockets of affluence in major urban areas, such as Mumbai, Karachi, Lagos, and Johannesburg. There, the middle classes will be a driving force behind the massification of higher education. So will their national governments and private businesses.

The "bigger picture"

The dynamics of global demand for higher education can be summarized as follows: this demand will be shaped by foreign individuals and entities that both aspire to U.S. higher education services and have the financial means to pay for them. Beyond Europe, North America, and Australia, many of these consumers live and work in the emerging markets of East and Southeast Asia, Latin America and the Caribbean, Central and Western Asia, and the Arab World.

As these markets expand, large segments of the population will join the workforce. In the process, they will look to acquire the skills necessary for well-paying jobs.[26] Simultaneously, local businesses will want to train their managers and staff in best commercial practices. They will also want to acquire cutting-edge technologies adaptable to large-scale production and commercialization. Local colleges and universities will seek academic advice on how to develop new courses and curricula. They will also seek experienced faculty who can train their instructors in best teaching and research practices.[27] Governments will want higher education expertise to build research institutes, laboratories, hospitals, and schools. They will also want to educate their citizens so as to improve their productivity, increase their prosperity, and enhance their personal well-being.

All this will fuel foreign demand for U.S. higher education talent. As economic growth gives rise to new wants and needs, it will have a multiplier effect.

---

[26] This demand will shape the nature of the courses and curricula offered by colleges and universities that cater to it. It is likely to prompt the development of applied academic and professional programs relating to economic expansion. By the same token, it could also encourage the development of liberal arts programs that impart core competencies, such as critical thinking, problem-solving, and analytical skills. Altbach, Reisberg, and Rumbley, *Trends in Global Higher Education*, 103–104.

[27] The Organization for Economic Cooperation and Development (OECD) estimates that international demand for faculty will surge through 2030. With the massification of higher education, countries with rising college-age population numbers will need qualified instructors with terminal degrees to prepare college-age individuals for entry into the workforce. OECD, *Higher Education to 2030 (Vol.1): Demography* (2008), 13–14.

6

Global Markets beyond the Horizon: Part II

This chapter focuses on higher education markets in the Arab World, East and Southeast Asia, South Asia, and Latin America. In addition, it discusses international branch campuses in emerging markets, the expansion of the global market for internationally mobile tertiary education students, and the responsiveness of a handful of U.S. colleges and universities to the immense foreign demand for American higher education talent. Lastly, the chapter identifies potential competitors in various higher education export markets, based on the national origin of branch campus sponsors, and the principal countries of destination for internationally mobile tertiary education students.

> Knowledge is power. Information is liberating. Education is the premise of progress, in every society, in every family. On its foundation rest the cornerstones of freedom, democracy, and sustainable human development.[1]
>
> Kofi Annan, seventh Secretary General of the United Nations

> Education is neither Eastern nor Western. Education is education and it's the right of every human being.[2]
>
> Malala Yousafzai, Pakistani gender and human rights advocate

Regional and national markets

Beyond the horizon, opportunities abound in four major markets: the Arab World, East and Southeast Asia, South Asia, and Latin America.[3]

---

[1] K. Annan, United Nations Press Release SG/SM/6268, June 23, 1997.

[2] M. Yousafzai, as quoted in J. Meikle, "Malala Yousafzai Urges British Girls Not to Take Education for Granted," *The Guardian*, October 7, 2013.

[3] In Central Asia, the principal market for U.S. higher education services is Kazakhstan. For the period 2012–2019, the value of contracts awarded by public and private entities in the region to U.S. colleges and universities approached $25 million. In Sub-Saharan Africa, the principal markets are

Bridging the Gap between the Abundance of American Higher Education Talent and the Immense Foreign Demand for It. Richard J. Joseph, Oxford University Press. © Richard J. Joseph (2022). DOI: 10.1093/oso/9780192848307.003.0007

The Arab World

In the Arab World, the largest national markets for higher education services lie in the oil-rich kingdoms of the Arabian Peninsula. With ambitious
social agendas, their rulers are dramatically shaping the structure of higher
education demand in the region. Their strategic goals are several. First,
faced with the prospect of natural resource depletion, they want to diversify their national economies and lessen their dependence on oil. They see
higher education as a means for doing so. Second, to ease the burden on
the state welfare system, they want to make their youth more financially
self-reliant. They believe that higher education will equip them with the
skills necessary for long and productive careers. Third, to reduce national
dependence on foreign expertise, they aspire to create a cadre of indigenous managers, engineers, scientists, and other professionals who can play
a greater role in the economy. In their view, higher education is integral
to the process. Finally, they regard entrepreneurship as a way to stimulate
economic growth. To promote and support entrepreneurial activities, they
seek instructors and programs that can impart the requisite skills.

Toward achieving these strategic goals, Arab rulers are pouring millions
of dollars into executive, technical, and professional training programs;
start-up colleges and universities; business incubators and accelerators;
and scientific and medical research institutes. To date, these ventures have
generated handsome fees for Western higher education service providers,
many of whom are based in the United States.

To cite a few examples: in 1997, the Qatar Foundation, funded by the
Emir of Qatar, launched Education City, a multimillion dollar development project near Doha.[4] The purpose of the venture is to create an
educational hub that will transform Qatar's energy-based economy into
one that is more knowledge-based. Through various financial incentives,
the foundation persuaded eight top-tier Western universities, including six
American, to establish branch campuses in the city. It asked each institution to develop courses and curricula in one or more areas of specialization.

South Africa and Nigeria. For this period, the corresponding figures were about $25 million for South
Africa and slightly more than $13 million for Nigeria. U.S. Department of Education, Office of Federal
Student Aid, "Foreign Gift and Contract Report" (annual reports, 2018–2020), https://studentaid.gov/
data-center/school/foreign-gifts (accessed August 1, 2021).

[4] For a description of the project see the official Qatar Foundation Education City website at
https://www.qf.org.qa/education/education-city (accessed July 15, 2021); also T. Mazzarol and
G.N. Soutar, "Revisiting the Global Market for Higher Education." *Asia Pacific Journal of Marketing
and Logistics*, vol. 24, no. 5 (2012): 717, 729.

The six American universities and their respective specializations are as follows:

- Virginia Commonwealth, the arts and design;
- Cornell, medicine;
- Texas A&M, engineering;
- Carnegie Mellon, biology, computer science, and business administration;
- Georgetown, international politics, economics, culture, and history;
- Northwestern, journalism and communication.

The two non-U.S. institutions are HEC Paris and University College, London. Their respective specializations are business/executive education and information studies/museum practice.

Education City is an innovative way for governments in developing countries to leverage off the strengths of top-tier Western academic institutions to build a first-class multidisciplinary university. The Qatari project has been successful, despite major challenges.[5]

A similar venture is Dubai International Academic City (DIAC). Its strategic goal is to transform Dubai into an international education center. DIAC was founded by TECOM, a subsidiary of a Dubai investment group. Though independent of the government, DIAC is backed by the government and aligns its commercial goals with the emirate's strategic goals. Since its founding in 2007, DIAC has evolved into the largest education hub in the Middle East.

It houses a common library and auditorium, three innovation centers, and the branch campuses of 27 colleges and universities. It hosts over 27,000 students from more than 150 countries. These students are enrolled in over 500 degree programs.

For many Western colleges and universities, DIAC serves as an offshore base for targeting the huge education markets of South Asia and Sub-Saharan Africa. Unlike higher education ventures in the latter regions, it operates in a free zone, and thus is less fettered by government regulation.

In 2016, Saudi Arabia unveiled *Vision 2030*, an ambitious plan to transform the Kingdom into an economic powerhouse connecting Europe,

---

[5] One of these challenges is discussed in *Gulf News Journal* Reports, "Roots of American Universities Grow Deeper in Qatar, Drawing Criticism," *Gulf News Journal*, June 8, 2015, https://gulfnewsjournal.com/stories/510548507-roots-of-american-universities-grow-deeper-in-qatar-drawing-criticism (accessed June 1, 2021).

Africa, and Asia.[6] Toward realizing this vision, the Saudi government has invested heavily in higher education programs and institutions. Its strategic goals include aligning program learning outcomes with the needs of the marketplace, equipping Saudi youth with the skills necessary for successful careers, elevating the social status of women,[7] and creating an entrepreneurial ecosystem in the Arabia Peninsula. Toward achieving these goals, the government allocated huge sums for a long list of projects.[8] They encompass:

- joint research,
- technology transfer,
- business incubators and accelerators,
- education programs for small- and medium-size enterprises,
- the expansion of existing colleges and universities,
- the establishment of new ones,
- career development and faculty training,
- the creation of online courses and curricula,
- women entrepreneurship programs.

The Saudi government has turned to U.S. colleges and universities for academic assistance. Those that have risen to the occasion include Tufts, Johns Hopkins, George Mason, and the Massachusetts Institute of Technology.

Despite the slashing of government budgets in recent years, the market for higher education in the Arabian Peninsula remains robust. Between 2014 and 2019, the total value of contracts awarded to U.S. colleges and universities was as follows: $2.7 billion in Qatar, $838 million in Saudi Arabia, $347 million in the United Arab Emirates (U.A.E.), $169 million in Kuwait, and $38 million in Oman[9] (see Figure 0.2 in the Introduction).

The challenges facing U.S. higher education service providers in this part of the world are numerous. They touch on the following:

---

[6] Kingdom of Saudi Arabia, *Vision 2030*, https://www.vision2030.gov.sa (accessed June 1, 2021). On recent developments in Saudi higher education see S. AllahMorad and S. Zreik, "Education in Saudi Arabia." *World Education News and Reviews*, April 9, 2020, https://wenr.wes.org/2020/04/education-in-saudi-arabia (accessed August 25, 2021).

[7] Notwithstanding this strategic goal, most tertiary education programs in the Kingdom are segregated by gender, a phenomenon that results in the duplication of costs and efforts.

[8] See A. McKie, "Vision or Mirage in Saudi Arabia?" *Inside Higher Ed*, July 5, 2018.

[9] U.S. Department of Education, *Foreign Gift and Contract Report, 2020*, https://studentaid.gov/data-center/school/foreign-gifts (accessed August 1, 2021).

- *Academic freedom*: Many Middle East officials pay lip service to academic freedom, without wholeheartedly endorsing it.
- *Administrative staff*: Non-academic staff with extensive experience in college or university affairs are few and far between.
- *Student quality*: Many local students have been spoiled by social entitlements. Some lack the motivation, drive, and interest to succeed in a rigorous tertiary education program.
- *Business partners*: Many investors in higher education projects are more interested in financial returns and co-branding than in scholarship and knowledge creation. Some lack an appreciation for the core values of the academy. Others bypass faculty in shared governance and judge professorial quality solely in terms of student satisfaction.
- *Commercial attitude*: In some circles, there is an overriding belief that Oxford-quality talent, like any other "commodity," can be bought at the "right" price. Needless to say, those who espouse this belief are naïve.

East and Southeast Asia

In the emerging markets of the Far East, governments see higher education as a means of developing the human talent necessary to support and sustain economic growth. In their view, higher learning, technological advancement, economic progress, and social transformation go hand-in-hand. This is particularly true of the People's Republic of China, where the Communist Party plays the dominant role in formulating higher education policy. To party leaders, higher education should serve the strategic goals of socialist modernization.[10]

This philosophy inspired a series of initiatives designed to mold the future "managers" of the communist revolution and improve the standing of Chinese academic institutions on the world stage. In 1995, the Ministry

---

[10] This philosophy is reflected in the Higher Education Law of the People's Republic of China, adopted August 29, 1998 at the Fourth Session of the Standing Committee of the Ninth National People's Congress, China Education Center, https://www.chinaeducenter.com/en/cedu/hel.php (accessed June 1, 2021). Article IV of the law states: "Higher education shall be conducted in adherence to the educational principles of the State, in the service of the socialist modernization drive and in combination with productive labour, in order that the educatees shall become builders and successors for the socialist cause, who are developed in an all-around way—morally, intellectually and physically." On higher education in China see Organization for Economic Cooperation and Development, *Education in China, a Snapshot* (2016), 14; and M. Gu, R. Michael, C. Zheng, and S. Trines, "Education in China." *World Education News and Reviews*, December 17, 2019, https://wenr.wes.org/2019/12/education-in-china-3 (accessed August 25, 2021).

of Education launched Project 211 with the aim of developing a cadre of professionals capable of implementing the party's plans for social and economic transformation.[11] In 1998, the General Secretary of the Communist Party inaugurated Project 985 toward improving the research capability and increasing the scholarly output of a select group of Chinese universities.[12] In 2015, the State Council unveiled the "Double First Class Project" intended to support and strengthen certain disciplines, elevate an elite group of universities to world-class status, and transform China into a higher education power by 2050.[13] Toward propelling these initiatives forward, the government allocated billions of yuan to 36 top-tier (Class A), six second-tier (Class B), and over 50 middle-tier (non-Class A and B) universities.[14] These measures are likely to raise the standards of Chinese academic institutions in the years ahead.[15]

They are also likely to segment the market into first-tier, second-tier, and third-tier universities. First-tier universities are those designated as such under Projects 211, 985, and "Double First Class." About 150 in number, they include prestigious public institutions, such as Tsinghua, Peking, Fudan, and Zhejiang. Second-tier universities are all others funded under Project 211 or the "Double First Class" initiative. They include highly specialized public universities, such as Beijing Sport University, Shanghai Conservatory of Music, Northeast Forestry University, and Tianjin University of Traditional Chinese Medicine; also, multidisciplinary public universities that are strong in certain areas. Third-tier universities are all other Chinese colleges and universities that are not specifically designated under any of the foregoing initiatives. They include over 2,500 government-sponsored higher education institutions and more than 300 private universities.

In the future, the nature and scope of market opportunities will depend on the relative standing of the Chinese institution. In light of the goals of Project 985 and the "Double First Class" initiative, first-tier Chinese universities are likely to seek research collaboration, faculty exchanges, and joint projects in all disciplines. Second-tier Chinese universities will want

---

[11] China Education Center, "Project 211 and 985," https://www.chinaeducenter.com/en/cedu/ceduproject211.php (accessed June 1, 2021).
[12] China Education Center, "Project 211 and 985."
[13] *People's Daily* (China), September 21, 2017, http://en.people.cn (accessed June 1, 2021).
[14] See, for example, L. Qingquan, "China's Double First Class Programme Should Open to Regional Universities." *Times Higher Education*, July 21, 2020.
[15] On higher education reform in China see H. Li, "Higher Education in China, Complement or Competition to U.S. Universities." In *American Universities in a Global Market*, edited by C.T. Clotfelter (2010), 278–281.

faculty, staff, and management training programs, research collaboration in specific disciplines, and joint projects in the social, economic, cultural, and scientific realms. Third-tier universities will want a wide array of services, including higher education advisory services, course and curriculum design and development, faculty training, and quality assurance.

This demand could benefit broad segments of the U.S. higher education sector. First-tier demand is likely to benefit top-ranked American colleges and universities; second-tier demand, U.S. academic institutions that are strong in the social, economic, cultural, and scientific disciplines; third-tier demand, colleges and universities in all subsectors. Eager to improve their standing in Chinese higher education hierarchy, third-tier universities will be receptive to advice and assistance from all types of academic institutions.

To date, several U.S. colleges and universities have taken advantage of these opportunities. In 2006, the University of Michigan partnered with Shanghai Jiao Tong University (then a Project 211 and 985 university, and later a "Double First Class" institution) to establish a joint engineering institute in Shanghai. In 2010, Duke University joined forces with Wuhan University (also a Project 211 and 985 university, and subsequently a "Double First Class" institution) to build a liberal arts and technical research university at Kunshan. In 2012, New York University embarked on a joint venture with East China Normal University (the same triple designation) to establish NYU Shanghai, a broad-based teaching and research university. In 2014, the University of California, Berkeley partnered with Tsinghua University (a triple designation) to create the research-oriented Shenzhen Institute.

In the context of a multimillion dollar higher education market, as well as the government's ambitious plans to improve the stature of Chinese universities globally, these ventures are just the tip of the iceberg. Despite a declining Chinese fertility rate, which portends a drop in college-age numbers, the national market remains huge. While U.S. colleges and universities have made inroads into the markets of Beijing, Shanghai, and Hong Kong, they have hardly put a dent in the massive markets of the interior.

Among the challenges that Western academic institutions are likely to face in the Chinese market are the following:

- *Language barriers*: Relative to their South and West Asian counterpart, few Chinese students, faculty, and administrators beyond Hong

Kong are fluent in English. By the same token, few American students, faculty, and administrators are fluent in Mandarin.

- *The appropriate level of authority*: In the various provincial markets, identifying which level of Communist Party officialdom to approach for project authorization can be tricky. In some locales, key decision-makers are local party leaders; in other locales, provincial party leaders; still in others, national party leaders. The lack of clarity creates confusion.

- *Intellectual property*: Many Western colleges and universities are apprehensive about foreign appropriation of their intellectual property. They fear that their state-controlled Chinese partners will acquire their intellectual property and then squeeze them out of the joint venture. Whether this fear is justified has yet to be seen.

- *Government controls*: Education authorities insist on controlling enrollment numbers, admissions criteria, tuition rates, and some program content. A high degree of control risks program viability and institutional autonomy.

- *Government restrictions*: For nationalistic and ideological reasons, the Ministry of Education has restricted the number and scope of foreign partnerships. In 2018, it annulled more than a fifth of them, including local partnerships with the University of Florida and the City University of Seattle.[16] U.S. academic institutions can still enter the Chinese market, but only if they sponsor single-degree joint programs or joint institutes and are hosted by an existing Chinese university;[17] also if the arrangement is sanctioned by local government authorities.[18]

- *Academic freedom*: While most Chinese academics profess to academic freedom, many party, government, and university officials do not.[19] Western scholars claim that the government is increasingly suppressing freedom of expression at local colleges and universities.[20] The recent crackdown on political dissent in Hong Kong could be a sign of things to come. Significantly, in 2015, the University of Groningen cancelled plans for a joint venture with China Agricultural

---

[16] E. Feng, "China Closes a Fifth of University Partnerships." *Financial Times*, July 17, 2018.

[17] Feng, "China Closes a Fifth of University Partnerships."

[18] I am grateful to China Education Consultant James Chen for this insight.

[19] See Scholars at Risk, *Obstacles to Excellence: Academic Freedom and China's Quest for World-Class Universities* (2019), https://www.scholarsatrisk.org/wp-content/uploads/2019/09/scholars-at-risk-obstacles-to-excellence_en.pdf (accessed July 15, 2021).

[20] See, for example, J. Ruth and Y. Xiao, "Academic Freedom and China" (American Association of University Professors, 2019), https://www.aaup.org/article/academic-freedom-and-china#.x9vtgi2cars (accessed June 1, 2021).

University over concerns about academic freedom. In 2018, Cornell terminated a partnership with Renmin University over similar concerns.

In Japan, South Korea, Singapore, Taiwan, Indonesia, Malaysia, and the Philippines, the private sector plays a major role in higher education.[21] In all these countries, rapid economic growth has fueled the rise of the middle class. Accompanying its ascendancy has been a corresponding rise in national demand for higher education, despite a tapering off in recent years.[22] Toward meeting this demand, private institutions have stepped forward where public universities have held back.

The markets for higher education in Japan and South Korea are the most advanced. They are also the most mature. The gross enrollment ratios of both countries are among the highest in the world.[23] So are their tertiary education attainment rates.[24] According to the OECD, Japan and South Korea rank among the top countries in the world for exceptional

---

[21] See the following reports in *World Education News and Reviews*: S. Chawala, "Education in Japan," February 18, 2021, https://wenr.wes.org/2021/02/education-in-japan (accessed August 25, 2021); N. Clark, "Education in Singapore," June 1, 2009, https://wenr.wes.org/2009/06/wenr-june-2009-feature (accessed June 15, 2021); D. Mani and S. Trines, "Education in South Korea," October 16, 2018, https://wenr.wes.org/2018/10/education-in-south-korea (accessed June 15, 2021); J. Magaziner, "Education in Taiwan," June 7, 2016, https://wenr.wes.org/2016/06/education-in-taiwan (accessed June 15, 2021); D.B. Dilas, C. Mackie, Y. Huang, and S. Trines, "Education in Indonesia," March 21, 2019, https://wenr.wes.org/2019/03/education-in-indonesia-2 (accessed June 15, 2021); N. Clark, "Education in Malaysia," December 2, 2014, https://wenr.wes.org/2014/12/education-in-malaysia (accessed June 15, 2021); and N. Clark, "Education in Vietnam," May 5, 2014, https://wenr.wes.org/2014/05/higher-education-in-vietnam (accessed June 15, 2021).
     As Albach, Reisberg, and Rumbley point out:

> "Now, private higher education institutions, many of them for-profit or quasi for-profit, represent the fastest-growing sector worldwide. Countries with over 70% private enrollment include Indonesia, Japan, the Philippines and the Republic of Korea."
> "In general, the private sector is 'demand absorbing', offering access to students who might not be qualified for the public institutions or who cannot be accommodated in other universities because of overcrowding. While some selective private universities exist, in general the private sector serves a mass clientele and is not seen as prestigious. Legally for-profit institutions constitute a small higher education sub-sector but there is notable growth in all developing regions. The sector is run mostly on a business model, with power and authority concentrated in boards and chief executives, faculty hold little authority or influence and students are seen as consumers." P.G. Altbach, L. Reisberg, and L.E. Rumbley, *Trends in Global Higher Education: Tracking an Academic Revolution* (UNESCO, 2009), xiv.

[22] As a result of domestic demographic trends, demand tapered off in the 2010s.
[23] According to UNESCO, South Korea's 2018 gross enrollment ratio is 96%. UNESCO Institute for Statistics, "Gross Enrolment Ratio by Level of Education," http://data.uis.unesco.org (accessed August 25, 2021). According to The World Bank, Japan's 2015 ratio is estimated at 63%. The World Bank, DataBank, "School Enrollment, Tertiary (percent gross)," https://databank.worldbank.org/home.aspx (accessed June 1, 2021).
[24] Based on the following reports in *World Education News and Reviews*: S. Chawala, "Education in Japan," February 18, 2021, https://wenr.wes.org/2021/02/education-in-japan (accessed August 25, 2021); and D. Mani and S. Trines, "Education in South Korea," October 16, 2018, https://wenr.wes.org/2018/10/education-in-south-korea (accessed August 25, 2021).

student learning outcomes.[25] Since 1990, the number of their colleges and universities has surged.[26] Yet, in both nations, fertility rates are on the decline; the college-age population as a percentage of the total population is decreasing; tertiary enrollments are falling; and demand for higher education is softening.[27]

Of all markets in Southeast Asia, Singapore is the most open. It is also the most competitive. Under the "Global Schoolhouse" initiative launched in 2002, the Government of Singapore attracted several world-class universities to the city-state. A few, however, such as the Chicago Booth School of Business and Johns Hopkins University (biomedical research facility) have since closed their doors. In 2006, the Singapore government launched the Campus for Research Excellence and Technological Enterprise ("CREATE") to promote research collaboration between Singaporean and Western universities. It played a major role in establishing research centers at CREATE, including the Singapore–MIT Alliance for Research and Technology, the Berkeley Education Alliance for Research in Singapore, and the Illinois–Singapore Advanced Digital Sciences Center.

Among the more lucrative opportunities in Southeast Asia are program design and development, faculty training, management education, and higher education advisory services. Opportunities for technology transfer are scant compared with those that exist in the more advanced economies of Japan, South Korea, and Taiwan.

In East and Southeast Asia as a whole, the nominal value of contracts awarded by governments, foundations, and businesses to U.S. colleges and universities is enormous (see Figure 0.2 in the Introduction). For the 2014–2019 period, country/regional totals are as follows: U.S. contracts with parties in China, $763 million; Japan, $437 million; Singapore, $191 million; South Korea, $179 million; Hong Kong S.A.R., $109 million; Malaysia, nearly $42 million; and Taiwan and Indonesia, $26 million each.[28] Principal among the U.S. contracting parties are large public and private research universities of all tiers. As the economies of East and

---

[25] OECD, Programme for International Student Assessment, 2018 results, https://www.oecd.org/pisa/publications/pisa-2018-results.htm (accessed August 25, 2021).

[26] D. Mani and S. Trines, "Education in South Korea," October 16, 2018, https://wenr.wes.org/2018/10/education-in-south-korea (accessed August 25, 2021).

[27] Based on data presented in United Nations, *World Population Prospects 2019*, and the following reports in *World Education News and Reviews*: S. Chawala, "Education in Japan," February 18, 2021, https://wenr.wes.org/2021/02/education-in-japan (accessed August 25, 2021); and D. Mani and S. Trines, "Education in South Korea," October 16, 2018, https://wenr.wes.org/2018/10/education-in-south-korea (accessed August 25, 2021).

[28] U.S. Department of Education, *Foreign Gift and Contract Report, 2020*.

Southeast Asia continue to grow, so will the opportunities available to American higher education service providers.

South Asia

In South Asia, the largest higher education market by far is India. Despite a retreat precipitated by the Global Pandemic, its economy remains one of the fastest growing in Asia. The vast majority of India's citizens speak English. Its gross enrollment potential is high.[29] By 2027, India will overtake China as the world's most populous nation.[30] More than 40% of its people are under age 25 and more than a quarter under age 14.[31] Its burgeoning middle class is rapidly shaping the structure of higher education demand.[32]

Toward meeting this demand, Indian colleges and universities have made great strides. Between 2010 and 2020, the number of students enrolled in Indian higher education institutions soared by 10 million.[33] The number of Indian universities increased by 380 and the number of affiliated colleges, by nearly 7,000. Accompanying this growth has been a widening of public access to higher education. Such access, however, has been uneven across castes, ethnicities, sects, and regions.[34]

Despite their past successes, Indian colleges and universities face major hurdles. Though fairly well funded, central universities, such as the University of Delhi, Banaras Hindu University, and the University of Hyderabad, lack the institutional capacity to accommodate incremental enrollments on a grand scale.[35] Endowed with greater capacity, state universities lack the financial resources. To some extent, the void left

---

[29] Currently estimated at 74%, based on a gross enrollment ratio of 26.3%. See Government of India, Ministry of Human Resource Development, Department of Higher Education, Executive Summary, *All India Survey on Higher Education 2018–19* (2019).

[30] United Nations, Department of Economic and Social Affairs, Population Division (hereinafter referred to as U.N. Population Division), Table A.9 "Total population at mid-year by region, subregion, country, and area." *World Population Prospects 2019: Highlights*. ST/ESA/SER.A/423. According to the United Nations, India's population is expected to grow from 1.38 billion in 2020 to 1.64 billion in 2050.

[31] U.N. Population Division, Tables A.9 and A.32 "Population in school ages by region, subregion, country and area." *World Population Prospects 2019: Volume I: Comprehensive Tables* (2020).

[32] On current trends in Indian higher education see S. Trines, "Education in India," *World Education News and Reviews*, September 13, 2018, https://wenr.wes.org/2018/09/education-in-india (accessed August 21, 2021).

[33] Government of India, Executive Summary, *All India Survey on Higher Education*.

[34] Ibid.

[35] See British Council, *Understanding India: The Future of Higher Education and Opportunities for International Cooperation* (2014), 6, https://www.britishcouncil.in/sites/default/files/understanding_india.pdf (accessed June 15, 2021).

by central and state universities has been filled by private institutions.[36] Their share of enrollments climbed from 61% in 2010–2011 to 66% in 2018–2019.

The constraints faced by Indian institutions leave ample room in the market for U.S. service providers. The challenges they face in entering this market, however, are daunting. Some areas of the country lack the physical and technological infrastructure necessary to support first-rate operations.[37] The vast majority of Indians lack the financial means necessary to defray the high cost of a U.S. college education. In addition, the country's higher education sector is greatly overregulated. The entanglement of rules and regulations issued by the University Grants Commission risks strangling the operations of international branch campuses.[38] That is why many U.S. colleges and universities have opted to target India from offshore bases in the Arabian Gulf.

American institutions can add value to Indian higher education in the following ways:

- *Faculty development*: Many Indian institutions are in dire need of qualified instructors.[39] U.S. colleges and universities can help them develop a world-class faculty. They can familiarize this faculty with pedagogical approaches that rely less on top-down lecturing, passive learning, and rote memorization and more on analytical reasoning, critical thinking, and faculty–student interaction.
- *Courses and curricula*: American colleges and universities can help their Indian counterparts design and develop courses and curricula that are more attuned to the needs of a developing society.
- *Quality assurance*: Through quality assurance reviews, they can help Indian institutions raise their academic standards, and perhaps also obtain Western accreditation.

---

[36] With 66% of total college enrollments in 2018–19, 78% of all Indian colleges are private. Government of India, Executive Summary, *All India Survey on Higher Education 2018–19*.

[37] See Trines, "Education in India," *World Education News and Reviews*.

[38] See, for example, University Grants Commission, Regulation of Admission and Fees in Private Non-Aided Professional Institutions, May 16, 1998, https://www.ugc.ac.in (accessed June 1, 2021), which places a cap on tuition and fees that private educational institutions can charge their students. Faced with the prospect of such regulations, many Western colleges and universities have found it more lucrative to set up shop in the free zones of Qatar and Dubai, where they can target the Indian market offshore. See also British Council, *Understanding India*, 16.

[39] See British Council, *Understanding India*, 16.

- *Entrepreneurial, managerial, and soft skills*: Indian labor markets are saturated with technicians and engineers who lack the entrepreneurial, managerial, and soft skills necessary to succeed in business.[40] U.S. academic institutions can play a major role in imparting these skills.
- *Online learning*: In the realm of online learning, Indian universities surpass their U.S. counterparts in terms of enrollments.[41] On the other hand, U.S. colleges and universities surpass their Indian counterparts in terms of subject matter expertise, instructional design, and e-learning support systems.[42] By providing services in these functional areas, they can help Indian institutions improve the quality of online education.

Between 2014 and 2019, the value of contracts awarded by Indian parties to American colleges and universities totaled $185 million[43] (see Figure 0.2 in the Introduction). A major beneficiary was Apollo Global (now Vanta Education), which received a $38 million contract to operate the Bridge School of Management in Gurgaon.

Latin America

A broadening of the middle class, a rise in personal income, an increase in high-school graduation rates, and the proliferation of student financial aid have all fueled higher education demand in Latin America.[44]

[40] Ibid., 6, 16, 30–31, 35.

[41] For example, enrollments at the Indira Gandhi National Open University exceed 4 million, nearly 40 times enrollments at the University of Phoenix. British Council, *Understanding India*, 35.

[42] Ibid., 37. Different types of Indian entities have contracted with Western colleges and universities for a variety of purposes. These entities and their respective purposes include (1) private Indian corporations to develop online programs for working professionals (see, for example, the Apollo Group project at https://www.vccircle.com/ht-media-buys-out-partner-apollo-globals-stake-in-education-jv/ (accessed July 15, 2021)); (2) Indian provincial governments to conduct agricultural and environmental research (see, for example, the Iowa State University project at https://www.seedlab.iastate.edu/files/fall2017l.pdf (accessed July 15, 2021)); and (3) Indian public health institutes for infectious disease control, staff training, and clinical practice (see, for example, the Columbia University project at http://water.columbia.edu/research-themes/water-food-energy-nexus/water-agriculture-livelihood-security-in-india/40unjab-india/ (accessed July 21, 2021)).

[43] U.S. Department of Education, *Foreign Gift and Contract Report, 2020*.

[44] M.M. Ferreyra, C. Avitabile, J.B. Álvarez, F.H. Paz, and S. Urzúa, *At a Crossroads: Higher Education in Latin America and the Caribbean* (The World Bank Group, 2017), 12, 24, 50, 149, 153.

Public and private institutions have responded to this demand by launching new programs, expanding existing programs, and establishing new schools, colleges, and universities. Demand is particularly robust in the emerging markets of Brazil, Chile, Colombia, and Mexico. There, the number of new programs and institutions has skyrocketed.[45] So have educational expenditures per student, with Chile and Mexico leading the way.[46]

The result has been an improvement in gross enrollment ratios throughout Latin America.[47] Some countries, however, have made greater strides than others. Relatively high ratios exist for the more affluent nations of South America, particularly Argentina, Uruguay, and Chile. Relatively low ratios exist for the poorer nations of Central America, most notably Honduras, Guatemala, and El Salvador. Access to higher education, particularly among women, low-income families, indigenous groups, and those residing in close proximity to major metropolitan areas, has improved. However, such access has been uneven across countries, provinces, and regions.[48]

Throughout Latin America, public universities play a major role in catering to market demand. This is particularly true of Argentina, Uruguay, and Ecuador.[49] Where demand for specialized skills is strong, private institutions have stepped in. They have gained significant market share in Brazil, Mexico, and Chile.[50]

Of all countries in the region, Mexico is a "natural" for U.S. colleges and universities, particularly those based in the American Southwest. Its government officials, college administrators, business managers, and university faculty all look to American academic institutions for leadership. Mexico is the tenth most populous country in the world.[51] More than

[45] Ibid., 7, 49, 200–204.

[46] In Mexico, most expenditures are publicly funded. In Chile, they are privately funded. Ibid., 58–59.

[47] Panama is the only country whose gross enrollment ratio declined from 2000 to 2017. Ibid., 49.

[48] Ibid., 7, 153. Since the start of the New Millennium, the rate of access has accelerated in Bolivia, Chile, Colombia, and Peru. It has decelerated in El Salvador, Argentina, and Guatemala. ·

[49] Ibid., 19.

[50] Ibid., 19, 204. According to Altbach, Reisberg, and Rumbley, the private sector educates more than half the student population in such countries as Mexico, Brazil, and Chile. See Altbach, Reisberg, Rumbley, *Trends in Global Higher Education*, chapter 6. In Colombia, government support for private institutions has been met with popular push-back. L. Carroll, A. Reyes, and S. Trines, "Education in Colombia." *World Education News and Reviews*, June 23, 2020, https://wenr.wes.org/2020/06/education-in-colombia-2 (accessed August 25, 2021).

[51] U.N. Population Division, File POP/1-1 "Total population (both sexes combined) by region, subregion, and country, annually for 1950–2100." *World Population Prospects 2019: Highlights, and Volume 1: Comprehensive Tables* (2020).

a quarter of its people are under age 15.[52] Relative to other Latin American countries, its GDP per capita is high.[53] With the introduction of compulsory high-school education in 2013, access to, and demand for, higher education has increased.[54]

Another economic powerhouse is Brazil. Its market potential is huge. The Brazilian economy is the largest in Latin America. Although the economy contracted during the Global Pandemic, it has since rebounded and is projected to grow steadily throughout the 2020s.[55] Brazil's income per capita and gross enrollment potential are fairly high.[56] Government educational expenditure as a percentage of GDP exceeds the ratios for most other countries in the region.[57] Brazil is rich in human and natural resources. As its economy expands, so will potential demand for Western, and in particular American, higher education talent.

Throughout Latin America, opportunities for U.S. colleges and universities lie primarily in the areas of faculty training, executive education, program design and development, academic advisory services, and quality assurance.[58] Financial returns, however, are low compared with those that can be generated in Arabia and East Asia. Holding down these returns are economic variables. On the demand side, the financial resources of those who seek U.S. higher education services are relatively modest. On the supply side, the U.S. cost of providing these services is relatively high.

[52] U.N. Population Division, File POP/8-1 "Total population (both sexes combined) by broad age group, region, subregion and country, 1950–2100." *World Population Prospects 2019.*

[53] The World Bank, DataBank, "GDP per capita (current US$)," https://databank.worldbank.org/home.aspx (accessed June 1, 2021).

[54] Inadequate funding, administrative challenges, and regional economic disparities, however, have constrained universal access. See C. Monroy and S. Trines, "Education in Mexico." *World Education News and Reviews*, May 23, 2019, https://wenr.wes.org/2019/05/education-in-mexico-2 (accessed August 25, 2021).

[55] The World Bank, "The World Bank in Brazil," https://www.worldbank.org/en/country/brazil/overview (accessed July 15, 2021).

[56] In 2018, Brazil's net national income per capita in current U.S. dollars stood at $7,483. The World Bank, DataBank, "GDP per capita (current US$)," https://data.worldbank.org/indicator/ny.gdp.pcap.cd (accessed July 15, 2021). In 2013, Brazil's tertiary education gross enrollment ratio was slightly above 50%, one of the lowest in the region. The World Bank, DataBank, "Gross enrolment ratio, tertiary education," http://data.un.org/data.aspx?d=unesco&f=series%3ager_56 (accessed July 15, 2021).

[57] The World Bank, DataBank, "Government expenditure on education, total (% of GDP)," https://data.worldbank.org/indicator/se.xpd.totl.gd.zs (accessed July 15, 2021).

[58] In the past, Latin American government agencies and non-profit entities engaged U.S. colleges and universities in teacher training (see the Kansas State University project in Ecuador at https://global.k-state.edu/dayofecuador/docs/go-teacher-fact-sheet.pdf (accessed July 15, 2021)); agricultural research (see Columbia University projects in South America at https://www.earth.columbia.edu/projects/sponsor/international%20center%20for%20tropical%20agriculture (accessed July 15, 2021)); and providing advisory services for students, faculty, and local universities (see Rice University project in Brazil at https://brazil.rice.edu/about-brazilrice/ (accessed July 15, 2021)).

Nonetheless, lucrative opportunities do exist, as is evidenced by the aggregate value of contracts awarded to U.S. colleges and universities (see Figure 0.2 in the Introduction). Between 2014 and 2019, for selected countries, this value was as follows: Brazil, $68 million; Mexico, $36 million; and Colombia, $20 million.[59]

International branch campuses

Indicative of the surge in foreign demand for Western higher education talent is the proliferation of international branch campuses (IBCs).[60] An IBC is an entity owned in whole or in part by an academic institution (the "sponsor" or "sponsoring institution") based in a country other than the country in which the branch operates (the latter being the "host country"). Substantially on site in the host country, it offers one or more programs that lead to a degree awarded by the sponsoring institution.[61] An IBC differs from a partnership or joint venture in that it adheres to the practices of the sponsor. It confers its degree(s) in the name of the sponsor, based on the latter's degree requirements.

According to the Observatory on Borderless Education, the number of IBCs stood at 99 in 2002. By 2017, the figure had risen to 257—an astounding 160% increase.[62] Although a handful of IBCs were established in Europe, Canada, and Australia, the vast majority were set up in the emerging markets of the Middle East, Far East, and Southeast Asia. During this timeframe, the number of sponsoring institutions tripled—from 11 in 2002 to 33 in 2017. Although a few sponsors are based in China and India, most are based in the United States, United Kingdom, France, Russia, Australia, and the Netherlands (see Figures 6.1 and 6.2).

---

[59] U.S. Department of Education, *Foreign Gift and Contract Report, 2020*.

[60] J. Spring, *Globalization of Education*, 2nd ed. (2015), 105–106; and Weisbrod, Ballou, and Asch, *Mission and Money*, 168–169.

[61] R. Garrett, K. Kinser, J.E. Lane, and R. Merola (The Observatory for Borderless Higher Education and Cross Border Education Research Team), "International Branch Campuses: Trends and Developments 2016" (2016), 2–5, https://www.academia.edu/30219182/international_branch_campuses_trends_and_developments_2016 (accessed July 15, 2021).

[62] Garrett et al., *International Branch Campuses*, 5–8. See also J.E. Lane and K. Kinser (Cross-Border Education Research Team and State University of New York, Albany), "A Snapshot of a Global Phenomenon: The Results of the First Global Survey of IBCs" (paper presented at the 2011 annual conference of ASHE); K. Kinser and J.E. Lane (The Observatory on Borderless Higher Education and Cross-Border Research Team), "International Branch Campuses: Evolution of a Phenomenon." *International Higher Education*, no. 85 (2016): 3; and C.T. Clotfelter, ed., *American Universities in a Global Market* (2010), 399.

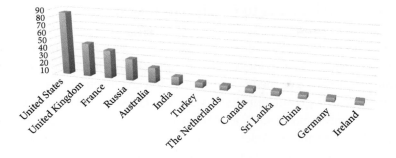

Fig. 6.1 International branch campuses by home country of sponsoring institution, 2020.

Source: Cross-Border Education Research Team, C-BERT Branch Campus Listing. (See Appendix for notes.)

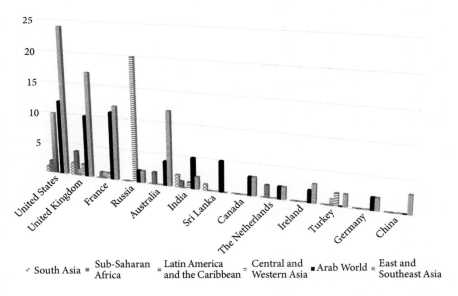

Fig. 6.2 Regional branch campuses by home country of sponsoring institution, 2020.

Source: Cross-Border Education Research Team, C-BERT Branch Campus Listing. (See Appendix for notes.)

Many IBCs offer undergraduate, graduate, and doctoral degrees. Some specialize in executive education. Program-related disciplines include business, computer science, engineering, education, healthcare, the social sciences, and the liberal arts. In total, IBCs enroll about 180,000 students from various countries around the world.

U.S. responsiveness to foreign demand

To say that U.S. colleges and universities have been unresponsive to the immense foreign demand for American higher education talent would be misleading. Some have made great strides toward meeting this demand. They include elite private universities, such as Harvard, MIT, and Cornell; large state universities, such as Michigan, Texas A&M, and the University of California, Berkeley; mid-size institutions such as Ball State, Arkansas, and Eastern Washington; and small private universities such as Rice and Franklin (see Figure 6.3). What they all have in common is a strong brand—some stronger than others. In addition, their leadership is more "export-oriented" in comparison with leaders of the vast majority of American colleges and universities.

Their foreign clientele includes government agencies, such as the Ecuador Ministry of Education; non-profit entities, such as the Shanghai National Accounting Institute; academic institutions, such as Kazakhstan's Nazarbayev University; oil companies, such as Petrobras Brazil; scientific firms, such as the Indian Institute of Tropical Meteorology; pharmaceutical companies, such as Takeda Japan; and academic–business–government partnerships, such as the AIDS Prevention Initiative of Nigeria. What all

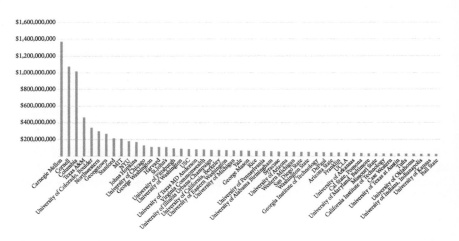

Fig. 6.3 Major U.S. service providers in global emerging markets for higher education, by nominal value of service contracts, 2014–2019.

Source: U.S. Department of Education, Office of Federal Student Aid, Foreign Gifts and Contracts Report, 2020. (See Appendix for notes.)

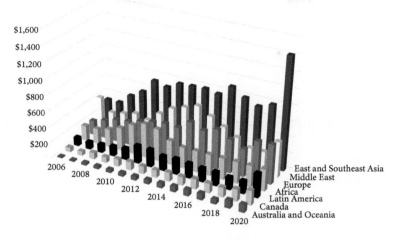

Fig. 6.4 U.S. exports of educational services by global region, in millions, 2006–2020.

Source: U.S. Department of Commerce, Bureau of Economic Analysis. (See Appendix for notes.)

these clients share in common is an ardent desire to tap American higher education talent. And they have all been influenced by the American value proposition.

According to the U.S. Department of Commerce, the total value of U.S. educational service exports climbed from nearly $1.3 billion in 2006 to almost $2.3 billion in 2019, despite a leveling off in recent years for most regions (see Figure 6.4). Of the total, Europe's import share grew from 14% to 22%, while that of East and Southeast Asia swelled from 25% to 33%; Latin America's share held steady at roughly 8%; Africa's share fell from 15% to 12%; and that of the Middle East plummeted from 33% to 12%. Changes in the compositional mix largely reflect broad economic trends. Since 2010, the economies of East and Southeast Asia and Europe grew at a faster pace than did the economies of many other regions. The volume of their trade with the United States grew accordingly.

Global competition

In international markets for higher education, the principal competitors of U.S. service providers are British, French, German, Canadian, and

Australian colleges and universities.[63] Since the start of the New Millennium, they have been joined by educational establishments in Russia, Japan, China, India, and South Korea.[64] The national origin of branch campus sponsors[65] sheds light on the nature of this competition (see Figure 6.2). Here are the data by region.

National origin of branch campus sponsors

The Arab World
Competitors of U.S. academic institutions in the Arab World are primarily European colleges and universities. In 2016, the total number of branch campuses established by institutions in the United Kingdom, France, the Netherlands, Germany, Russia, Ireland, and Switzerland were more than twice those for the United States—28 versus 13. While U.S. institutions had a strong showing in Qatar, British universities dominated the U.A.E. market, while French universities dominated the North African market.

East and Southeast Asia
In this expansive arena, the competitive position of U.S. colleges and universities is weaker than that of their European and Australian counterparts as a whole. Here, sponsoring institutions in the United Kingdom, France, the Netherlands, Australia, and other countries set up a total of 45 branch campuses, compared with 26 for those in the United States. While no one player dominated the market in East Asia, Australian, British, and French institutions dominated the market in Southeast Asia.

Latin America and the Caribbean
Lying in America's "backyard," Latin America and the Caribbean is the only regional market in which American institutions have a clear competitive advantage. Here, U.S. sponsors set up nine branch campuses, compared with a total of five for European and South American sponsors.

---

[63] E. Han Kim and Min Zhu, "Universities as Firms: The Case of US Overseas Programs." In *American Universities in a Global Market*, edited by C.T. Clotfelter (2010), 178; R.B. Freeman, "What Does Global Expansion of Higher Education Mean for the United States?" In *American Universities in a Global Market*, edited by C.T. Clotfelter (2010), 399; and Mazzarol and Soutar, "Revisiting the Global Market," *Asia Pacific Journal of Marketing and Logistics*, 719.

[64] Mazzarol and Soutar, "Revisiting the Global Market," *Asia Pacific Journal of Marketing and Logistics*, 719, 722.

[65] Garrett et al., *International Branch Campuses*, 5–8.

Other regions of the world

In other regional markets, the American presence is overshadowed by that of other global players. As of 2016, Russian institutions dominated markets in the former socialist republics of Central Asia. British and Dutch universities outnumbered their African, Asian, and Australian counterparts in Sub-Saharan Africa. Only two European sponsors, one British, the other Italian, had established branch campuses in South Asia. Significantly, American colleges and universities lacked a significant presence in all three regions.

Principal countries of destination for international students

No scholarly work on the globalization of higher education would be complete without a review of IMTE student markets. These markets are a huge source of revenue for hundreds of American colleges and universities. Though shaped primarily by the preferences of IMTE students for study abroad, they shed light on the national identity of potential competitors of U.S. colleges and universities in higher education *export* markets.[66] The reasoning is this: if academic institutions in the principal countries of destination are able to attract IMTE students to their home campuses, they are likely to have a competitive advantage in the export markets of the IMTE countries of origin. Thus, they are potential competitors with one another in these export markets. To some extent, this reasoning is supported by data on the national origin of branch campus sponsors. The principal countries of destination for IMTE students tend to overlap with the home countries of the sponsors of international branch campuses.[67]

East and Southeast Asia

The leading destinations for IMTE students from East and Southeast Asia[68] are the United States, Australia, the United Kingdom, Canada, and South

---

[66] Though not the only segment of the broader market for higher education services, this is an important segment. Depending on their academic strengths and organizational capabilities, these institutions could also be key players in other segments of the market, such as program design and development, technology transfer, academic advisory services, and project development and management.

[67] Notable exceptions are South Asia and Sub-Saharan Africa. Although the United States is a principal destination for IMTE students from these regions, American colleges and universities lack a substantial branch campus presence there. A major reason is financial. As has been pointed out, nations in these regions generally lack the financial resources to cover the high cost of U.S. operations.

[68] The analysis in this section is based on data available in the UNESCO Institute for Statistics, "Inbound Internationally Mobile Students by Region of Origin" and "Inbound Internationally Mobile Students by Country of Origin," http://data.uis.unesco.org (accessed November 1, 2021), for the East

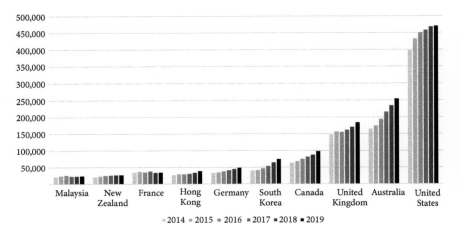

Fig. 6.5 Principal countries of destination for IMTE students from East and Southeast Asia, 2014–2019.

Source: UNESCO Institute for Statistics. (See Appendix for notes.)

Korea (see Figure 6.5). By implication, colleges and universities in the latter four countries are potential competitors of American institutions in the export markets of the Asian countries of origin. In terms of 2019 numbers, over 470,000 IMTE students from East and Southeast Asia pursued their studies in the United States; 254,000, in Australia; about 184,000, in the United Kingdom; 98,000, in Canada; and close to 75,000 in South Korea.

In terms of 2014–2019 average market shares, major players are the United States, with a 36% share; Australia, with 16%; the United Kingdom, with 13%; Canada, with 6%; and South Korea, with 4% (see Figure 6.6). Surprisingly, despite its inexorable rise on the world stage and central location, Mainland China is not a leading destination.[69] On the other hand, the Special Administrative Region (SAR) of Hong Kong, under the sovereignty of the People's Republic, ranks among the top ten.

Asia and Pacific region of origin and countries of origin therein. For an elaboration of the methodology used to derive the underlying numbers see notes to Figures 6.5 and 6.6 in Appendix.

[69] For the period 2014-2019, IMTE students from East and Southeast Asia who pursued their course of study in the People's Republic of China are not reported in the UNESCO database.

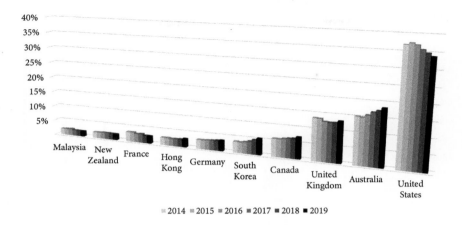

Fig. 6.6 and bar chart legend:
≡ 2014 ≡ 2015 ≡ 2016 ≡ 2017 ≡ 2018 ≡ 2019

Fig. 6.6 Estimated market shares of principal countries of destination for IMTE students from East and Southeast Asia, 2014–2019.
Source: UNESCO Institute for Statistics. (See Appendix for notes.)

South Asia

Potential competitors in the export markets of South Asia[70] are colleges and universities in Australia, Canada, and the United Kingdom. Together with the United States, they are the principal destinations for IMTE students from the region (see Figure 6.7). Their ranks are joined by institutions in Malaysia, which attract IMTE students primarily from Muslim-majority countries. Principal among these countries are Iran, Pakistan, and Bangladesh.[71] In terms of 2019 numbers, more than 170,000 students from South Asia pursued their studies in the United States; about 158,000 in Australia; over 84,000 in Canada; an estimated 35,000 in Malaysia; and close to 34,000 in the United Kingdom.

In terms of average market shares, the United States leads the pack, with 28% of the market, followed by Australia with 16%; Canada with 8%; and Malaysia and the United Kingdom each with 6% (see Figure 6.8). Notwithstanding America's dominant position, its market share has markedly declined since 2017. By contrast, Australia's has sharply risen.

---

[70] The analysis in this section is based on data available in the UNESCO Institute for Statistics, "Inbound Internationally Mobile Students by Region of Origin" and "Inbound Internationally Mobile Students by Country of Origin," http://data.uis.unesco.org (accessed November 1, 2021), for countries of origin in South Asia. For an elaboration of the methodology used to derive the underlying numbers see notes to Figures 6.7 and 6.8 in Appendix.
[71] UNESCO Institute for Statistics, "Inbound Internationally Mobile Students by Country of Origin" for countries of origin in South Asia.

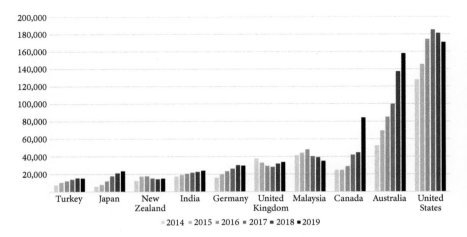

Fig. 6.7 Principal countries of destination for IMTE students from South Asia, 2014–2019.

Source: UNESCO Institute for Statistics. (See Appendix for notes.)

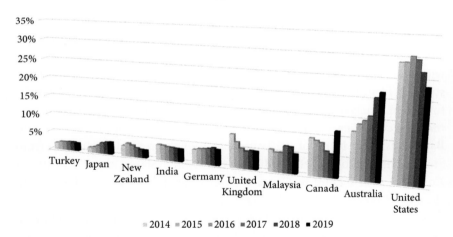

Fig. 6.8 Estimated market shares of principal countries of destination for IMTE students from South Asia, 2014–2019.

Source: UNESCO Institute for Statistics. (See Appendix for notes.)

The Arab World

In the Arab World, key players are the United States, France, Saudi Arabia, U.A.E., and Jordan[72] (see Figure 6.9). By implication, academic institutions

---

[72] The analysis in this section is based on data available in the UNESCO Institute for Statistics, "In-bound Internationally Mobile Students by Region of Origin" and "Inbound Internationally Mobile

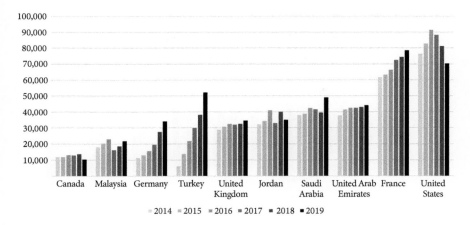

Fig. 6.9 Principal countries of destination for IMTE students from the Arab World, 2014–2019.
Source: UNESCO Institute for Statistics. (See Appendix for notes.)

in these countries are potential competitors in the export markets of the region. Saudi Arabia, U.A.E., and Jordan are major destinations because many Arab students prefer to pursue their studies in a familiar cultural environment. France is a principal destination because of its past colonial ties to the Levant and North Africa. In terms of 2019 numbers, France leads the pack, with over 78,000 IMTE students compared with slightly more than 70,000 for the United States, close to 49,000 for Saudi Arabia, 44,000 for the U.A.E., and roughly 35,000 for Jordan. Since 2016, the number of IMTE students who pursued their studies in the United States has significantly declined, while the number who pursued their studies in Turkey and France has skyrocketed.

With respect to 2014–2019 average market shares, of the total pool of IMTE talent from the Arab World, about 18% pursued their studies in the United States, 15% in France; 9% each in Saudi Arabia and the U.A.E., and 8% in Jordan (see Figure 6.10). Since 2014, America's share has contracted, while Turkey's and Germany's respective shares have expanded.

Latin America and the Caribbean
Potential competitors in the higher education markets of Latin America and the Caribbean are academic institutions in the United States,

Students by Country of Origin," http://data.uis.unesco.org (accessed November 1, 2021), for individual Arab states. For an elaboration of the methodology used to derive the underlying numbers see notes to Figures 6.9 and 6.10 in Appendix.

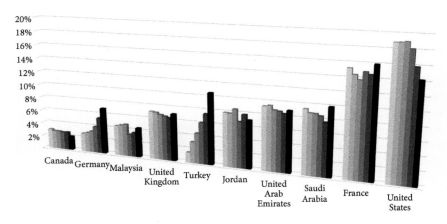

Fig. 6.10 Estimated market shares of principal countries of destination for IMTE students from the Arab World, 2014–2019.
Source: UNESCO Institute for Statistics. (See Appendix for notes.)

Argentina, Spain, France, and Germany[73] (see Figure 6.11). In 2017, Argentina surpassed the United States as the top destination for IMTE students from the region. Two years later, Argentina attracted nearly 106,000 students, compared with 80,000 for the United States. Working in Argentina's favor are cultural factors, low tuition rates, and less stringent visa restrictions. Working against the United States are high tuition rates, more stringent visa restrictions, and rising anti-immigration sentiment. As for other major IMTE destinations, Spain attracted close to 35,000 students; Canada, 17,000; Germany, nearly 16,000; and France, a little more than 15,000. Since 2017, IMTE enrollments in Argentina, Spain, Canada, Australia, and Portugal have risen, while those in the United States have been relatively flat.

In terms of 2014–2019 average market shares, America's is slightly more than 25%; Argentina's slightly less than 25%; Spain's, 8%; France's, 5%; and Germany's and Canada's, each about 4% (see Figure 6.12). Since 2014, the shares of Argentina, Spain, Canada, and Australia have swelled, while those of the United States, France, and the United Kingdom have shrunk.

---

[73] The analysis in this section is based on data available in the UNESCO Institute for Statistics, "Inbound Internationally Mobile Students by Region of Origin" and "Inbound Internationally Mobile Students by Country of Origin," http://data.uis.unesco.org (accessed November 1, 2021), for the Latin America and Caribbean region of origin. For an elaboration of the methodology used to derive the underlying numbers see notes to Figures 6.11 and 6.12 in Appendix.

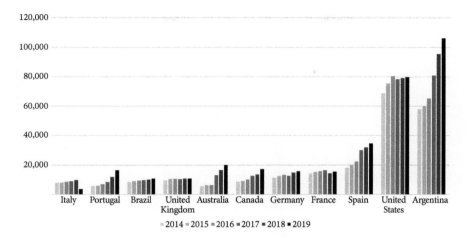

Fig. 6.11 Principal countries of destination for IMTE students from Latin America and the Caribbean, 2014–2019.
Source: UNESCO Institute for Statistics. (See Appendix for notes.)

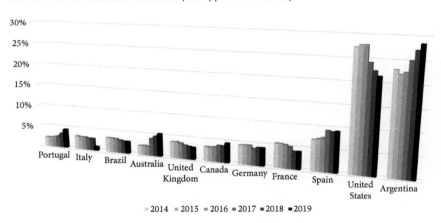

Fig. 6.12 Estimated market shares of principal countries of destination for IMTE students from Latin America and the Caribbean, 2014–2019.
Source: UNESCO Institute for Statistics. (See Appendix for notes.)

Sub-Saharan Africa

In Sub-Saharan Africa, potential competitors of U.S. institutions are colleges and universities in France, South Africa, the United Kingdom, Malaysia, and Canada.[74] Together with the United States, these

---

[74] The analysis in this section is based on data available in the UNESCO Institute for Statistics, "Inbound Internationally Mobile Students by Region of Origin" and "Inbound Internationally Mobile Students by Country of Origin," http://data.uis.unesco.org (accessed November 1, 2021), for the African region of origin and countries lying therein. For an elaboration of the methodology used to derive the underlying numbers see notes to Figures 6.13 and 6.14 in Appendix.

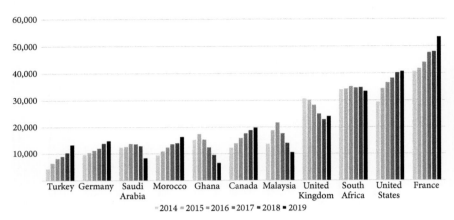

Fig. 6.13 Principal countries of destination for IMTE students from Sub-Saharan Africa, 2014–2019.

Source: UNESCO Institute for Statistics. (See Appendix for notes.)

countries are the principal destinations for IMTE students from the African continent (see Figure 6.13). Underling this order are cultural and geographical factors. Students from Francophile countries have a cultural affinity for France; those from Anglophile countries, the United Kingdom, Canada, and the United States. South Africa is a convenient location for students residing in the southern part of the continent; Malaysia, for students residing in the eastern part. In 2019, IMTE enrollments were as follows: France, 53,000; the United States, roughly 41,000; South Africa, slightly more than 33,000; the United Kingdom, 24,000; Canada, close to 20,000; and Malaysia, a little over 10,000. Significantly, IMTE enrollments in France, the United States, and Canada have increased, while those in the United Kingdom and Malaysia have decreased.

For the 2014–2019 period, average market shares were as follows: France, 13%; the United States and South Africa, 10% each; the United Kingdom, 8%; Malaysia and Canada, 5% each (see Figure 6.14). As with the numbers, the shares of France, the United States, and Canada have been on the rise, while those of the United Kingdom and Malaysia have been on the decline.

Central and Western Asia

In the IMTE markets of Central and Western Asia, the dominant player by far is Russia.[75] Turkey occupies a distant second, followed by the Ukraine.

---

[75] The analysis in this section is based on data available in the UNESCO Institute for Statistics, "Inbound Internationally Mobile Students by Region of Origin" and "Inbound Internationally Mobile

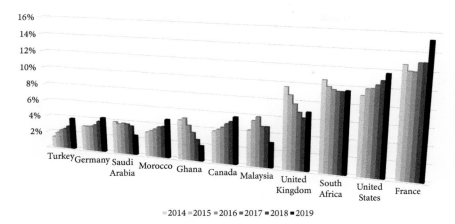

Fig. 6.14 Estimated market shares of principal countries of destination for IMTE students from Sub-Saharan Africa, 2014–2019.

Source: UNESCO Institute for Statistics. (See Appendix for notes.)

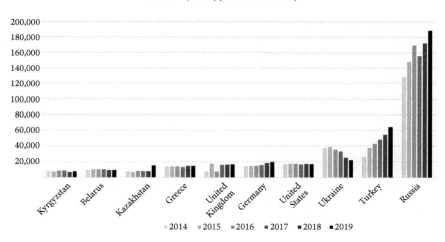

Fig. 6.15 Principal countries of destination for IMTE students from Central and Western Asia, 2014–2019.

Source: UNESCO Institute for Statistics. (See Appendix for notes.)

Lagging far behind are the United States and Germany (see Figure 6.15). This order largely reflects geopolitical, cultural, and geographic factors. Most states in the region are former Soviet Socialist Republics; hence, they

Students by Country of Origin," http://data.uis.unesco.org (accessed November 1, 2021), for the Central Asian region of origin and individual non-Arab countries of origin located in Western Asia. For an elaboration of the methodology used to derive the underlying numbers see notes to Figures 6.15 and 6.16 in Appendix.

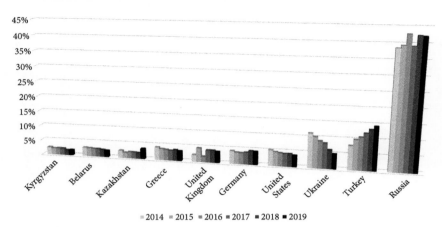

Fig. 6.16 Estimated market shares of principal countries of destination for IMTE students from Central and Western Asia, 2014–2019.
Source: UNESCO Institute for Statistics. (See Appendix for notes.)

are drawn to Russia. Many of their citizens are Turkic, and therefore have a cultural affinity for Turkey. They are situated near Eastern Europe; hence, the geographic pull of the Ukraine. In terms of 2019 numbers, Russia attracted over 188,000 IMTE students; Turkey, slightly over 64,000; the Ukraine, 22,000; Germany, a little more than 19,000; and the United States and United Kingdom, about 17,000 each.

In terms of 2014–2019 average market shares, Russia takes the lead, with 41% of the IMTE market; followed by Turkey, with 11%; Ukraine, 8%; the United State and Germany, 4% each (see Figure 6.16). In recent years, Turkey's share has ballooned, while the shares of Ukraine and the United States have diminished.

Summary and implications

These findings and their broader implications can be summarized in the following points:

- Globally, the United States is the top destination for IMTE students from all over the world. In 2019, the total number of IMTE students who pursued their studies in the United States approached 850,000

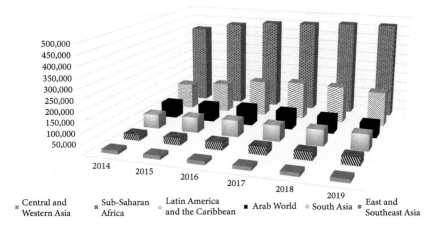

Fig. 6.17 IMTE students enrolled in institutions in the United States by global region, 2014–2019.

Source: UNESCO Institute for Statistics. (See Appendix for notes.)

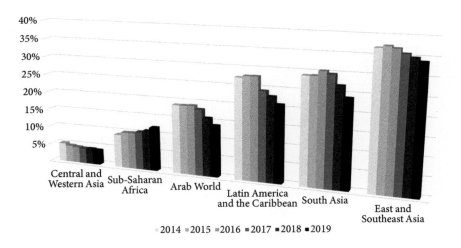

Fig. 6.18 U.S. market share of IMTE students by global region, 2014–2019.

Source: UNESCO Institute for Statistics. (See Appendix for notes.)

(see Figure 6.17). For the six-year period ending 2019, America's global market share averaged 20% (see Figure 6.18).

- Regionally, the United States is the leading destination for IMTE students from both East and Southeast Asia and South Asia. Despite Argentina's ascendancy, the U.S. is still a major player in Latin America and the Caribbean, and is second to France in Sub-Saharan

Africa and the Arab World. In Central and Western Asia, however, the United States lags far behind Russia, the undisputed leader.

- Despite America's strong presence in most regional IMTE markets, its competitive position has eroded in all but Sub-Saharan Africa. In 2017 the United States was overtaken by Argentina in Latin America and the Caribbean. In 2019, it was overtaken by France in the Arab World. In recent years, it has been losing ground to Australia and Canada in South Asia. This development is most likely due to a tightening of U.S. visa restrictions, growing perceptions of a less welcoming America, and an intensification of regional competition. As for Sub-Saharan Africa, the fortification of America's position is attributable to lower market concentration, less intense competition, and greater room for expansion.

- Globally, the principal competitors of U.S. colleges and universities in IMTE markets are educational institutions in Australia, Canada, France, and the United Kingdom. Regionally, in addition to the foregoing, major competitors are institutions in Russia in Central and Western Asia; Argentina in Latin America and the Caribbean; South Africa in Sub-Saharan Africa; Saudi Arabia and the U.A.E. in the Arab World; and Malaysia in South Asia.

- The strong presence of U.S. colleges and universities in the IMTE markets of South Asia and Sub-Saharan Africa contrasts with their weak presence in terms of branch campuses there. This disparity is largely a function of economics. The vast majority of South Asians and Sub-Saharan Africans lack the resources necessary to defray the cost of a U.S. education. This cost is relatively high, while their resources are relatively meagre. (Recall the low GDP/NNI per capita of nations in these two regions.) By implication, operating a branch campus in either region is not financially feasible for a great many American colleges and universities. The cost of deploying U.S. higher education talent in either region exceeds the upside potential for service-related revenues. These costs (e.g., travel, accommodations, amenities, insurance, overseas support) are *incremental* to those incurred by American institutions at their home U.S. campuses. On the other hand, bringing residents of South Asia and Sub-Saharan Africa to these campuses *is* financially feasible, because, in doing so, U.S. colleges and universities effectively save on the incremental deployment costs, while generating economies of scale. Moreover, the wealthy minority of South Asians and Sub-Saharan Africans who pursue their studies in the United States generally have the financial means to defray the high cost of a U.S. education.

- U.S. colleges and universities can leverage off America's dominant position in many regional IMTE markets to enter the higher education export markets of the IMTE countries of origin. One strategy for doing so is to target countries with (1) relatively high GDP/NNI per capita, and (2) high gross enrollment potential, where (3) America's IMTE competitive position is strong. On the other hand, several factors weigh in favor of targeting other markets. They include relatively low barriers to entry (Sub-Saharan Africa), the presence of a sizeable English-speaking population (South Asia), and an opportunity to profoundly impact the social and economic development of the region (both Sub-Saharan Africa and South Asia). They also include the moral imperative to educate and enlighten, regardless of commercial opportunity, financial means, or market position.
- This analysis is focused more on U.S. *non-profit* institutions than on U.S. *for-profit* institutions. Yet, the latter institutions are poised to fill the void left by traditional non-profit American colleges and universities that are either unable or unwilling to expand into foreign markets. The for-profits' doing so could leave them with the lion's share of global markets for degree and non-degree programs.[76] It could also divide this market into two segments: a fast-growing segment dominated by the for-profits, and a slower-growing segment dominated by the non-profits. Despite this possibility, public and private non-profit colleges and universities will still have a competitive edge in global markets for technology transfer, project design and development, and higher education advisory services. What matters most in these segments is research capability, academic expertise, a reputation for academic integrity, and longstanding relationships.

Taking American higher education to all the world . . .

These findings attest to the powerful allure of the American value proposition. Non-U.S. nationals want and seek American higher education. They are willing to travel to the United States from the far corners of the Earth

---

[76] Specifically, the design, development, and delivery of degree and non-degree programs.

to obtain it. Yet, as has been pointed out, U.S. social, political, and regulatory barriers stand in the way of their doing so—which brings us back to the central question: *If all the world cannot come to America for higher education, then why not take American higher education to all the world?* The human need is great, and the market potential is enormous.

To date, only a handful of traditional American colleges and universities have succeeded in "going global"—a small fraction of the 4,000-institution-strong U.S. higher education sector. Evidently, their leaders are keenly aware of the vast opportunities that lay beyond the horizon. More export-oriented than not, they have been willing to take risks. Yet, in light of the enormity of international markets, they can do a great deal more.

Remarkably, the vast majority of American colleges and universities have been either unable or unwilling to tap the immense foreign demand for American higher education talent. The quintessential questions are "*Why?*" and "*What would it take for them to do so?*" Let us turn to these questions.

7

Institutional Barriers to International Expansion

The Great Chasm creates opportunities for U.S. academic institutions to extend their global reach, for the benefit of both themselves and non-U.S. nationals who value their services. Hence, it would seem logical for them to do so. Bridging the Great Chasm, however, is not an easy feat for the vast majority of American colleges and universities. It is complicated by a multitude of factors, including a traditional culture that is averse to commercialization, an organizational structure that is operationally slow, and a system of governance that often leads to indecision, conflict, and paralysis. In a highly competitive, rapidly changing economic environment, these factors often work to the detriment of American academic institutions. This chapter explores why they stand in the way of international expansion, and what it would take to remove them.

> [L]ooking on the universities as competitive business concerns, and speaking in terms applicable to business concerns generally, the assets of these seminaries of learning are in an exceptional degree intangible assets . . . [T]his collective body of "immaterial capital" that pertains to the university at large is made up in great part of the prestige of diverse eminent persons included among its personnel and incorporated in the fabric of its bureaucratic departments, and not least the prestige of its executive head; in very much the same way as the like will hold true, e.g., for any company of public amusement, itinerant or sedentary, such as a circus, a theatrical or operatic enterprise, which all compete for the acclamation and custom of those to whom these matters appeal.[1]
>
> Thorstein Veblen, American economist and philosopher

> Today, it is primarily the capitalist market economy which demands that the official business of the administration be discharged precisely, unambiguously, continuously, and with as much speed as possible . . . Business management

---

[1] T. Veblen, *The Higher Learning in America: A Memorandum on the Conduct of Universities by Business Men* (1918), 109.

Bridging the Gap between the Abundance of American Higher Education Talent and the Immense Foreign Demand for It.
Richard J. Joseph, Oxford University Press. © Richard J. Joseph (2022). DOI: 10.1093/oso/9780192848307.003.0008

throughout rests on increasing precision, steadiness, and above all, the speed of operations . . .[2]

Max Weber, sociologist, historian, and political economist

On methodology

To support the existence of subjective phenomena is much more difficult than substantiating objective facts, for the subjective is associated with attitudes, beliefs, interests, and values, which are less capable of measurement than are tangible, physical, or finite objects. Yet, the subjective is important because it influences behavior that has a bearing on the objective, such as the collectivity of students, instructors, classrooms, and buildings that support the operations of a traditional American college or university.

Shedding light on the subjective can be achieved by means of a Weberian ideal-typical construct, the elements of which are drawn from real-world experience. In Chapter 1, we explained how this heuristic tool can be used to explore various facets of reality. The ideal-typical construct used in the present chapter pertains to the culture, organization, and governance of traditional American colleges and universities (the "traditional model"). These features are relevant, because they impact the ability and willingness of an institution to expand into foreign markets. They are influenced by a number of subjective variables, including the attitudes, beliefs, interests, and values of major stakeholders.

Institutional obstacles

Culture

Aversion to commercialization

In terms of institutional outcomes, traditional academic culture is a double-edged sword. On the one hand, it engenders a high degree of educational quality, academic integrity, and intellectual advancement—all hallmarks of American higher education. On the other hand, its adherents are suspicious of anything that smacks of commercialism. Many of them react vehemently to any insinuation that a college or university

[2] M. Weber, "'Objectivity' in Social Sciences and Social Policy." In *The Methodology of the Social Sciences*, edited by E.A. Shils and H.A. Finch (1949), 197.

should be more "business-like" in character. In their view, interjecting business principles in an academic culture goes against the very mission and purpose of a college or university. Epitomizing this view is the exhortation of the eminent scholar Thorstein Veblen:

> [T]he intrusion of business principles in the universities goes to weaken and retard the pursuit of learning, and therefore to defeat the ends for which a university is maintained. This result follows, primarily, from the substitution of impersonal, mechanical relations, standards and tests, in the place of personal conference, guidance and association between teachers and students; as also from the imposition of a mechanically standardized routine upon the members of the staff, whereby any disinterested preoccupation with scholarly or scientific inquiry is thrown into the background and falls into abeyance.[3]

Former Harvard President Derek Bok gives us this explanation of why members of a university are averse to commercialism:

> Members of the university who resist commercial influences have several concerns. They fear that money and efficiency may gradually come to have too dominant a place in academic decision making and that the verdict of the market will supplant the judgment of scholars in deciding what to teach and whom to appoint. They suspect that commercialization and those who favor it will strengthen the forces that look at teaching and research chiefly as means to some practical end rather than as ends in themselves. Most of all, they worry that business methods, with their emphasis on accountability and control, may encroach upon the exceptional personal freedom that is such a cherished part of academic life.[4]

No doubt, such concerns are legitimate. Members of a college or university have a vital stake in safeguarding the academic integrity of the institution. However, these concerns become counterproductive, and even dysfunctional, when they prevent the organization from adopting business-like practices to ensure its financial well-being. At the end of the day, financial resources make possible the proliferation of teaching, scholarly, and other intellectual activities that make an institution *academic*. Diminish these resources, or keep them constant in the face of

---

[3] Veblen, *The Higher Learning in America*, 192.
[4] D. Bok, *Universities in the Marketplace: The Commercialization of Higher Education* (2003), 19.

flat enrollments, declining revenues, and escalating costs, and the entire ideological superstructure of American higher education will be at risk.

Supply-side driven

From a market perspective, this culture is supply-side driven. Far too many courses are offered on the basis of what professors want to teach, not what learners want and need for their professional development. Most of these learners are "big kids," with extensive practical experience and a good idea of what they need to succeed in life. To assume that only the erudite know what is best for them, or what they need for personal or professional success, is unfounded.

What market information is brought to bear on the design of courses and curricula is frequently local or regional in nature. In the past, this approach made sense because most U.S. colleges and universities drew most of their students from within a 500-mile radius. In addition, local and regional markets were large enough to sustain these institutions financially.[5] In the future, however, such an approach will not make sense because local markets are not as broad or robust as they were in the past. Shifting demographics and intensifying competition are diminishing the quantity and quality of students recruited from the institution's backyard.

Aversion to change

This culture is averse to change.[6] Often, the aversion is couched in lofty terms, such as

> Rather than take advantage of lucrative market opportunities, we prefer to remain a small college, with high academic standards, that delivers a first-rate education.

However altruistic, such a sentiment is laden with an inherent contradiction. In the changing landscape of American higher education, few colleges and universities will be able to maintain high academic standards or deliver a first-rate education without taking advantage of lucrative market opportunities.

---

[5] Hawawini offers an additional explanation for the domestic market orientation of U.S. academic institutions, specifically business schools: "Lower degrees of internationalization for US schools can be explained by two primary factors: the first is the large size of the US domestic market that supplies large numbers of candidates to business schools, and the second is the historical mission of US schools that is primarily focused on developing domestic talent." G. Hawawini, *The Internationalization of Higher Education and Business Schools* (2016), 13.

[6] As noted by J. Denneen and T. Dretler, *The Financially Sustainable University* (2012), 9.

For some stakeholders, the only way to deal with escalating costs is to bring in a rainmaker and leave things the way they are. Cost-cutting is laudable, so long as it does not slash departmental budgets, reduce staff benefits, eliminate faculty perks, or demolish academic fiefdoms. Merging, divesting, or reorganizing administrative units, however redundant be their programs, services, assets, or personnel, is to be avoided at all costs. Downsizing, dismantling, or restructuring is unfathomable, even where it gives rise to efficiencies that improve the long-term viability of the enterprise, and even where it enhances the long-term employment prospects of faculty, administrators, and staff. Discontinuing pet projects, however unsustainable they may be, is *ipso facto* "unwise." And weak enrollments stem from the inability of the student to recognize the program's intrinsic worth, not from defective design, outdated content, or irrelevance to real-world experience.

Organization

Misaligned rewards

Traditional American colleges and universities are bureaucratic, inward-looking, and procedurally slow. Operationally, they resemble public agencies more than private enterprises. In terms of pace, they rival the post office. Underlying this *modus operandi* is a system of rewards that produces suboptimal results relative to organizational goals. Far too often, brilliant scholars are promoted to senior administrative positions on the basis of outstanding teaching and research, not necessarily the skills or expertise demanded by the job.[7] No doubt, the vast majority have the intellect and capability to do the job. However, managing people, budgets, and operations is not their passion, competency, or forte. Moreover, the skills required to excel at management are entirely different from the skills required to excel at teaching and research.

This unassailable practice has come at the cost of organizational efficiency. It has transformed what should be an executive role into something more honorific. Here's what President Bok has to say about it:

---

[7] A traditional view expressed by Veblen: "From the circumstances of the case it also follows that they [i.e., aids and advisors to the university president] will commonly occupy an advanced academic rank, and so will take a high (putative) rank as scholars and scientists . . . Experience teaches that scholarly or scientific capacity does not enter in any appreciable measure among the qualifications so required for responsible academic office, beyond what may thriftily serve to mask the conventional decencies of the case." Veblen, *The Higher Learning in America*, 100.

Presidents and deans lack the experience of most corporate managers in administering large organizations. Because the principal purposes of their universities are academic, they must be intellectual leaders more than administrators. For this reason, their backgrounds and training are almost always in research and teaching rather than administration. Once in office, their success is measured much more by their accomplishments in building academic programs than by their record in achieving greater efficiency.[8]

And the wise Max Weber gives us this word of caution:

Honorific arrangements make administrative work an avocation and, for this reason alone, honorific service normally functions more slowly; being less bound to schemata and being more formless.[9]

As for non-academic staff, typically, they are rewarded on the basis of their faithful adherence to standard practices, policies, and procedures, not service innovation, customer satisfaction, or revenue generation. Conduct that reinforces an internal focus, such as planning, processing, advising, budgeting, and assessing, is highly valued. Less valued is conduct with an external focus, such as sales, marketing, recruiting, and business development.

In some academic circles, moreover, highly competent practitioners with exceptional technical skills and extensive industry experience are treated as mere "support staff," not accomplished professionals in their own right. Sadly, they are often judged on the basis of what they have not done and what they have failed to achieve in the past, not on the basis of what they have accomplished outside of academia or what they are capable of doing for the organization in the future.[10]

---

[8] Bok, *Universities in the Marketplace*, 24.

[9] M. Weber, "Bureaucracy." In *From Max Weber*, edited by H.H. Gerth and C. Wright Mills (1958), 214.

[10] Expressing the traditional view toward non-academic staff is Veblen: "Yet these more unscholarly members of the staff will necessarily be assigned the more responsible and discretionary positions in the academic organization; since under such a scheme of standardization, accountancy and control, the school becomes primarily a bureaucratic organization, and the first and unremitting duties of the staff are those of official management and accountancy. The further qualifications requisite in the members of the academic staff will be such as make for vendibility, volubility, tactful effrontery, conspicuous conformity to the popular taste in all matters of opinion, usage and conventions." Veblen, *The Higher Learning in America*, 190.

Steep hierarchies

Reinforcing this bias are sharp distinctions in rank and status.[11] In some college and university environments, steep hierarchies engender a sort of caste system that impedes cross-functional teamwork and upward mobility. Academic diehards insist that laymen should never be empowered within the organization, or entrusted with substantial authority, especially over those who possess the "right" credentials, have taught in the classroom, and have published in peer-reviewed journals. Indeed, practitioners should never be allowed to "run the show," even where the "show" requires skills, experience, and competencies that most academics lack, and even where the scope of authority is confined to the layman's specific professional expertise.

Self-contained silos

Then there are administrative silos and bureaucratic dinosaurs. On the one hand, administrative units demarcate functional boundaries, define the scope of managerial authority, and reinforce academic disciplines. For the most part, they facilitate communication, interaction, and collaboration *within* their institutional confines. On the other hand, these units often rigidify into self-contained silos that operate in isolation. When they do so, they tend to slow communications, impede interaction, and discourage collaboration *beyond* their institutional confines.

Rigid bureaucracies

As for college and university bureaucracies, on the one hand, they clarify roles and responsibilities, set employee expectations, and give structure and order to groupings predisposed to chaos. On the flip side, they set up psychological barriers between and among personnel, and foster a bureaucratic mindset that is antithetical to teamwork. If overly structured, they are prone to leaving major gaps in the work chain, either because the intervening task falls outside anyone's job description, or because it cannot be performed within the standard nine-to-five workday.

In the most bureaucratic of institutional orders, every employee has a place, dares not transcend it, and feels no ethical responsibility or moral imperative to trespass into the space of others. The most obstinate refuse

---

[11] See Denneen and Dretler, *The Financially Sustainable University*, 6–7. Cf. Weber: "The principles of office hierarchy and of levels of graded authority mean a firmly ordered system of super- and subordination in which there is a supervision of the lower offices by the higher ones . . . The principle of hierarchical office authority is found in all bureaucratic structures: in ecclesiastical structures as well as in large party organizations and private enterprises." Weber, "Bureaucracy." In *From Max Weber*, 197.

to do more than what the job requires. The most complacent excel at process but not execution. When asked about the feasibility of a novel idea, especially one that risks disrupting their daily routine, the most entrenched either shrug their shoulders or recite a litany of excuses as to why it will not work in practice. Of course, that is their right and prerogative. Such is the nature of bureaucracy. As Weber points out,

> For this bureaucracy rests upon expert training, a functional specialization of work, and an attitude set for habitual and virtuoso-like mastery of single yet methodically integrated functions . . . The discipline of officialdom refers to the attitude-set of the official for precise obedience within his habitual activity, in public as well as in private organizations. This discipline increasingly becomes the basis of all order . . .[12]

Regardless of right and prerogative, far too often the end-result is dysfunctionality.[13] Innovation is stifled. Responsibility is curtailed. Job inflexibility becomes the norm. Essential tasks fall through the cracks. Redundancies and inefficiencies abound. So do turf wars.

Governance

Traditional shared governance is conducive to three positive outcomes. First, it ensures that stakeholders who contribute to the success of the enterprise have an important say in institutional decision-making. Second, it enhances the likelihood that academic considerations will take

---

[12] Weber, "Bureaucracy." In *From Max Weber*, 229.

[13] Veblen had nothing but disdain for this order, which he attributed to an invasion of business principles in the academic enterprise, likened to a house of correction. "Business principles take effect in academic affairs most simply, obviously and avowably in the way of a businesslike administration of the scholastic routine; where they lead immediately to a bureaucratic organization and a system of scholastic accountancy . . . Such a system of authoritative control, standardization, gradation, accountancy, classification, credits and penalties, will necessarily be drawn on stricter lines the more the school takes on the character of a house of correction or a penal settlement; in which the irresponsible inmates are to be held to a round of distasteful tasks and restrained from (conventionally) excessive irregularities of conduct. At the same time this recourse to such coercive control and standardization of tasks has unavoidably given the schools something of the character of a penal settlement." Veblen, *The Higher Learning in America*, 189. The "inmates" to which Veblen refers are "immature and reluctant students." Of course, Veblen was less concerned about impediments to teamwork, operational efficiency, and client servicing than about obstacles in the way of scholastic pursuits, which obstacles he viewed as incidental to centralization, control, and standardization. Nonetheless, his comments shed light on the creeping bureaucratization of American colleges and universities that tends to stifle creativity, spontaneity, and efficiency.

precedence over business considerations in teaching, research, and scholarship. Third, it safeguards the values of the academy.

By the same token, shared governance sometimes—oftentimes— contributes to three negative outcomes: indecision, resistance to change, and conflict.

Indecision

As a general principle, where too many stakeholders are involved in the decision-making process, the end-result frequently is no decision at all. Consensus becomes difficult, if not impossible to achieve. The process gets bogged down in interminable debate without closure, finality, or execution. On the other hand, where too few stakeholders are involved in the decision-making process, the end-result frequently is uninformed, impractical, and poor decisions. Implementing these decisions becomes difficult, if not impossible to achieve. Occasionally, the process gets bogged down by foot-dragging and subtle resistance.

Without effective controls, traditional shared governance can be a factor in the first outcome. Major proposals, such as degree requirements or curriculum reform, get mired in a tangle of administrative proceedings and committee deliberations.[14] There, they are debated *ad infinitum* by a cadre of brilliant, accomplished, and strong-willed individuals, each with a different, yet valid point of view. Consequently, an issue seemingly as simple as changing a course title or delaying a semester start date could take months, if not years, to sort out. Routine operational matters acquire political significance, as they are taken up by factions on opposite sides of the fence. In the worst of all cases, the end-result is stalemate, inertia, paralysis, and/or no decision at all. Alternatively—and what is practically the same—it is the appointment of a special task force to investigate the matter and report back to the key decision-maker in a few months' time.

Resistance to change

In any higher education environment, some stakeholders resist change out of a genuine concern for educational quality and institutional well-being.

---

[14] Bok observes: "[C]ommittees often have too few professors possessing relevant knowledge and experience and too many who are appointed for other reasons. Under these conditions, faculty governance can easily sink into longer and longer debates about less and less, accomplishing little of real importance for professors while causing frustration and delay for the administration . . ."

"This unfortunate state of affairs already exists on a number of campuses. Impatient at the thought of being mired in endless debate, enterprising presidents and deans are increasingly tempted to bypass faculty review when launching new entrepreneurial ventures." Bok, *Universities in the Marketplace*, 190–191.

Others do so because they have a vested interest in perpetuating the status quo. Whatever the reason or motive, traditional shared governance empowers both types of stakeholders. It amplifies their voice in organizational decision-making, thus giving them the power to stall and even thwart meaningful change.

This contrasts with corporate governance. Through their firm grip on the decision-making apparatus, more centralized and authoritarian than not, corporate executives can quash the machinations of employees who, in their view, stand in the way of "progress." As a result, they can realize their will in pursuit of their strategic goals, often in the absence of rank-and-file opposition. In academia, by contrast, administrators, faculty, and trustees all must come to terms with "the opposition" by virtue of a decentralized and inclusive system of governance.[15] Lest they unwittingly invite mutiny, they must defer to the will of the minority—typically, a handful of vocal, yet enfranchised stakeholders—often at the expense of strategic objectives. To ethical purists, the result is good, because the process is good. Indeed, it strengthens the moral fiber of the institution. To utilitarian managers, on the other hand, the result is suboptimal. It risks subverting the long-term strategic goals of the institution.

Conflict

Effective shared governance is premised on a division of authority between and among key stakeholders. Where this division is unclear, or where there are no boundaries on the exercise of this authority, the result is often confusion, chaos, and conflict.[16] At an extreme, it is institutional paralysis.

Within an ill-defined order of governance, transgressions can be subtle and inadvertent. Administrators and trustees invade the space of academics when they interject non-academic considerations into teaching and learning, second-guess an instructor's academic assessment, dictate topics worthy of faculty research, and/or criticize the quality of scholarly output. Conversely, academics delve into the realm of business managers when they arrogate to themselves the task of setting the strategic goals of the institution, prescribe how non-academic resources should be utilized,

---

[15] Denneen and Dretler, *The Financially Sustainable University*, 9. On decentralized decision-making in academic institutions see Toutkoushian and Paulsen, *Economics of Higher Education*, 263. In addition, by emboldening those who express resistance to change, tenure could strengthen such resistance.

[16] Regarding limiting faculty power in institutional decision-making, Bowen points out, "There is a self-evident need for consultation with those who are expert in their disciplines and experienced in teaching—but this is not the same thing as giving faculty veto power over change." W.G. Bowen, *Higher Education in the Digital Age* (2013), 76.

attempt to supervise or terminate non-academic staff, and insist on what suppliers should be engaged, what sports facilities should be built, what markets should be targeted, and how business affairs in general should be conducted.

Of course, in a collaborative and collegial environment, every stakeholder has a right and is at liberty to provide thoughtful and constructive input in the form of *recommendations*. However, recommendations do not rise to the level of *decisions*, which are incidental to proper decision-making authority. The challenge posed by shared governance is not whether to include major stakeholders in organizational decision-making, but rather how to empower them, limit the scope of their authority, and prescribe the manner in which it should be exercised. Authority without borders gives rise to conflicts, tensions, misunderstandings, and tugs-of-war. These, in turn, could debilitate the organization and/or distract it from its mission, purpose, and objectives.

Though not the root cause of these dysfunctionalities, shared governance can be a contributing factor. In contrast to corporate governance, it empowers a multitude of stakeholders and engages them in organizational decision-making, sometimes—oftentimes—without individual accountability. It gives them a broad platform from which they can pursue personal agendas, frequently at the expense of the institution as a whole. This is not to say that in light of this possibility, shared governance should be scrapped altogether and replaced with a more centralized and authoritarian mode of decision-making. Not at all. Rather, it is to say that where shared governance prevents the organization from achieving its strategic goals, especially in the face of threats to its financial viability, the system should be reformed to produce a better result. Where shared governance functions in a spirit of collegiality and cooperation, its advantages are inclusiveness, transparency, and sound oversight. It gives key stakeholders an opportunity to vet their ideas, express different points of view, and air legitimate grievances. Unquestionably, these outcomes contribute to the health of the organization and the vitality of the academic community.[17] As advantages, they far outweigh potential disadvantages.

[17] "Throughout, the aim should be to build a system of governance that uses the strengths of both the faculty and administration by educating the former about the larger needs and opportunities of the university while keeping the latter attentive to the essential values and standards that are required to maintain the highest attainable intellectual quality." Bok, *Universities in the Marketplace*, 193.

Roadblocks to international expansion

So, why do these factors stand in the way of international expansion? Indeed, why are they obstacles in the way of bridging the gap between the abundance of American higher education talent and the immense foreign demand for it? Let us begin with culture.

Cultural roadblocks

An institutional culture that is supply-driven is unresponsive to the needs of consumers, be they domestic or foreign. If it is averse to change, its adherents will find it difficult to discontinue unprofitable programs, adopt new modes of delivery, develop innovative services, and/or reinvent the organization to meet foreign demand. If it is loath to commercialization, they will have no financial incentive to do so. If the culture is too inward-looking, self-absorbed, and isolationist, the faithful will be blind to the enormous opportunities that lie beyond the horizon. They will be incapable of shifting gears to take advantage of these opportunities. In the context of an impending drought in enrollments, they will be unable to find water should the well run dry.

Organizational roadblocks

Traditional organizational structure can be equally problematic. If the organization is too rigid, bureaucratic, and procedurally slow, it will lack the nimbleness required to take advantage of fleeting opportunities that arise in a highly competitive, rapidly changing economic environment.[18] It will not be able to move fast enough to make timely decisions necessitated by sudden, unforeseen movements in the market. Nor will it be able to implement these decisions in an effective, efficient, and expeditious manner. Moreover, to the extent that structural rigidity fosters a bureaucratic mindset, it will impede effective teamwork across departmental lines. It will create gaps in the work chain, leaving tasks critical to international expansion unattended. It will hinder the integration of academics, logistics, marketing, and operations.

---

[18] As noted by Hawawini, "[Internationalization] calls for changes in the institution's existing structure, operating modes, and mindset in order for the institution to join and contribute to the shaping of the global knowledge economy." Hawawini, *Internationalization*, 5.

A major initiative, such as expanding into a foreign market, requires cross-functional teamwork, swift execution, effective delivery, and employee flexibility. "All hands on deck" should be the charge of the day. Every team member should be willing to step in, fill the void, and take up any slack left by others. He or she should be willing to do whatever it takes to get the job done. Needless to say, cubically isolated individuals, working independently of one other, impervious to time constraints, defending their turf against potential intruders, and guided by the maxim *"why it cannot be done"*, as opposed to *"how can we make it happen?"* fall short of this standard.

As for managerial expertise, if academic merit is the primary criterion for appointments to senior administrative positions, then there is likely to be a disconnect between organizational needs and executive competencies. Roles critical to international expansion will be reserved for accomplished scholars, who may excel at teaching and research, but often lack the experience, skills, and expertise needed for developing new business, penetrating foreign markets, inventing new services, and managing growth. Practitioners adept at marketing, selling, branding, business execution, client servicing, logistics, technology, and operations—all critical for the initiative—will be sidelined. Academic considerations will trump business considerations in functional areas that relate primarily to business.

As for staff incentives, if faithful adherence to conventional practices and procedures is rewarded to a greater extent than product innovation, customer satisfaction, and client servicing, the end-result will be mediocre services, limited in scope, and unattuned to the needs of the consumer. Unbending rules and regulations will take precedence over reasonable flexibility in dealing with the client. Innovation, customization, and entrepreneurship will be discouraged, if not stifled altogether. Moreover, if conduct with an internal focus is rewarded more than conduct with an external focus, the end-result will be a more inward-looking, less market-oriented enterprise. This, in turn, could adversely affect the ability of the organization to attract and retain business talent; the efficacy of its sales, marketing, and recruiting efforts; the scope of its customer base; and the magnitude of its service-related revenues.

Poor communication and coordination among self-contained units can be equally debilitating. From a strategic perspective, they often place these units at cross-purposes with one another in the marketplace. From an operational perspective, they sometimes result in a duplication of efforts. From a marketing perspective, they send mixed signals to current and prospective clients.

Several years ago, different units of the same American college ("U.S. College") targeted Client One in an overseas market. Unbeknownst to the international programs office, the executive education office offered Client One a set of low-price open-enrollment programs. Unbeknownst to the executive education office, the international programs office offered Client One a series of high-price customized programs. Preferring the lower price, Client One opted for the first offer. Thereupon, the executive education office proceeded to deliver the goods.

In so doing, it inadvertently breached an agreement that the international programs office had concluded with Client Two. As part of the agreement, the international programs office promised Client Two that all U.S. College programs delivered in the overseas market would be co-sponsored and co-branded exclusively with Client Two. Because Client Two was a major competitor of Client One, its waiving the exclusivity clause was totally out of the question. This placed U.S. College in a predicament. When representatives of Client Two learned about the agreement with Client One, they hit the ceiling. They charged U.S. College with breach of contract and vowed never to deal with it again.

It took a lot of skill and diplomacy for U.S. College to extricate itself from the predicament. In the end, the college president struck a deal with both parties. The bargain, however, cost U.S. College a considerable amount of money, as well as the trust and confidence of both Client One and Client Two. The lesson to be learned is this: if one arm of the organization knows not what the other arm is doing, the end-result is likely to be miscommunication, misunderstanding, and misalignment. These, in turn, could damage the institution's reputation, relationships, and business.

Governance

In a major global initiative, if too many chiefs are involved in decision-making, there is a risk that no consensus will be reached on business strategy, target markets, services to be rendered, and which units will deliver them. The lack of alignment, in turn, could debilitate the organization in the face of time-sensitive opportunities and intense competition.[19] Furthermore, if a handful of disgruntled, yet enfranchised stakeholders oppose the initiative, they could stall or block it altogether. They could throw

---

[19] See Weisbrod, Ballou, and Asch, *Mission and Money*, 172–173.

obstacles in the way of its implementation. They could foot-drag in the face of critical deadlines. Finally, where boundaries on decision-making authority are unclear, governing bodies could clash on the nature of the initiative and its strategic direction.[20] This, in turn, could give rise to conflict and confusion, which could derail the project altogether.

Here's a scenario that might strike a chord with trustees, faculty, and administrators. It is "hypothetical in the extreme," intended to prove a point, not point a finger.

Ivory Tower College is in dire financial straits. To turn it around, trustees with a business mindset adopt a strategy to expand into an overseas market whose growth promises a high rate of return. They express the belief that, in light of its institutional strengths, Ivory Tower will have a distinct competitive advantage in this market. The move is adamantly opposed by a few influential faculty members, who denounce the host country's foreign policy. Any engagement in the country, they contend, will signal to all the world that Ivory Tower endorses this policy.

Soon, other constituencies join in the fray. Traditionalists in the faculty senate protest that the initiative will transform their small regional college into a large global university. Humanities scholars on the administrative council voice concern that the initiative is beyond the college's technological and operational capability. Entrenched college bureaucrats declare that the tasks associated with the initiative "just cannot be done."

Cognizant of mounting opposition, the faculty senate convenes an emergency session and endorses an alternative strategy. That strategy calls for the development of distance-learning programs for local working professionals and the earmarking of profits for a fine arts center. Senate members threaten the college president with a vote of no confidence if he refuses to go along.

Alarmed by the escalating tensions, trustees step in and insist that only the board has authority to set the strategic direction of the college. Emeritus professors counterargue that as a vital partner in shared governance, the faculty senate has equal authority. All parties dig in their heels and refuse to compromise. To break the deadlock, Ivory Tower President intervenes and appoints a special task force to "look into the matter" and report back to him in six months' time. In a flash of expediency, he figures that

---

[20] Similar clashes occur where the goals of an academic unit of a university conflict with those of the broader university. Hawawini, *Internationalization*, 29–30.

fixing Ivory Tower's financial problems must take a back seat to solving its political problems, at least for the time being.

After a prolonged summer break, the task force finally meets and debates each strategic alternative *ad infinitum*. In the meantime, a major competitor establishes a branch campus in the foreign market, thus wiping out the college's once-held competitive advantage.

What would it take to bridge the Great Chasm?

Bridging the Great Chasm calls for the antithesis of the traditional model. Specifically, it calls for the following.

A change in culture

A major international initiative that is both academic and commercial in nature requires a broad understanding of, and profound respect for, both the academic and the commercial. Academic values are essential for ensuring the quality of the services to be rendered. Commercial values are vital for the delivery of these services in markets that are new, competitive, and untested. An initiative inspired by academic values alone could flounder as a result of inadequate business planning, ineffective marketing, poor execution, and weak operationalization. An initiative inspired by commercial values alone could falter by virtue of destroying the institution's academic integrity. To be successful, the initiative must be animated by both sets of values, each placed in proper perspective.

Academic values should supply *educational substance* in activities such as the design, development, and delivery of services. Commercial values should shape *business form* in the organization, management, financing, marketing, and pricing of these services. It follows, logically, that the former activities should be overseen by credible academics who have the skills, experience, and expertise to ensure educational quality, while the latter should be directed by competent managers who have the skills, experience, and expertise to ensure effective execution. For the initiative to succeed, both types of professionals should be engaged. And in terms of empowerment, they should be on equal footing within the organization.

Where academic and commercial activities overlap or require close coordination, matters should be handled by a cross-functional team, consisting of both academics and practitioners. The former can shed light on the educational aspects of the endeavor, while the latter can give advice on the commercial aspects. Such a team could provide valuable guidance on

- consumer preferences as they relate to higher education talent;
- how to leverage off the strengths of the institution to create new and innovative services geared to the needs of the consumer;
- how to marshal the human and material resources necessary to deliver these services effectively, efficiently, and expeditiously;
- how to reconfigure administrative units to facilitate effective delivery and seamless operations, without, however, compromising the academic integrity of the institution or the educational quality of its programs;
- how to maximize financial value in a manner consistent with the institution's mission and values.

These measures are likely to transform a culture that is internally oriented and supply-side driven into one that is externally oriented and demand-driven. They are likely to create a milieu more conducive to commercial pursuits that advance the institution's mission and purpose.

A change in organization

Beyond teaching and research, the institution should move in the direction of cross-functional teams, similar to the one previously described. It should tear down bureaucracies, hierarchies, and silos that stand in the way of effective teamwork. It should create a flatter organizational structure, a more fluid work environment, and an entrepreneurial mindset, all conducive to greater collaboration, communication, and innovation.

In this new institutional order, non-academics with skills essential for international expansion should be given primary authority over functional areas specific to their expertise. Academics, whose talents are critical for the undertaking, should be given broad authority over educational content and learning outcomes. The aims of this arrangement are two-fold: first, to ensure faculty oversight in the educational aspects of the endeavor; and second, to give practitioners full, adequate, and appropriate authority over the commercial aspects. Achieving these dual aims will give rise to synergies. It will complement the conceptual skills of academics with the practical skills of laymen.

Here's an example of how the arrangement would work: in the chain of activities incidental to providing higher education services to international clients, a marketing team would be charged with managing the client relationship,[21] determining client preferences as to the type of service to be rendered (i.e., when, where, and how it should be delivered; client budget constraints; and the intended beneficiaries), and conveying this information to members of other teams. A faculty advisory council would be charged with designing the service in line with client preferences, supplying educational content, recruiting subject-matter experts to deliver the service, and ensuring educational quality. A finance team would be charged with assessing the financial feasibility of the service, costing and pricing it, and budgeting for its design, development, and delivery. An operations team would be tasked with evaluating the operational feasibility of the service, adapting it to the client's preferred mode of delivery, managing logistics and technology, and providing backroom support.

This *international market-oriented model* differs from the traditional model (illustrated in Figure 7.1) in that it would streamline operations, expedite decision-making, generate efficiencies, integrate core functions, and be more attuned to the needs and preferences of the consumer. It would be flexible enough to meet these needs and preferences, fluid enough to facilitate the continuous flow of information, lean enough to ensure efficient operations, and nimble enough to accommodate sudden and unforeseen movements in the market. The contours of this model are illustrated in Figure 7.2. How it would work in practice is illustrated in Figure 7.3.

As for teaching and research, because these activities require freedom, independence, and reflection to flourish, the institutional framework in which they are conducted should remain open, flexible, and conducive to *individual* thought and action, as well as consensual *group* collaboration. The relatively loose structure in which these activities are conducted is what makes them appealing to those who are intellectual, individualistic, and independent by nature. Accordingly, in these functional areas, freedom, individualism, and autonomy should be the norm, not the exception.

Finally, to signal to internal constituencies that it attaches value to a market orientation, the institution should demonstrably reward customer satisfaction, service innovation, and revenue generation to the same extent as it does effective planning, processing, advising, budgeting, and

---

[21] Alternatively, because many clients prefer dealing directly with the chief executive officer, a marketing team could support the president who would be primarily responsible for managing the client relationship.

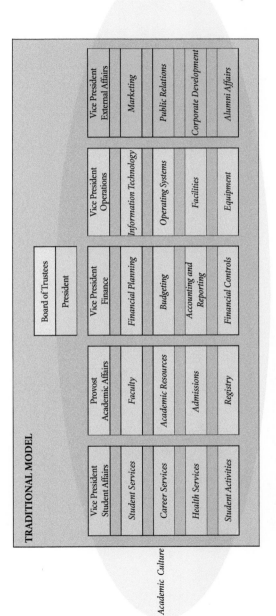

Fig. 7.1 The traditional model.

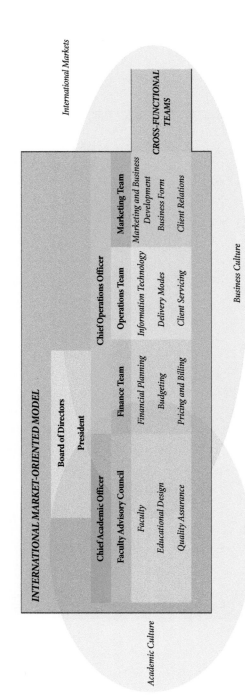

Fig. 7.2 The international market-oriented model.

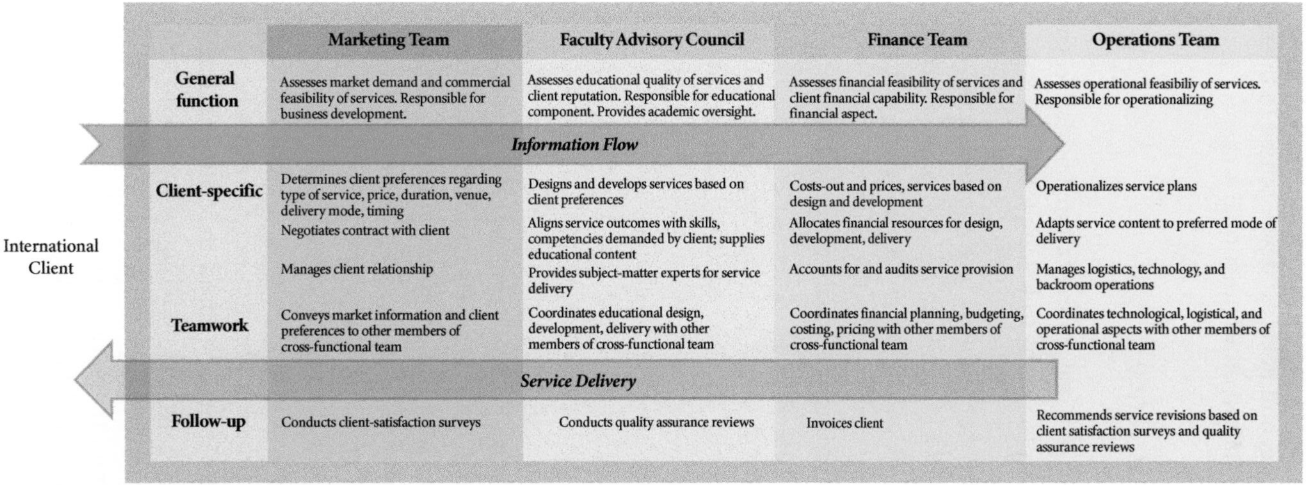

	Marketing Team	Faculty Advisory Council	Finance Team	Operations Team
General function	Assesses market demand and commercial feasibility of services. Responsible for business development.	Assesses educational quality of services and client reputation. Responsible for educational component. Provides academic oversight.	Assesses financial feasibility of services and client financial capability. Responsible for financial aspect.	Assesses operational feasibility of services. Responsible for operationalizing
		Information Flow		
Client-specific	Determines client preferences regarding type of service, price, duration, venue, delivery mode, timing	Designs and develops services based on client preferences	Costs-out and prices, services based on design and development	Operationalizes service plans
	Negotiates contract with client	Aligns service outcomes with skills, competencies demanded by client; supplies educational content	Allocates financial resources for design, development, delivery	Adapts service content to preferred mode of delivery
	Manages client relationship	Provides subject-matter experts for service delivery	Accounts for and audits service provision	Manages logistics, technology, and backroom operations
Teamwork	Conveys market information and client preferences to other members of cross-functional team	Coordinates educational design, development, delivery with other members of cross-functional team	Coordinates financial planning, budgeting, costing, pricing with other members of cross-functional team	Coordinates technological, logistical, and operational aspects with other members of cross-functional team
		Service Delivery		
Follow-up	Conducts client-satisfaction surveys	Conducts quality assurance reviews	Invoices client	Recommends service revisions based on client satisfaction surveys and quality assurance reviews

International Client

Fig. 7.3 Operationalization of the international market-oriented model.

assessment—professionally, if not monetarily. In addition, it should formally recognize the career achievements of those engaged in sales, marketing, client servicing, and business development to the same extent as it does with respect to staff in other functional areas.

A change in governance

To ensure the success of a major international initiative, traditional governance should be modified in the following ways:

First, it should be streamlined. In the process, the institution should strike a balance. On the one hand, it should keep the number of participants large enough to ensure adequate representation and informed decision-making. On the other hand, it should reduce this number to a minimum to facilitate close collaboration and expeditious decision-making.[22]

Second, to prevent gridlock where time is of the essence, the system should incorporate internal controls. Limits should be set on the length of official debate. Governing bodies should be required to meet throughout the year. Mechanisms should be in place for *ad hoc* decision-making, in the event that a majority fails to reach a decision, deliberations are stalled, or implementation is hindered. A fair and expeditious appellate procedure should be established.

Third, to avoid conflict and confusion, decision-making authority should be based on a clear separation of powers. Consistent with well-established tenets of corporate governance, the board, working closely with the president, should have primary authority over strategy, including *global* strategy. The president should have primary authority over global execution. Faculty should have primary authority over the educational aspects of the venture. Business managers should have primary authority over the business aspects. This separation of powers should be based on relative skills and competencies. As a maxim, ultimate functional authority should reside with primary functional expertise.

Finally, to integrate the various components of the system, a "social pact" of sorts should be concluded among key stakeholders. This

---

[22] To ensure sound oversight, the institution might create, for each constituency, an advisory council or board, elected for a fixed term by their respective colleagues. The delegates would be accountable to their colleagues for recommendations made within their scope of authority. They would be removable from office only "for cause," which would exclude making informed decisions in good faith.

pact should delineate each governing body's scope of authority, provide for continuous and ongoing consultation, set forth protocols for internal communication, and define a fair procedure for dispute resolution.

A new business model

The process of streamlining operations, expediting decision-making, generating efficiencies, integrating core functions, and responding effectively to the needs and preferences of the client requires a new business model. The optimal configuration is the *international market-oriented model*, which integrates essential service-providing functions. There are several versions of this model. In one version, cross-functional activities with an international market focus are housed in the traditional entity. Such positioning, however, is not ideal, because marketing, finance, and operations would be expected to produce results in a cultural milieu that is not particularly conducive to business. At an extreme, it could give rise to internal tensions that could impede the progress of the initiative, if not stifle it altogether. Accordingly, activities essential to the design, development, financing, operationalization, and marketing of higher education services should be taken out of the traditional organization and placed in a separate entity.[23] This entity would be subject to the control of the main college or university. However, it would be relatively autonomous.

Specifically, it would have its own corporate charter, system of governance, organizational structure, budget, facilities, management, staff, and faculty. It might even seek accreditation as a branch of the main institution if it meets applicable accreditation requirements. This "stand-alone" version is preferable to the "in-house" version because activities essential for the service provision would be housed in an entity whose very purpose would be the conduct of such activities and whose culture would be more conducive to it. The corporate structure associated with the "stand-alone" version would isolate business risks, insulate the parent from legal liability, and preserve the parent's tax-exempt status.

In the final analysis, creating a separate entity with its own culture, organization, and governance is the key to success. A major attempt to restructure a traditional organization, transform its culture, and reform

---

[23] This is consistent with the "de novo internationalization principle." Hawawini, *Internationalization*, 9.

its governance is likely to be disruptive, costly, and ultimately ineffective. "Gutting it out" to make room for a different *modus operandi* would be impractical, if not impossible to achieve. Appending a new administrative unit to the existing organizational structure would likely perpetuate the traditional way of doing things. With time, the unit would be bureaucratized, like other units of the organization. Its culture would be infected with the biases of the dominant culture. Its entrepreneurial spirit would be stifled. Its pace of operations would be slowed. The better way to go, therefore, is to create a separate entity that is relatively autonomous, yet subject to the control of the traditional institution. This approach has the distinct advantage of enabling the creation of a new culture, organization, and governance more attuned to the needs of the consumer, with the least possible cost, disruption, and dysfunctionality.

So, what is really new about this model?

Several features of the international market-oriented model are novel.

- *Modus operandi.* Its mode of operation is based on the deployment of flexible and fluid cross-functional teams devoid of steep hierarchies, cumbersome bureaucracies, and self-contained silos. As a result, the organization is likely to be nimbler in the face of changing market conditions.
- *Functional integration.* Relative to the traditional model, the new model better integrates functions essential for the provision of higher education services (i.e., academics, marketing, finance, and operations). Consequently, it is likely to improve communications, information flow, and coordination.
- *Alignment of authority with expertise.* The new model aligns ultimate functional authority with primary functional expertise. As a result, it promises to strengthen business execution and improve operational efficiency.
- *Empowerment of non-academic staff.* More so than the traditional model, the new model empowers business, technical, and other non-academic staff, whose skills are essential for international expansion.
- *Blend of cultures.* The new model reconciles academic and business values in a cultural milieu that is conducive to both academic and business pursuits.

- *Market orientation.* Relative to the traditional model, the new model is more client-focused, demand-driven, and market-oriented.

Add to these features a more streamlined system of governance, and the end-result is likely to be swifter decision-making and stronger execution. Such a system would reduce the possibility of deadlocks, conflict, and confusion, all the while preserving academic integrity.[24]

Leadership, mission, and values

To function properly, an organization based on the international market-oriented model should have exceptional leadership. This leadership should respect differences in roles, responsibilities, competencies, and authority. It should be able to balance competing interests. It should be adept at managing a variety of functional activities. It should be sensitive to the fine nuances of the academic and business cultures, not to mention the foreign cultures prevailing in overseas markets. This is not the type of leadership that will have risen through the ranks of traditional academia. Rather, it is a new genre of leadership whose outlook and style will have been shaped by experience in both business and academia.[25]

[24] For-profit corporations, such as Laureate International, have pioneered a "conglomerate model." This model is essentially the international market-oriented model turned "upside down." In the latter model, a traditional academic institution creates a new entity to spearhead its global initiative. In the conglomerate model, a new entity spearheads the global initiative by acquiring traditional academic institutions located in different parts of the world.
The advantages of the "conglomerate model," relative to the international market-oriented model, are these: first, in the conglomerate model, the parent corporation is likely to be client-focused and demand-driven. Second, its subsidiaries have longstanding academic credibility. Third, as pre-existing institutions, they already have a cadre of students, faculty, staff, and administrators; a portfolio of courses, curricula, and programs; short- and long-term assets; licenses, accreditation, and brand. Fourth, the corporate structure associated with this model is sufficiently decentralized to accommodate the needs of clients in various locales. Finally, this corporate structure creates opportunities for joint programs and faculty/student exchanges among institutional affiliates.
The relative disadvantages are these: first, the culture, operations, and governance of constituent institutions remain "traditional," thus posing institutional obstacles in the way of local expansion. Second, as a collectivity, functional areas and program portfolios are likely to overlap, giving rise to redundancies throughout the broader enterprise. Third, institutional affiliates cannot leverage off the business brand of the parent to enhance their academic credibility. Finally, the conglomerate is held together through strong business control, which could translate into weak academic oversight.
[25] As for market strategy, the works of Mazzarol and Soutar are relevant. They developed a model of how educational institutions can gain a competitive advantage in international markets. Shaping the contours of this model are five principles: first, the institution should examine its market environment, including industry structure, market outlook, and its own market experience. Second, it should assess its strategic resources, including staff, facilities, programs, and finances. Third, it should formulate a "generic enterprise strategy." This strategy should emphasize how the institution can achieve market

Finally, in pursuing its strategic goals, the institution should be true to its mission and purpose. Its international pursuits should be consonant with this mission and purpose. They should also be consonant with the organization's core values. These values both define the organization and differentiate it from other types of enterprises. They are the heart and soul of the institution, which makes it essentially *academic*.

differentiation. Fourth, it should develop distinctive competencies, including a strong brand, a broad range of programs, a solid alumni base, financial strength, international strategic alliances, offshore teaching programs, and possibly also forward integration. Fifth, it should minimize factors that could inhibit market success.

Mazzarol and Soutar cite two such factors: (1) the organizational expertise and quality of staff, and (2) the presence of a client-oriented, innovative culture. They base their finding on the results of a 1998 survey of 315 higher education institutions, including 11 in the United States. This finding is anomalous, in light of the highly entrepreneurial, specialized, and market-oriented nature of the undertaking, and also the reluctance of the vast majority of traditional institutions to venture into markets beyond their own backyard. Nonetheless, it is based on empirical data—specifically, the subjective beliefs of international marketing administrators.

Mazzarol and Soutar admit that the finding is "at odds with previous studies that suggest that people and organizational culture can be a source of competitive advantage." They point out, "As the globalization of higher education increases the level of commercial competition among institutions, it is anticipated that the role of people and culture within institutions will change." In light of these qualifications, their finding highlights the need for further research. It also makes our ideal-typical construct all the more relevant and useful. T. Mazzarol and G.N. Soutar, *The Global Market for Higher Education* (2001).

8
How to Bridge the Great Chasm

What are the practicalities of "going global"? What are the mechanics? What are the inherent risks? This chapter discusses (1) preconditions that must be met before an institution can successfully "go global," (2) collaborative arrangements that can facilitate the endeavor, (3) the pitfalls of some of these arrangements, and (4) how they can be managed through quality controls. The chapter also discusses ways to finance the venture, the outsourcing of operational tasks, and the delivery of higher education services online. It offers "nuts-and-bolts" advice on how to bridge the gap between the abundance of American higher education talent and the immense foreign demand for it.

> For the everyday work of the higher learning, as such, little of a hierarchical gradation, and less of bureaucratic subordination, is needful or serviceable . . .[1]
>
> Thorstein Veblen, American economist and sociologist

> This is not to say that university officials must necessarily work within the existing structures of faculty governance and put up with all of its frustrations. New procedures and new entities may be called for to fit the special circumstances of new entrepreneurial ventures . . . Still, the central point remains that universities will do a better job of upholding essential values if faculty members help design and oversee all profit-making or commercial activities that affect the academic life of the university . . .[2]
>
> Derek Bok, former President of Harvard University

It is cliché, but change in the private sector often comes at a much faster rate than it does in academe. A university's partners may want to move at speeds outside a typical university's comfort zone. Therefore, the success of a university partnership with an entity in the private sector may depend in part on the university's structuring the partnership in such a way that it can be executed

---

[1] T. Veblen, *The Higher Learning in America: A Memorandum on the Conduct of Universities by Business Men* (1918), 104.
[2] D. Bok, *Universities in the Marketplace: The Commercialization of Higher Education*, (2003), 192–193.

Bridging the Gap between the Abundance of American Higher Education Talent and the Immense Foreign Demand for It.
Richard J. Joseph, Oxford University Press. © Richard J. Joseph (2022). DOI: 10.1093/oso/9780192848307.003.0009

faster than new initiatives are typically completed on campus. Different ways of thinking and acting may be necessary.[3]

> Task Force on University Partnerships, American Association of State Colleges and Universities

Introduction

"Going global" is not easy. It is likely to encounter resistance from a multitude of stakeholders who are fixated on the domestic market. After all, this is the market that they know and trust. Before rejecting "internationalization," however, they should consider the changing landscape of American higher education. They should consider its likely impact on enrollments, revenues, costs, and profit margins. They should carefully weigh the feasibility of other options. And they should think twice about the costs and benefits of doing nothing.

Preconditions

To proceed on firm footing, the leadership of the institution should be confident that several preconditions have been met. The first is stakeholder "buy-in."

Stakeholder "buy-in"

The decision to "go global" should not be made arbitrarily or unilaterally. Rather, it should be made deliberately in concert with major stakeholders, all of whom should be engaged in the process.[4] It is ill-advised for college or university leaders simply to declare that the initiative is in the best interests of the organization. Such a move is almost certain to invite opposition from skeptics. Instead, the leaders should demonstrate, to the satisfaction of all, that the initiative is in the best interests of *every constituency*. And they should be prepared to address the legitimate concerns of *every constituency*.

---

[3] American Association of State Colleges and Universities (AASCU), *Making Partnerships Work: Principles, Guidelines, and Advice for Public University Leaders* (2017), 23.

[4] P.G. Altbach, "The Complexities of Global Engagement." In *Global Opportunities and Challenges for Higher Education Leaders*, edited by L.E. Rumbley, R. Matross Helms, P. McGill Peterson, and P.G. Altbach (2014), 21.

For example, to procure faculty "buy-in," the leaders should demonstrate that the initiative will not compromise either academic integrity or educational quality. They might point out that the new organizational structure will give faculty an important say in the services to be delivered, who will deliver them, and to whom they will be delivered. They might describe the quality controls they intend to install to ensure academic integrity and educational quality. They might earmark a portion of the profits for faculty research, professional development, teaching assistance, and additional faculty hiring. They might commit to engaging faculty in overseas teaching, research, program coordination, project development, and academic advising. They should emphasize that by generating additional resources for the institution, the initiative will do for faculty what "business as usual" failed to do for them in the past. And they should be prepared to back up their claims with evidence.

Here's an example of how not to proceed. Several years ago, the president of a prominent northeastern college launched a multimillion dollar initiative to expand overseas. He did so by fiat, without seeking the advice and consent of the faculty. Although most faculty members were indifferent to the initiative, a few vehemently opposed it. The forceful hand of the president, however, kept their resistance at bay.

The opposition remained subdued so long as the president was in power. When he stepped down, however, what had long been simmering under the surface suddenly gushed to the fore. The opportune moment was the installation of a new president. Lacking experience in higher education, she also lacked the stature of her predecessor. Sensing political "weakness," foes of the initiative renewed their effort to kill it. They did so by threatening the new president with a vote of no confidence unless she "reorganized the project out of existence."

Caving in to the opposition, the president ultimately did so. Her expedient move, however, left the college in dire straits. By forfeiting millions of dollars in revenues to be generated by the project, the chief executive left a gaping hole in the college budget. Faced with mounting operating costs, her successor had no choice but to cut faculty salaries, lay off administrative personnel, and discontinue unprofitable programs. In the end, opponents of the initiative had been triumphant, but their triumph had come at the cost of the financial well-being of the organization as a whole.

An important takeaway is this: never launch a major international initiative without key stakeholder "buy-in." Consultation and engagement are not just recommended, but essential for the success of the venture.

A comprehensive business plan

Second, a comprehensive business plan should be in place. The "master plan" should incorporate subsidiary strategic, marketing, and financial plans that build on each other's assumptions and projections. The strategic plan should address the institution's strengths and weaknesses, as related to prospective market opportunities. It should also address the risks associated with expanding abroad, as well as how these risks can be minimized. The marketing plan should include a thorough market analysis. It should identify target markets, prospective clients, services to be rendered, and potential competition. It should also set forth a coherent strategy for penetrating these markets, developing new business, and gaining a competitive advantage. The financial plan should incorporate a schedule for funding start-up costs, operating expenses, and capital expenditures. It should also set forth long-term projections based on reasonable and defensible assumptions.

Intellectual property policy

Third, intellectual property issues should be sorted out. If the proposed services are higher education advisory, technology transfer, course design and development, or project development and management, a coherent intellectual property policy, acceptable to faculty, administrators, staff, and trustees, should be in place. This policy should spell out what constitutes "intellectual property," whether title to it belongs to the institution or the innovator, whether ownership is exclusive or concurrent, and terms of licensing and profit-sharing. It should be based not only on the law of intellectual property, but also on best practices in higher education.[5] One of the last things that stakeholders would want in the midst of a major international initiative is to get embroiled in in a fight over royalties.

---

[5] These practices are discussed in Association of American University Professors, *Defending the Freedom to Innovate: Faculty Intellectual Property Rights after Stanford v. Roche* (2014).

Such a battle could well occur, unless intellectual property issues are sorted out beforehand.

Institutional capability

Fourth, the institution should assess its overall capability. It should be confident that it has adequate organizational, technological, and financial capability for both start-up and operation. Organizationally, the institution should be confident that it has sufficient academic expertise to design, develop, and deliver the proposed services; sufficient financial expertise to cost, price, and budget for them; sufficient operational expertise to provide logistical, technological, and backroom support; sufficient marketing expertise to develop new business and to service existing clients; and sufficient management bandwidth to plan, coordinate, and execute the project. Technologically, it should be confident that it has the requisite facilities, equipment, infrastructure, processes, and software for the undertaking. Financially, it should be assured that it has sufficient financial resources, or access to such resources, to fund the venture. If after a thorough analysis it concludes that it lacks adequate capability, it might explore ways to make up for the deficiency, such as partnering with another entity.

On a related note, if it is expected that the unit or entity that will provide the services will draw on the human or physical resources of the broader enterprise, an orderly process for doing so should be in place. This process should incorporate a procedure for seconding college or university personnel to the service unit or entity; utilizing the main institution's infrastructure, equipment, and facilities; and accounting for both actual use and foregone opportunities. For example, if a new service subsidiary is formed and it borrows faculty from the parent organization, it should compensate the parent for actual and opportunity costs. (Rationale: if the parent organization loses faculty, it might have to hire additional instructors to perform their duties.) If the subsidiary occupies physical space of the parent organization, it should pay imputed rent to the parent. (Rationale: if the parent organization gives up existing space, it might have to acquire additional space to perform basic functions.) Such a system of internal accounting and transfer pricing would more accurately reflect real and opportunity costs. It would also more accurately reflect total *net* costs to the enterprise as a whole.

A presence on the ground

Finally, the institution should be willing to establish a presence on the ground in any foreign market that it enters. Doing so is important because it signals to local residents (a.k.a. potential clients) that the service provider is "here to stay." It also indicates the service provider's long-term commitment to the educational advancement of their respective communities. A "fixed base" would give the service provider a distinct advantage over those competitors who propose to service local clients only remotely. It would enable the provider to supplement any service that it provides remotely, with visible on-the-ground support. A U.S. college or university can establish a presence on the ground by stationing an employee (perhaps a recruiter or marketer) in the target market. Alternatively, this can be done by commissioning a local agent to handle its affairs. Ideally, the institution should set up an office in every country in which it provides services.

Collaborative arrangements

In launching a global initiative, a U.S. college or university can pursue one of several courses of action. First, it can go it alone, if it has sufficient capability. Second, it can forge an alliance with another academic institution.[6] Third, it can elicit the support of a foreign government agency or educational foundation.[7] Lastly, it can partner with a multinational corporation.[8] Each alternative has its advantages and disadvantages.[9]

---

[6] T. Mazzarol and G.N. Soutar, *The Global Market for Higher Education* (2001), 91–92. Insofar as they involve a degree of marketing and operational integration, these alliances would go beyond loose associations such as the Worldwide Universities Network.

[7] An example of the latter is the Qatar Foundation, which provides facilities and infrastructure for eight international branch campuses in Education City near Doha.

[8] J. Spring, *Globalization of Education*, 2nd ed. (2015), 52–54; J. Berman, "Connecting with Industry: Bridging the Divide." *Journal of Higher Education Policy & Management*, vol. 30, no. 2 (2008): 165–174; and T. Mazzarol, and G.N. Soutar, "Revisiting the Global Market for Higher Education." *Asia Pacific Journal of Marketing and Logistics*, vol. 24, no. 5 (2012): 717, 724–726.

[9] On partnering with U.S. institutions, agencies, and corporations see B.A. Weisbrod, J.P. Ballou, and E.D. Asch, *Mission and Money, Understanding the University* (2008), 207–208. On international higher education partnerships with an emphasis on leadership development see B. Barnett and S.L. Jacobson, "Higher Education Partnerships for Studying and Improving Leadership Preparation and Development Around the World." In *Globalization and Internationalization in Higher Education*, edited by F. Maringe and N. Foskett (2010), 255–272.

Going it alone

The advantages of going it alone relate to control, income, and self-reliance.

- The sponsoring institution retains control over all aspects of the venture, including business strategy, client selection, and service quality.
- It is entitled to 100% of the income.
- It can rely on its own trusted staff for service delivery.

As for disadvantages,

- The sponsoring institution defrays the full cost of the undertaking.
- It bears all the risks, including the risk of loss.
- It consumes its own human and material capital.
- It cannot leverage off the institutional strengths of others.

Alliance with another academic institution

The advantages of forging an alliance with another academic institution are as follows:

- Both institutions are likely to have similar normative values, which reduces the risk of conflict over academic goals.
- They can pool their human and material resources and share operating costs.
- They can spread financial, market, and operational risks.
- They can complement and enhance each other's academic capabilities.

The disadvantages are several:

- Managerially, the sponsoring institution loses full control.[10]
- Financially, it loses profit share.
- Operationally, it must rely on another entity's culture, organizational structure, system of governance, policies, practices, and procedures.[11] Doing so could slow down decision-making and blunt execution.

---

[10] Mazzarol and Soutar, *The Global Market for Higher Education*, 91–92.
[11] G. Hawawini, *The Internationalization of Higher Education and Business Schools* (2016), 41–42.

Moreover, if the modus operandi of the sponsoring institution is based on the international market-oriented model, while that of the partnering institution is based on a more traditional model, such an arrangement would defeat the very purpose of adopting the new model. That purpose is to streamline operations, expedite decision-making, generate efficiencies, integrate essential functions, and be more attuned to the needs and preferences of the client.

Foreign government agency support

Eliciting the support of a foreign government agency or educational foundation is advantageous in many ways:

- By lending its full faith and credit to the undertaking, the agency or foundation can increase the likelihood of its success.
- The sponsoring institution might be able to tap its partner's budgetary resources, thus lessening the need for self-financing.
- The agency or foundation might be able to provide valuable technical and logistical support, thus enhancing the sponsor's operational capability.
- It might open the door to other opportunities in the public sector.

The drawbacks are as follows:

- Procuring public support can be tedious, time-consuming, and all-encompassing. The process could drag on for months.
- The arrangement is likely to impose a layer of bureaucracy on an undertaking that, in principle, should be entrepreneurial. Governmental rules and regulations could stifle innovation and agility.
- The sponsoring institution could lose control of the venture to a public entity with greater political clout. Political considerations could come to outweigh academic considerations in the selection of clients and the delivery of services.
- Finally, the sponsoring institution incurs reputational risk. If the conduct, policies, or practices of the foreign government or foundation are the least bit reprehensible, any affiliation with it could sully the sponsor's reputation.

Partnering with a multinational corporation

The advantages of partnering with a multinational corporation are numerous:

- For one, the sponsoring institution can complement its academic capability with the business savvy, market knowledge, client network, technological know-how, and operational capability of a transnational enterprise. These intangibles are critical for international expansion.
- It can leverage off the human, financial, technological, and physical resources of the multinational. Doing so could help it fund and staff the project, penetrate new markets, develop new business, service existing clients, and provide backroom support.
- The arrangement would allow the sponsoring institution to align its operations with those of an enterprise that is likely to be results-oriented, market-driven, swift at decision-making, and strong at execution.
- It would allow the sponsor to create two pipelines: one for placing its graduates in the multinational corporation, and the other for training the multinational's employees.
- Finally, the arrangement would give the sponsor an opportunity to forge an alliance with an entity that is not a direct competitor. Doing so would increase the likelihood of its gaining full control over all educational aspects of the venture.

Then, there are disadvantages:

- For public colleges and universities, this option might be limited or unavailable. The laws and regulations of some states restrict the nature and scope of partnerships with business enterprises.[12]
- The sponsoring institution risks losing control to an entity whose directors, officers, and staff have a business mindset and who might not understand, appreciate, or respect the values of academia.
- The sponsor could forego income, depending on the partner's relative stake in the venture.
- It incurs reputational risk, which is linked to the brand, conduct, policies, and practices of the multinational.[13]

---

[12] AASCU, *Making Partnerships Work*, 27–28.
[13] Hawawini, *Internationalization*, 31.

- Its affiliation with a business enterprise could diminish its standing in the academic world.
- Finally, without adequate controls, the arrangement could result in the subordination of academic goals to business goals. This, in turn, could subvert the sponsor's mission and purpose.[14]

Table 8.1 summarizes the advantages and disadvantages of each arrangement.

Despite its drawbacks, partnering with a multinational is worth considering. It creates synergies in functional areas that are vital for international expansion: namely, *academics*, *finance*, *marketing*, and *operations*. It complements the sponsor's academic credibility with the multinational's organizational capability. In addition, it is likely to give the sponsor greater latitude in overseeing all educational aspects of the venture. How can it be accomplished?

Safeguarding academic interests
In forging the partnership, the institution should craft an agreement that maximizes potential advantages while minimizing potential disadvantages. It should also proceed with caution. It should choose a trustworthy partner that is not a potential competitor. That way, it can retain control over all educational aspects of the venture. It should be willing to trade a greater share of the profits for a larger voice in decision-making—perhaps by giving the multinational a non-voting preferred share. Most importantly, it should insist on stringent controls. Specifically, it should demand adequate representation on all governing boards, with exclusive authority over academic and faculty affairs; primary responsibility for admissions, academic assessment, and educational quality; and an important say in marketing, branding, and client selection. All this should be a "deal-breaker."

In addition, the sponsoring institution should insist that rights to any intellectual property that it contributes remain with the author or inventor, consistent with its internal intellectual property policy.

---

[14] In some Arab countries, the service provider must partner with a local citizen or corporation to do business there. Under this practice, which is often codified, all licenses, contracts, and title to property must be held in the name of the local intermediary, or *wasta*, whose role is to facilitate the conduct of business in the country. In return for this "favor," the *wasta* usually takes a cut of the profits. Because the *wasta* is the nominal owner of the foreign beneficiary's assets in the country, the beneficial owner incurs the risk of losing control of them. Thus, it is important for the beneficial owner to select a trustworthy intermediary. "Know thy *wasta*" is an adage that should not be taken lightly.

Table 8.1 Advantages and disadvantages of various arrangements for "going global"

Type of arrangement	Income share	Organizational capability	Degree of control	Organizational structure	Principal advantages	Principal disadvantages
Sole sponsorship	100%	Primarily academic	Full	Traditional or market-oriented structure	Management control; quality control; no profit sharing	Limited marketing, operational, and financial capability
Academic partner	Less than 100%	Enhanced academic and financial	Partial	Traditional or market-oriented structure of sponsor combined with traditional structure of partner	Similar academic values; increased financial capability; some risk-sharing	Additional process and slower decision-making; limited marketing capability; potential loss of control
Government partner	Less than 100%	Enhanced technical, logistical, and financial	Partial	Traditional or market-oriented structure of sponsor combined with government bureaucracy	Enhanced technical, logistical, financial capability; access to governmental resources; some risk-sharing	Bureaucratic red tape and slower decision-making; limited marketing capability; potential loss of control; reputational risk
Business partner	Less than 100%	Enhanced marketing, logistical, operational, and financial	Partial	Traditional or market-oriented structure of sponsor combined with business organization	Commercial pace of partner; enhanced marketing, logistical, operational, and financial capability; some risk-sharing; operational synergies	Dissimilar cultural values; potential loss of control; subordination of academic values to business values; reputational risk; state regulatory restrictions

Such a provision would safeguard the interests of both the sponsoring institution and those among its constituencies who created the intellectual property, which encompasses courses, curricula, scholarly works, syllabi, lectures, exams, computer codes, lab reports, research methods, new technologies, and academic blueprints.[15]

Also, the sponsor should obtain ironclad guarantees of academic freedom. These guarantees should be incorporated in the partnership agreement. If a new entity is formed, they should also be incorporated in the entity's charter and by-laws.

Finally, the sponsoring institution should be realistic, given the potential disparity in bargaining power between an academic institution rich in ideas and a business enterprise rich in resources; furthermore, given their different mindsets, values, and goals, a handshake alone will not suffice to protect the sponsor's fundamental interests. Such a deed will only be as strong as the word of the parties and their willingness to hold each other accountable. As is often the case in business dealings, the non-academic partner could have a change of heart later in the game and stage a "takeover." Or it could develop its own in-house academic capability, and then squeeze the sponsor out of the venture. Such a contingency should be anticipated and provided for from the very onset.

Government guidelines

To minimize the likelihood of such a takeover, government agencies, such as the U.S. Department of Education, should step in to oversee academic–business partnerships. These agencies should issue rules and regulations that govern their formation, operation, and dissolution. They should set forth normative standards of ethical behavior and best practices. They should safeguard the academic integrity of the sponsoring institution. After all, they have a vital interest in doing so.

U.S. higher education is a multimillion dollar business. The exportation of U.S. higher education services promises to reduce the foreign trade deficit and spread American goodwill, ideas, and values throughout the world. The value of U.S. higher education services is inextricably linked to academic integrity. Academic integrity hinges on strong academic values,

---

[15] Consider the following advice offered by the AASCU: "[I]n partnerships that affect academic programs, a university needs to make a point of saying that it retains full control over such programs—assuming that is the desired goal. Provisions for ownership of intellectual property that may result from partnerships should be stated from the onset. Partnerships in which partners may have direct contact with students need to be explicit about the parameters of that contact." AASCU, *Making Partnerships Work*, 21.

which prevail only in the cultural milieu of a credible academic institution. This is the essence of the American value proposition.

Outsourcing

An alternative to partnering is outsourcing; i.e., subcontracting logistical, marketing, or operational functions to another entity, such as an online program manager or commercial marketing firm.[16] This type of arrangement, however, has its drawbacks. For one, the cost of outsourcing is likely to be high. For another, the sponsoring institution, as principal, bears all the costs and risks. In addition, the subcontractor has no ownership stake in the venture. Lastly, in pursuing this alternative, the sponsor must rely on its own financial resources.

At the end of the day, an academic institution must decide which alternative best suits its needs, objectives, and interests. Any decision will invariably involve trade-offs.

Sources of financing

Aside from capital contributions, several sources of financing are available. Domestic banks might be willing to lend to the sponsor, based on its general creditworthiness. If the project is "stand-alone," they might be willing to lend directly to the entity that houses it, depending on the value of its assets, its projected earnings, and its expected cash flow. The sponsor might issue bonds in the open market, if its credit rating is high enough. Or it might borrow from a few wealthy investors, if it inspires their confidence. Private donors are also a source of capital. While domestic donors generally prefer to fund activities in the United States, foreign donors are willing to underwrite an overseas project, especially if it bears their name and operates in their backyard. Another potential source is international development banks.[17] One such source is the International Finance Corporation. In 2013, it invested $150 million in Laureate Education,

---

[16] J. Denneen and T. Dretler, *The Financially Sustainable University* (2012), 8.
[17] See, in general, R.M. Bassett, "International Organizations and the Tertiary Education Sector: Understanding UNESCO, the OECD, and the World Bank Linking-pin Organizations." In *Globalization and Internationalization in Higher Education*, edited by F. Maringe and N. Foskett (2010), 277–898; and Spring, *Globalization*, 35.

Inc., with the aim of increasing access to higher education in emerging markets.[18]

Some sources are unavailable. State legislatures are averse to allocating public funds for services that benefit primarily non-state residents. Although U.S. government agencies, such as the U.S. Agency for International Development, are willing to fund certain types of education projects, for policy reasons they are unlikely to finance the general expansion of U.S. colleges and universities.

Because providing higher education to non-U.S. nationals is a multimillion-dollar "service export," it would seem reasonable for the U.S. government to provide export finance assistance. Such assistance could take the form of low interest rate loans or loan guarantees to export-oriented U.S. colleges and universities. It could also take the form of credit facilities for the foreign consumers of their services. In addition, the U.S. government might provide additional sales and marketing support to U.S. services providers, similar to that provided by the Australian government to its service providers.[19] These and other options are worth exploring.

Unlike many other Western countries, the United States lacks a coherent higher education export strategy. To some extent, this shortcoming is attributable to the fragmentation of the U.S. higher education sector, and also to the domestic market focus of American colleges and universities. Until the onset of the Great Recession, U.S. demand for higher education was strong enough to sustain the operations of thousands of participants. Because the domestic market had been expanding for decades, American colleges and universities felt no compulsion to look elsewhere for their "bread and butter." As a result of unfavorable demographic trends, a slowdown in sectoral growth, and the disruptive effects of the Global Pandemic, many institutions have since had a change of heart. Now is the time to formulate a coherent U.S. higher education export strategy.

---

[18] International Finance Corporation, "IFC Invests $150 Million in Laureate to Expand Higher Education in Emerging Markets," January 23, 2013, https://www.ifc.org/wps/wcm/connect/news_ext_content/ifc_external_corporate_site/news+and+events/news/feature_laureate (accessed July 15, 2021).

[19] In Australia, such support is provided through a government program called AUSTRADE, the services of which are described at https://www.austrade.gov.au/australian/education/services (accessed July 15, 2021).

Beyond bricks-and-mortar

Two forces are propelling the broad move to online learning. The first is cost: specifically, the rising cost of residential, in-person delivery. As this cost continues to escalate, it is increasingly rendering the traditional mode of delivery beyond the reach of families of modest means. The second is the Global Pandemic. By disrupting in-person classroom delivery, it has forced almost every U.S. educational institution to deliver its courses online.

Despite the inconvenience of course adaptation, online delivery has had a number of positive effects. For one, it has given American colleges and universities an opportunity to extend their reach beyond the local market. For another, it has given them an opportunity to innovate and experiment in areas previously left untouched. Finally, it has given them pause to rethink the traditional way of doing things.

Online delivery promises to facilitate the exportation of U.S. higher education services to the far corners of the Earth. Right now, however, such a feat remains more a possibility than a reality. It is hindered by capacity constraints in developing countries: specifically, inadequate equipment, personnel, financial resources, and technological infrastructure.[20] As the economies of these countries expand, such constraints are likely to be lifted.

That which can be achieved through online delivery is mind-boggling.[21] Here are a few examples, most of which are familiar to experts in the field.[22]

---

[20] See, in general, S. Guri-Rosenblit, *Digital Technologies in Higher Education: Sweeping Expectations and Actual Effects* (2009).

[21] For a general discussion of the role of information and communication technology in higher education see W.G. Bowen, *Higher Education in the Digital Age* (2015). On the expansion of online and distance learning see Weisbrod, Ballou, and Asch, *Mission and Money*, 171–174.

Online programs offered by local colleges and universities in emerging markets play a major role in mass education. For example, the number of students enrolled in online programs offered by the Gandhi National Open University in India exceeds 1.8 million. The University of South Africa caters to a market of over 250,000 distance learners based in countries throughout the African continent. Altbach, Reisberg, and Rumbley, *Trends in Global Higher Education*, 123–137. See also C. McIntosh and Z. Varoglu, *Perspectives on Distance Education. Lifelong Learning & Distance Higher Education* (2005).

[22] The following passages are intended for the intelligent layman, who is not familiar with cutting-edge or highly technical developments in the field.

Enhancing academic capability

By pooling resources for online delivery, U.S. colleges and universities can enhance their overall academic capability. They can create world-class programs that draw on the best intellectual talent within each organization. They can create interdisciplinary offerings in which the academic strengths of one institution are complemented by those of another. They can create transnational forums for comparing research results, discussing best teaching practices, and sharing local experiences. They can join forces to create full-service, multidisciplinary universities that build on the specializations of the various partners. The challenges of an online joint venture are daunting,[23] but the possibilities are endless. Such collaborative efforts can amplify the educational impact of a group of institutions by combining their professional talent and leveraging off their academic strengths.

Navigating a virtual universe

In the world of cyberspace, colleges and universities can create a virtual reality. It can encompass classrooms, conference rooms, auditoriums, bookstores, libraries, bursaries, help desks, and even sports facilities.[24] Thanks to Internet technology, this reality can be accessed by way of a smart phone on the other side of the planet.

In the realm of cyberspace, virtual students (a.k.a. "avatars") with real-life identities can walk virtual hallways, congregate in virtual lounges, assemble in virtual lecture halls, and interact in virtual classrooms. They can consult real-life instructors in virtual offices; meet with team members in virtual break-out rooms; and take tests in virtual exam halls monitored remotely by real-life proctors. They can obtain medical advice, diagnosis, and professional counseling in virtual healthcare centers. They can even do yoga in virtual exercise rooms. In this creative universe, real-life instructors can appear via hologram at multiple locations at the same time. At each location, they can interact with students able to perceive their virtual

---

[23] See, for example, the challenges faced by the consortium of universities in the online course pool initiative launched by 2U in 2014. C. Straumsheim, "2U Ends Semester Online." *Inside Higher Ed* (April 3, 2014), https://www.insidehighered.com/news/2014/04/03/online-education-provider-2u-disband-semester-online-consortium (accessed August 15, 2021).

[24] See, for example, the various features of the software tools developed by Second Life, http://go.secondlife.com/landing/education/?lang=en (accessed July 15, 2021). These tools have been adopted for educational use by Texas A&M University and Florida Institute of Technology.

presence with a sense of the "here and now".[25] Virtuality can be used to not only attract students, but also retain them. By sparking their imagination, it can increase the level of their participation, engagement, interaction, and learning.[26]

Transcending space, time, and language

When course delivery is in-person and on-site, differences in space and time pose obstacles in the way of achieving scale. These differences can be overcome through the creation of online courses and programs that span different time zones and locales. Through the instrumentality of an online platform, lectures in Boston can be delivered synchronously to students in Winnipeg (−1 time zone away), Sao Paulo (+2 time zones away), Accra (+5 time zones away), Rome (+6 time zones away), Cairo (+7 time zones away), and Moscow (+8 time zones away). Teamwork can be conducted asynchronously in various parts of the world. Internet technology allows U.S. colleges and universities to overcome spatial and temporal barriers to access distant markets. It also gives them an opportunity to develop innovative programs that allow participants to exchange ideas.

Assembled in the same cyberspace, experts around the world can share with one another their unique local experiences. They can offer diverse social, cultural, and political perspectives on the same theme, issue, or phenomenon. For example, in an online seminar on disease control, epidemiologists in various parts of the world can share their insights into how a global pandemic can be contained through preventative measures at the local level. Or in an online social forum, advocates of gender equality can share their cultural perspectives on the challenges facing women in the local workplace.

Aside from space and time, language can pose a barrier to the globalization of higher education. Yet, even linguistic differences can be overcome through the use of technology. For example, incorporating sound recognition equipment in an online operating system could enable the

---

[25] I am grateful to Professor Steve Limberg of the University of Texas at Austin for this novel idea.

[26] In this virtual world, moreover, instructors can closely monitor student progress. Through learning analytics, they can track course attendance, class participation, and the attainment of "learning milestones." Through the mechanism of automated alerts, they can find out when a student skips class, fails to upload an assignment, or falls short of a particular milestone. They can interact with students synchronously during class time and asynchronously outside of class time. They can post assignments on electronic bulletin boards, explore relevant issues in topical discussion groups, administer quizzes with software controls, and inform students collectively and individually of their course progress.

instantaneous translation of speech from one language to another. Adding "drop-down" foreign-language dictionaries could facilitate the translation of written materials. To be sure, integrating various types of technologies in online courses could amplify their educational impact. It could also open up to U.S. higher education service providers previously untapped markets.

Courses without borders

The traditional classroom has borders. They are demarcated by physical walls and a finite set of students. The walls insulate the classroom from the "noises" of the real world. The finitude defines the class: typically, a set of individuals with the same level of knowledge, maturity, and experience. The permanent contours of the traditional classroom add constancy and predictability to the learning experience. By the same token, they limit it. They confine the learning experience to a fixed space and time. And they insulate it from the fluidity, openness, diversity, and practicality of the "real world."

So, why not tear down the walls and open up the classroom to the "real-world"?—not just for the sake of scale, but also to add perspective, relevance, and practicality to the learning experience. These qualities could be imparted by subject-matter experts with superior knowledge, skills, and experience. Situated in different parts of the world, they could drop into the classroom virtually—perhaps holographically—to share their experiences with online learners.

So here's the vision: why not plug an online course into the professional networks of the world? Why not bring into the classroom prominent leaders of government, business, industry, and the arts? Indeed, why not open its doors to the "noises" of the real world. For example, a consortium of colleges and universities could create an online course on International Finance for synchronous delivery to students in Europe and North America. The course could be plugged into the financial networks of New York and London, as well as governmental networks in Europe and North America. At regular intervals, Wall Street traders and Lombard Street bankers could drop in virtually to discuss current developments in global capital markets. They might be joined on occasion by central bank officials, who could brief participants on fundamental economic trends.

To take another example, environmental experts could create an online seminar on Global Warming to be delivered synchronously to students in North and South America. The seminar could be plugged into the scientific networks of the United States, Canada, Brazil, and Ecuador. Periodically, oceanographers in the Arctic, biologists in the Amazon, and ecologists in the Galapagos could drop into the classroom virtually to offer their perspectives on climate change. They could be joined on occasion by officials at the U.S. National Oceanic and Atmospheric Administration, who could discuss the policy implications of their scientific findings.

Courses without borders can transcend the bricks-and-mortar confines of the traditional classroom. They can tear down the conceptual, temporal, spatial, and geographic walls that limit and constrain the learning experience. They can open up the classroom to the fluidity, openness, diversity, and practicality of the "real world." As a concept for taking American higher education to all the world, it is limited only by the imagination.

9

Ethical Dilemmas in International Expansion

This chapter focuses on a key challenge facing U.S. colleges and universities in their effort to "go global": how to preserve their academic integrity, while generating the financial resources needed to support their activities in the realm of ideas. Incidental to this challenge are four ethical dilemmas that occasionally arise in the course of international expansion: namely, the righteousness of (1) providing international higher education services only to those who can afford them; (2) engaging in foreign practices that contravene U.S. normative standards; (3) providing services in countries whose policies conflict with American liberal values; and (4) compromising academic freedom to remain in good standing with a repressive regime. The chapter offers a few thoughts on how the dilemmas can and should be addressed. It concludes by placing academic freedom in a broader philosophical context.

> How can university governance take greater advantage of the best qualities of faculty and administration while guarding against their weaknesses? How can it combine the desire of energetic university leaders to innovate and adapt to new pressures and opportunities with the faculty's sensitivity to the importance of preserving basic academic values? Solving this problem creatively and well represents the principal challenge to the modern university in trying to benefit from the opportunities of the commercial marketplace without losing its integrity in the process.[1]
>
> Derek Bok, former President of Harvard University

> You can't have a university without having free speech, even though at times it makes us terribly uncomfortable. If students are not going to hear controversial ideas on college campuses, they're not going to hear them in America.
>
> Donna Shalala, former U.S. Secretary of Health and Human Services

[1] D. Bok, *Universities in the Marketplace: The Commercialization of Higher Education* (2003), 189–190.

Bridging the Gap between the Abundance of American Higher Education Talent and the Immense Foreign Demand for It.
Richard J. Joseph, Oxford University Press. © Richard J. Joseph (2022). DOI: 10.1093/oso/9780192848307.003.0010

The central challenge

For many U.S. colleges and universities, international expansion will heighten the tension between the practical need to generate financial resources and the ethical imperative to preserve the institution's academic integrity. This tension will never go away, even in an endeavor so noble as "taking American higher education to all the world." It is amplified by the weight of the institution's financial stake in the venture. As the unfortunate case of Babson College illustrates[2], the greater the stake, the more acute the tension. Often, college and university leaders must choose between a lucrative opportunity that promises to generate substantial returns and the moral obligation to uphold the institution's mission, purpose, and values. Sometimes, the only way out of the impasse is to forego the opportunity altogether, even if this means leaving a gaping hole in the college or university budget.

Thus, the central challenge facing these institutions is figuring out how to generate the resources necessary to support their activities in the realm of ideas without compromising their academic integrity. Meeting this challenge requires ethical fortitude, reason, flexibility, and pragmatism.

It also requires adeptness at dealing with four ethical dilemmas that occasionally arise in the course of global expansion. These dilemmas concern the justice of providing international higher education services only to those who can afford them, engaging in foreign practices that contravene U.S. normative standards, providing services in countries whose policies conflict with American liberal values, and compromising academic freedom to remain in good standing with a repressive regime.

Ethical dilemmas

1. Providing services only to those who can afford them

Targeting markets at the intersection of high GDP/NNI per capita and high gross enrollment potential implies that that U.S. colleges and universities should focus their attention primarily, if not exclusively, on

---

[2] According to one public account, confronted with allegations of gender discrimination and bullying by administrators at an overseas institution (conduct not sanctioned by the leadership of the overseas institution) that a Babson subsidiary had helped build, Babson College officials faced a major dilemma: either risk a \$52.2 million contract, or intervene on behalf of the alleged victim. See M. Vasquez, "A Professor's Year Teaching in Saudi Arabia Was a Nightmare. Should an American College Have Stepped In?" *The Chronicle of Higher Education*, November, 6, 2019, https://www.chronicle.com/article/a-professors-year-teaching-in-saudi-arabia-was-a-nightmare-should-an-american-college-have-stepped-in/ (accessed August 15, 2021).

the more affluent nations of the world that can shape market demand. This proposition makes sense from a financial perspective, but not necessarily from an ethical perspective. It raises the perplexing question, "*What about the rest of the world?*"

The "rest of the world" includes the poorer nations of Sub-Saharan Africa and South Asia, who want and need these services but lack the financial resources to pay for them. Are these nations any less worthy of access to U.S. higher education talent than the wealthier nations of the world? If the principal criterion for attracting this talent is "ability-to-pay," then the poorer nations are simply out of luck.[3]

Granted, it is unreasonable to expect U.S. colleges and universities to render services gratuitously, at a loss, or at a cost that risks their financial well-being. However altruistic, such an endeavor would be self-defeating, if not self-destructive. On the other hand, it *is* reasonable to expect these institutions to fulfill their mission to educate and enlighten. Their doing so, in principle, should not be contingent on ability-to-pay.

So, how can American colleges and universities meet their financial needs while simultaneously meeting the educational needs of those who cannot afford their services? Indeed, how can they improve their financial condition at home while fulfilling their educational mission abroad? One way is by engaging U.S. government agencies, multinational corporations, international banks, and private investors in the endeavor. After all, they have a vital stake in promoting the educational advancement of less-developed nations.[4] To the extent that such advancement contributes to economic prosperity and political stability around the world, it ultimately benefits American government and business.

So, let us put forth a simple proposal. To close the gap between the high cost (let's say "C") of delivering U.S. higher education services abroad and the meagre financial resources (let's say "R") of the poorer nations of the world, why not forge a partnership between U.S. academic institutions, on the one hand, and American government and business, on the other? Financially, the partnership would cover the difference between C and R,

[3] S. Stein, "Rethinking the Ethics of Internationalization: Five Challenges for Higher Education." *InterActions: UCLA Journal of Education and Information Studies*, vol. 12, no. 2 (2016) (unpaginated), https://escholarship.org/content/qt2nb2b9b4/qt2nb2b9b4.pdf?t=obfpwa&v=lg (accessed July 15, 2021).

[4] J. Spring, *Globalization of Education*, 2nd ed. (2015), 87–88. Many such entities already finance educational projects in less-developed countries. For example, in 2008, under the leadership of the Clinton Global Initiative Forum, the Deutsche Bank Americas Foundation, the Kellogg Foundation, and Gray Matters Capital provided financial support to New Globe Schools toward bringing low-cost education to Africa. New Globe Schools later became affiliated with Bridge International Academies, which received a "philanthropic investment" from eBay founder Pierre Omidyar.

perhaps by expending public and private resources to defray the cost of deploying U.S. higher education talent in the poorer nations of the world.

Such a collaborative effort would serve a variety of purposes, including:

- giving the poorer nations of the world greater access to American higher education talent;
- allowing U.S. colleges and universities to cover their break-even costs;
- promoting economic development and political stability throughout the world, thereby fostering a climate conducive to American business;
- spreading American goodwill, liberal values, and democratic ideals around the world, consistent with the aims of U.S. foreign policy.

These purposes are at once altruistic and self-serving. Leaders of U.S. business, government, and higher education should take heed.

2. Engaging in foreign practices that contravene U.S. normative standards

In some foreign countries, practices that are unlawful or unethical from an American viewpoint are commonplace, normal, and acceptable from the local perspective. They include bribing government officials to obtain commercial favors, using child labor to produce goods and services, plagiarizing copyrighted material, transacting with entities that support terrorism, and discriminating against individuals on the basis of race, religion, nationality, gender, age, or sexual orientation.[5] To rationalize these practices in terms of "ethical relativism" (i.e., that normative standards are cultural and contextual) misses the point. For the actors in the present case are U.S. colleges and universities that profess to high American ethical standards, which are supposed to inspire the conduct of their affairs.

---

[5] Take, for example, the case of Professor Marwa Mohsen. Recruited by a subsidiary of Babson College to teach at an overseas start-up college, she accused Babson officials of refusing to come to her aid in the face of gender discrimination and on-the-job bullying (conduct not sanctioned by the leadership of the start-up college). According to Professor Mohsen's account, which was published in *The Chronicle of Higher Education*, she had pleaded with Babson officials to intervene on her behalf with officials of the overseas institution—a $52.2 million Babson client—only to discover a reluctance on their part to do so. In her public account, Professor Mohsen alleged that Babson College had failed to live up to the standards of American higher education, thereby risking its reputation as an academic institution. M. Vasquez, "A Professor's Year Teaching in Saudi Arabia Was a Nightmare. Should an American College Have Stepped In?" *The Chronicle of Higher Education*, November, 6, 2019, https://www.chronicle.com/article/a-professors-year-teaching-in-saudi-arabia-was-a-nightmare-should-an-american-college-have-stepped-in/ (accessed July 15, 2021).

Two such standards are codified in U.S. law. The Foreign Corrupt Practices Act[6] prohibits bribing foreign government officials to obtain or retain business or steer business to a particular individual or entity. It applies to U.S. citizens and residents, as well as entities that are organized under federal or state laws or that have their principal place of business in the United States. Covered transactions include any offer, payment, gift, promise to pay, or authorization to pay money or anything else of value. Prohibited purposes include intending to (1) influence an act or decision of a foreign government official; (2) induce the official to do an act or omission in violation of his or her duty; (3) secure an improper advantage; and (4) induce the official to use his or her influence with the foreign government to affect or influence an act or decision. Oddly, such purposes exclude any attempt to secure or expedite the performance of routine government deeds, as in the case of "grease payments."

This statute is far-reaching. It can be invoked where, in connection with the award of a contract, a U.S. college or university (1) compensates a foreign government agency, above the market rate, for sales or services, (2) allows the agency to use its premises without paying adequate rent, or (3) provides tuition discounts to government officials or their families. Because of its far reach and serious ramifications, U.S. higher education service providers should bear it in mind before engaging in a transaction with any foreign government official. When in doubt, they should consult legal counsel.

The second standard is embodied in Executive Order 13,224.[7] This law prohibits transacting or otherwise dealing with a foreign person who has committed a terrorist act or who poses a significant risk of doing so. It also prohibits contributing or receiving funds, goods, or services to or from or for the benefit of any such person.

This law is not as straightforward as it seems. In practice, its application can be tricky. The objects of the prohibition are not just actual or potential terrorists, but also individuals acting on their behalf and entities that they own or control. Identifying the culprits in a casual social setting can be difficult, if not impossible. They might appear to be nice, decent, and respectable, and the entities they control might seem bona fide,

---

[6] 15 U.S. Code § 78dd–2.

[7] 82 F.R. 16474. Issued on September 23, 2001 by George W. Bush, pursuant to the authority vested in him as President of the United States by the International Emergency Economic Powers Act (50 U.S.C. 1701 et seq.), the National Emergencies Act (50 U.S.C. 1601 et seq.), Section 5 of the United Nations Participation Act of 1945, as amended (22 U.S.C. 287c), and Section 301 of Title 3, United States Code.

professional, and reputable. Yet, lurking behind the façade is an insidious motive. Coming to the realization can be unnerving. To take a nightmarish scenario, a U.S. college president might wake up one day to discover that the overseas classroom that her college is leasing is owned by the "reputable" real-estate company, controlled by that "nice, decent, and respectable" person, who just blew up a bridge.

So, before authorizing the lease, what should the president have done? How could she have discovered beforehand that the deceptively "nice, decent, and respectable" person is a potential terrorist or that the "reputable" real-estate company is controlled by such an evildoer? Indeed, how can *any* U.S. college or university official in similar circumstances find out if a party to a proposed transaction is an actual or potential terrorist?

To facilitate discovery, and thus prevent blindsiding, the U.S. Treasury Department has published a list of individuals and entities that have committed or pose a significant risk of committing a terrorist act.[8] These persons are affectionately called "Specially Designated Global Terrorists" (SDGT). Their identities can be discovered through a simple online search. The failure to conduct a search could be costly. If the person's name is on the SDGT list, the omission could result in civil and criminal penalties, not to mention irreparable harm to the reputation of the transacting institution.[9]

So, returning to our scenario, before authorizing the lease, the president should have asked a colleague to consult the SDGT database. Had the colleague done so and discovered the name of that "nice, decent, and respectable" person and/or the "reputable" real-estate company on the SDGT list, the president would have been obligated to forego the transaction.

3. Providing services in countries whose policies conflict with American liberal values

The policies and practices of some foreign governments are offensive to American sensibilities.[10] They include discriminating against religious,

---

[8] This list is available at the Office of Foreign Assets Control website, https://sanctionssearch.ofac. treas.gov (accessed July 15, 2021).

[9] Other practices violate normative standards embodied in the Civil Rights Act of 1964 (42 U.S.C. 2000d et seq.) and the Age Discrimination in Employment Act of 1976 (29 U.S.C. 621 et seq.). In one real-world case, a U.S. college had contracted to recruit faculty for a start-up university in Asia. University officials had asked the college not to recruit faculty over the age of 60. College officials refused to comply with the request, because doing so would have rendered their institution complicit in age discrimination.

[10] For example, several years ago, the Government of Qatar's political and financial support for Hamas sparked the criticism of U.S. lawmakers and academics. The criticism placed the eight

ethnic, or racial minorities, using excessive force against civilians, denying detainees due process, press censorship, quashing peaceful protests, psychological or physical torture, and other human rights abuses.[11] Thus arises the question, if the citizens of these countries want American higher education talent and are willing to pay for it, should U.S. colleges and universities satisfy their demand, notwithstanding the reprehensible policies and practices of their government?

Opinions differ. Some would say that doing so is tantamount to endorsing or condoning the reprehensible behavior. A few might go further to argue that it renders the academic institution complicit in what are essentially criminal acts. For many in this camp, the "right" course of action is to boycott the country. Doing so would send a potent message to the repressive regime, thus forcing it to rethink its unacceptable practices and policies.

Others would say that the primary duty of any college or university is to fulfill its mission. That mission is to educate and enlighten, not "engage in foreign policy." Besides, they might contend, most citizens of the foreign country probably had nothing to do with the deplorable acts of their government. Indeed, they may well be the victims. Thus, in a sense, to educate and enlighten them is to empower them—to equip them with ideological weapons to combat government repression.

There is no simple answer to the question. Every institution must decide for itself and all of its stakeholders must be comfortable with the decision. In addition, they should weigh the potential consequences of whatever they decide.

A few years ago, officials of a prominent U.S. college agreed to help a foreign start-up university develop an MBA program. The university operated in a conservative Islamic country. The agreement drew the ire of the U.S. college faculty, who claimed that the government of the country had done little to improve the status of women. To support their claim, they cited evidence to the effect that relatively few women there had earned a college degree. Thus, they insisted, the "right" course of action was to boycott the country.

Despite faculty opposition, college officials went forward with the agreement. They advised their foreign counterpart on admissions policy,

university sponsors of branch campuses in Qatar in an awkward position. *Gulf News Journal* Reports, "Roots of American Universities Grow Deeper in Qatar, Drawing Criticism." *Gulf News Journal*, June 8, 2015, https://gulfnewsjournal.com/stories/510548507-roots-of-american-universities-grow-deeper-in-qatar-drawing-criticism (accessed June 1, 2021).
[11] Another issue pertains to equal access to education. See R. Arnove and B.L. Bull, "Education as an Ethical Concern in the Global Era." *FIRE: Forum for International Research in Education*, vol. 2, no. 2 (2015): 76–87, http://preserve.lehigh.edu/fire/vol2/iss2/6 (accessed July 15, 2021).

student recruiting, financial aid, and enrollment management. They urged their foreign clients to respect the principle of gender equality, despite the contrary sentiment prevailing in some circles of the broader society. Though seemingly minor, these measures had an impact, which was more symbolic than transformational. As it later turned out, most of the graduates of the foreign MBA program (53% to be exact) were women.

4. Compromising academic freedom to remain in good standing with a repressive regime

Like the political ideals that inspired the founding of the American republic, academic freedom is a fundamental liberal value. Because it inheres in the constitution of most U.S. colleges and universities, it deserves special attention here.

In some foreign countries, U.S. colleges and universities face a dilemma: either curtail academic freedom or invite foreign interference in their local affairs.[12] If the powers-that-be oppose the aims of those who exercise academic freedom, they can withhold resources from the institution, stifle its local operations, shut down its branch campuses, and/or appropriate its assets. Typically, this has occurred where participants in a program sponsored by the college or university have criticized the policies, practices, or actions of the host government, questioned the sanctity of mainstream religious beliefs, or challenged official party ideology. College or university leaders might raise the banner of academic freedom to defend the actions of the participants. Such a defense, however, will be useless where freedom of expression is not enshrined in the constitution of the foreign state.

Expressing oneself freely can be costly not only for the academic institution, but also for its stakeholders. Consider the following example.

Several years ago, a prominent American college committed to developing a start-up college in a foreign country. By agreement, the start-up college was to be independent of the U.S. institution. However, it was to be imbued with the values, or "DNA," of the U.S. college, principal among which was academic freedom.

Faithful to the agreement, the U.S. college recruited faculty for the start-up college, versed them in best teaching practices, and hosted them at

---

[12] See G. Hawawini, *The Internationalization of Higher Education and Business Schools (2016)*, 29; and S. Wilkins, "Ethical Issues in Transnational Higher Education: The Case of International Branch Campuses." *Studies in Higher Education*, vol. 42, no. 8 (2017): 1385–1400.

its home campus. There, the visiting faculty witnessed first-hand how academic freedom could work in practice. After spending a semester at the U.S. college, the visiting faculty returned to the foreign country, where they assumed their duties. Highly idealistic, they vowed to instill in members of their own community the liberal values of the American college. Were they naïve?

During her first semester of teaching, one of the newly installed faculty members delivered a lecture on marketing. In the course of the lecture, she criticized in passing the practices and conduct of the host government. A few days later, the president of the foreign college received a call from a senior government official complaining about the instructor's remarks. Shortly thereafter, the instructor was sacked. The president cited "poor teaching evaluations" as the reason for the termination. Facts and circumstances suggest otherwise.

As it later became known, an attendee at the lecture had close ties to the foreign government. Rumor has it that he informed its officials of the instructor's derogatory remarks. Upon investigating the incident, a quality assurance team from the U.S. college demanded the resignation of the start-up college president. His irresponsible move under the guise of responsibility struck a serious blow at academic freedom, the team charged.

The incident highlights the perilous path traversed by faculty in countries that lack a liberal tradition. It also highlights a major dilemma faced by American colleges and universities that want to expand into these countries.

Safeguarding academic freedom

Let us place the issue in a broader philosophical context.[13] In higher education, intellectual progress is predicated on academic freedom—for only in a free environment are individuals at liberty to exchange ideas, challenge conventional wisdom, create knowledge, and innovate. In democratic societies, such as the United States, colleges and universities that safeguard academic freedom are at the forefront of intellectual progress. They have fostered an environment in which disagreements are tolerated, debate is encouraged, and contradiction is transcended through a dynamic synthesis of opposing ideas.

---

[13] The passages that follow are based on R.J. Joseph, "Globalisation Can Threaten Liberal Traditions." *Financial Times*, March 27, 2014, © 2014 The Financial Times Ltd. All rights reserved.

As these institutions "go global," as they expand into authoritarian countries, the very precondition for intellectual progress is placed at risk. Prevailing in these countries is an overriding belief that disagreements should not be tolerated and debate should not be encouraged, for there is no apparent "contradiction," only economic opportunity within the existing status quo. What matters most is value creation in a static and unassailable political order. What matters least is knowledge creation in a free and flourishing academic community.

In the most despotic of political orders, government officials expect U.S. colleges and universities to dissuade students, faculty, and staff from "questioning the unquestionable." The "unquestionable" includes repressive government policies, mainstream religious beliefs, official party ideology, and even unethical business practices. Or they signal their willingness to grant the institutions a license to broach any topic of "educational value"—with the implicit understanding that "questioning the unquestionable" is of no educational value. Either way, if U.S. colleges and universities succumb to these pressures, academic freedom will become a hollow principle, and a core value of American higher education, the *sine qua non* for intellectual progress, will lose its vibrancy.

So, as U.S. colleges and universities "go global," as they expand into countries that lack a liberal tradition, how can academic freedom be safeguarded? No doubt, the leaders of American higher education can, and should, do their best to cultivate a culture of tolerance. In addition, they should stand firm in their defense of colleagues who express themselves freely in pursuit of the truth. By the same token, these officials should not be left to fend for themselves. Given the intensity of competition in foreign markets, the enormous pressure placed on college and university leaders to "make ends meet," and the precarious position of their institutions vis à vis their foreign host governments, international accreditation bodies should step in to strengthen their hand.[14] What can the accreditors do?

For one, they can insist on ironclad guarantees of academic freedom in foreign service contracts. For another, they can issue accreditation guidelines aimed at protecting academic freedom in overseas engagements. They should never assume that academic freedom exists because an American

---

[14] A concerted effort by U.S. colleges and universities to formulate a coherent "foreign policy" on academic freedom will be ineffective, unless the measure is endorsed by other Western colleges and universities. Rather than "cave in" to American institutional pressure, some repressive regimes would likely give preferential treatment to other Western colleges and universities that do not endorse the American position. For a discussion of the latter approach to academic freedom see K. Fischer, "Do Colleges Need a Foreign Policy?" *The Chronicle of Higher Education*, June 22, 2021.

college or university is a party to the contract. Indeed, they should always proceed with a healthy degree of skepticism. At a very minimum, they should require academic freedom at every degree-granting unit or branch of a global institution. They should make the accreditation status of every unit and branch separable from that of the principal college or university, and should condition this status, as well as the awarding of degrees in the name of the principal college or university, on academic freedom. The foreign unit or branch could still award degrees, but not in the name of the main institution.[15] The degrees would be unaccredited, and therefore of diminished market value. Such a state of affairs would more accurately reflect the value added by academic values to the market value of a U.S. college/university degree. It would also more accurately reflect the value of an educational experience devoid of full freedom of expression.

Measures such as these would have a far-reaching effect. They would bolster the position of American college and university officials in the face of repressive regimes. They would give these officials political leverage: "If we cannot operate in a free environment," U.S. educators can tell their foreign hosts, "then we cannot serve your people as an accredited branch. Nor can the branch award them degrees in the name of our American college/university." Such a posture would give the foreign hosts pause to rethink their repressive practices, without unduly penalizing either the main institution or recipients of degrees awarded by its units or branches.

Such measures would also safeguard the type of culture and climate that is conducive to intellectual progress. This result, in turn, would strengthen the American value proposition, which is predicated on the vitality of academic values, as is signified by accreditation. Because these values add value to the services that U.S. colleges and universities provide in the international marketplace, they play a critical role in generating financial benefits for American colleges and universities and educational benefits for other members of the world community. Indeed, to the extent that they enhance the real and perceived value of these services, they are an essential link in bridging the gap between the abundance of American higher education talent and the immense foreign demand for it.

---

[15] On the other hand, other units or branches, where academic freedom flourishes, could award degrees in the name of the principal college or university.

Parting Thoughts: Relevance for Other Western Institutions

These closing remarks summarize key points made in the book. They also place them in a broader perspective. In this section, we explore the possibility of extending our conclusion to other Western colleges and universities. What assumptions are necessary to do so soundly?

> Our world is at an inflection point. Global dynamics have shifted . . . I believe we are in the midst of an historic and fundamental debate about the future direction of our world. There are those who argue that, given all the challenges we face, autocracy is the best way forward. And there are those who understand that democracy is essential to meeting all the challenges of our changing world.[1]
> Joseph R. Biden, Jr., Forty-sixth President of the United States

> Democracy cannot succeed unless those who express their choice are prepared to choose wisely. The real safeguard of democracy, therefore, is education.[2]
> Franklin Delano Roosevelt, Thirty-second President of the United States

A narrow conclusion

As has been pointed out, to bridge the gap between the abundance of American higher educational talent and the immense foreign demand for it, fundamental reforms in the institutional culture, organizational structure, and governance system of traditional U.S. colleges and universities are necessary. Without these reforms, the financial viability of these institutions will be at risk, as will be the economic foundation of the U.S. higher education sector as a whole. This foundation supports the critical role that America plays, or should play, globally in knowledge creation, the dissemination of ideas, the pursuit of the truth, and the propagation of liberal, democratic ideals. In the context of a shifting international balance of power and a war in Europe, this role should never be taken for granted.

Our conclusion is specific to American institutions of higher learning. But what about other Western colleges and universities, particularly those

---

[1] President Joseph R. Biden, Jr., *Interim National Security Strategic Guidance*, March 2021, 3.
[2] President Franklin Delano Roosevelt, message for American Education Week, September 27, 1938.

Bridging the Gap between the Abundance of American Higher Education Talent and the Immense Foreign Demand for It.
Richard J. Joseph, Oxford University Press. © Richard J. Joseph (2022). DOI: 10.1093/oso/9780192848307.003.0011

in Europe, Canada, and Australia? Does the conclusion apply to them as well? Can it be extended to them by analogy? These questions require further reflection, deliberation, and research. Nonetheless, here are a few preliminary thoughts.

Extending the conclusion by analogy

In general, other Western colleges and universities face challenges similar to those faced by U.S. institutions.[3] They operate in mature, slow-growth markets. They encounter adverse demographic trends, the residual effects of the Global Pandemic, the scaling back of government funding, and rising anti-immigration sentiment. They are seeing flat enrollments, declining revenues, escalating costs, and narrowing margins. They are coping with a slower rate of expansion. If these institutions cannot rely on the revenue sources of the past, then they must seek out new sources for the future. Many of these sources lie beyond the horizon. They can be found in the emerging markets of East and Southeast Asia, Latin America and the Caribbean, Central and Western Asia, and the Arab World. To date, only a handful of European, Canadian, and Australian colleges and universities have succeeded in tapping these sources. In light of the preferred destinations of internationally mobile tertiary education students (as discussed in Chapter 6), global demand for their services appears to be robust.

But what about their institutional culture, organizational structure, and system of governance? Are they essentially similar to their U.S. counterpart? If so, then we can extend our conclusion to them by analogy.

It would be naïve to believe that there is a "traditional model" common to all of Europe, Canada, and Australia. Indeed, there is reason to believe that there are several such models. They evolved from a variety of institutional configurations—the medieval universities of Bologna, Paris, and Oxford; the Humboldtian institutions of Germany; and les Grandes Écoles de France. What they all have in common is a scholarly emphasis on critical thinking, scientific investigation, and free inquiry—though not necessarily organizational features.

---

[3] See, for example, E. Bennetot Pruvot, T. Estermann, and H. Stoyanova, *Public Funding Observatory Report 2020/2021*, Part 1 (October 2020) and Part 2 (April 2021); E. Bennetot Pruvot, T. Estermann, and V. Kupriyanova, *Public Funding Observatory Report 2019/2020* (February 2020); and A. Labi, "European Universities Consider How to Adapt to the New Economic Climate." *The Chronicle of Higher Education*, June 12, 2012.

So, with this complication in mind, let us put forth a "conditional" conclusion: if traditional academic institutions in Europe, Canada, Australia, and other Western countries are less inward-looking, rigid, bureaucratic, hierarchical, loathe to commercialization, procedurally slow, and averse to change than their U.S. counterparts, then our conclusion does not apply to them, and any attempt to generalize from the American experience would be unsound. On the other hand, if they resemble traditional U.S. academic institutions in these essential respects, then in light of the similar challenges they face, our conclusion can be extended to them by analogy. In the latter case, the broader implication is this: to bridge the gap between the abundance of *Western* higher educational talent and the robust foreign demand for it, fundamental reforms in the culture, organization, and governance of traditional Western colleges and universities may be needed. Without these reforms, the financial viability of these institutions will be at risk, as will be the economic foundation of *Western* higher education in general.

Points of discovery

Bridging the Gap between the Abundance of American Higher Education Talent and the Immense Foreign Demand for It has taken us to the far corners of the Earth. Our journey has been enlightening. Here are the principal points of discovery.

- Non-U.S. nationals want American higher education because of its perceived quality, which results from an institutional culture of academic freedom, knowledge creation, and the pursuit of truth. These normative values enhance the market value of American higher education. This is the essence of the "American value proposition."
- U.S. higher education services go well beyond course offerings, degree programs, faculty exchanges, and study abroad. They also encompass activities such as program design and development, higher education advisory services, project development and management, and technology transfer. These services are a "natural" for U.S. colleges and universities, because in providing them, they can leverage off their institutional strengths. At the same time, they can contribute to the economic, social, and political well-being of less-developed nations.
- The "abundance" of American higher education talent stems in part from a slackening of U.S. economic growth, following the expansion

of the higher education sector in the twentieth century. Contributing to the slowdown are several factors, including adverse demographic trends, flat enrollments, and the scaling back of government funding. A shrinking domestic market has given rise to intensified competition, as is indicated by rising discount rates and narrowing profit margins.

- Long-term demographic trends do not bode well for the future of the sector. They portend declining domestic enrollments, even sharper competition, a drop in net tuition revenues, and possibly also economic stagnation.
- Risks to the financial well-being of American institutions of higher learning include a steep decline in the level of disposable income, a reduction in the volume of student financial aid, cutbacks in public and private funding, and lower investment returns. These risks heighten in periods of contraction, when escalating operating costs rise above faltering operating revenues. Such occurred in the Great Recession of 2008 and the Global Pandemic of 2020.
- As the world economy grows, so will foreign demand for U.S. higher education services. This demand is shaped by the pressing need in developing countries to create a cadre of competent managers, teachers, and government officials versed in best professional practices; to prepare women, indigenous groups, and the disadvantaged for the workplace; and to build institutions that contribute to the economic, social, and political well-being of the nation as a whole.
- Demand for higher education may be *potential* or *actual*. Potential demand is linked to "gross enrollment potential" or the capacity for incremental enrollments. Actual demand is linked to gross enrollment potential, backed by adequate financial resources. It follows, logically, that greatest demand for higher education services lies in those regions of the world with high gross enrollment potential and high GDP/NNI per capita. Foremost among these regions are East and Southeast Asia, Latin America and the Caribbean, Central and Western Asia, and the Arab World.
- Conditions are ripe for a more export-oriented U.S. higher education sector. Foreign access to higher education in the United States has been restricted by tighter U.S. visa restrictions. Anti-immigration sentiment has deterred many foreign nationals from pursuing their studies in the United States. These basic conditions are unlikely to change dramatically in the near future. Hence, if all the world cannot

come to America for higher education, then why not take American higher education to all the world?

- In the case of traditional U.S. colleges and universities, several obstacles stand in the way of doing so. They include an institutional culture that is averse to commercialization, an organizational structure that is operationally slow, and a system of governance that often leads to indecision, conflict, and paralysis. It follows, logically, that to take American higher education to all the world, these obstacles must be removed. Doing so requires fundamental changes in the culture, organization, and governance of traditional U.S. colleges and universities.

- New business models embody these changes. One such model is the *international market-oriented model.* Functionally, its purposes are to streamline operations, expedite decision-making, generate efficiencies, integrate essential functions, cater to the needs and preferences of international clients, and facilitate global expansion.

- The international market-oriented model differs from the traditional model in six major respects: first, it relies on the deployment of cross-functional teams to design, develop, and deliver higher education services; second, it better integrates functions essential for the provision of these services; third, it aligns ultimate functional authority with primary functional expertise; fourth, it empowers non-academics whose skills are essential for global expansion; fifth, it complements an academic culture with a business culture that is conducive to business-related activities; finally, it is more client-focused, demand-driven, and market-oriented.

- To successfully "go global," U.S. colleges and universities must have sufficient organizational, financial, and technological capability, as well as management bandwidth. To enhance this capability, they can pursue one of several alternatives. First, they can forge an alliance with another academic institution. Second, they can elicit the support of a foreign government agency or educational foundation. And third, they can partner with a multinational corporation. In addition, they can outsource operational functions. The advantages and disadvantages of each alternative touch on the degree of management control; profit-, cost-, and risk-sharing; cultural compatibility; organizational synergies; and co-branding. Before pursuing a particular alternative, the sponsoring institution should weigh the advantages and disadvantages of each, in light of its own peculiar circumstances.

- To proceed on firm footing, the institution should be confident that several preconditions have been met. First, there should be stakeholder "buy in." Second, a comprehensive business plan should be in place. Third, intellectual property issues should be sorted out. Fourth, the institution should have adequate organizational, financial, and technological capability. And fifth, it should consider establishing a "presence on the ground" in every foreign market that it enters.

- The institution should be prepared to deal with ethical dilemmas that occasionally arise in the course of international expansion. They concern the righteousness of providing international higher education services only to those who can afford them, engaging in foreign practices that contravene U.S. normative standards, providing services in countries whose policies conflict with American liberal values, and compromising academic freedom to remain in good standing with a repressive regime. These dilemmas are associated with the central challenge facing all institutions of higher learning: figuring out how to preserve their academic integrity, while generating sufficient resources to support their activities in the "realm of ideas."

Summary

We are at a crossroads in the history of American higher education. Its economic substructure is at risk. Its ideological superstructure could be as well. Bridging the gap between the abundance of American higher education talent and the immense foreign demand for it could fortify this substructure. It could also improve the economic, social, and political well-being of less-developed nations.

This story is not just about seizing an historic opportunity to "clinch a deal" between the U.S. providers of higher education services and non-U.S. nationals who want and value these services. Nor is it just about achieving the utilitarian goal of meeting both the financial needs of American colleges and universities and the educational needs of other members of the world community. Rather, it is also about strengthening the critical role that America plays, or should play, globally in the realm of ideas. It is also about preserving the vitality of liberal, democratic ideals in the context of a changing domestic landscape and a shifting world order.

Notes to figures

Introduction

Figure 0.1. Annual growth rates in aggregate revenues net of aggregate expenditures per U.S. post-secondary degree-granting institution, 1990–2018.

Based on fiscal year data presented in U.S. Department of Education, Institute of Education Sciences, National Center for Education Statistics (NCES), Table 333.10 "Revenues of public degree-granting postsecondary institutions, by source of revenue and level of institution;" Table 333.40 "Total revenue of private non-profit degree-granting postsecondary institutions, by source of funds and level of institution;" Table 334.10 "Total expenditures of public degree-granting postsecondary institutions, by purpose and level of institution;" Table 334.30 "Total expenditures of private non-profit degree-granting postsecondary institutions, by purpose and level of institution;" and Table 317.10 "Degree-granting postsecondary institutions, by control and level of institution," *Digest of Education Statistics* (annual issues, 1990–2020), https://nces.ed.gov/programs/digest/ (accessed August 1, 2021). Because of differences in accounting standards, as well as periodic changes in these standards, total amounts are approximate and represent an "order of magnitude."

For public institutions:

Accounting standards:

- Accounting standards are set by the Government Accounting Standards Board (GASB).
- GASB Statement No. 34 (issued in June 1999 to be effective for all public entities after June 2003) changed the manner in which capital assets are reported, as well as the content and format of financial statements. See GASB Statement No. 34 "Basic Financial Statements—And Management's Discussion and Analysis—For State and Local Governments," June 1999. This change impacts the comparability of pre- and post-2003 data for accounts relating to these items.

Revenues:

- Data are for current-fund revenues. The total amount excludes non-operating revenues.
- Figures for the fiscal years beginning in 2001 and 2002 are estimates.

Expenditures:

- For fiscal years beginning in 2003 through 2008, figures for Other Expenses have been extrapolated from the total.
- Figures for fiscal years beginning in 2001 and 2002 are estimates.

For private institutions:

Accounting standards:

- Accounting standards are set by the Financial Accounting Standards Board (FASB).

- FASB Statement No. 124 (issued in November 1995 to be effective after December 1995) changed the manner in which investments and unrealized gains and losses are reported. See FASB Statement No. 124 "Accounting for Certain Investments Held by Not-for-Profit Organizations," November 1995. This change impacts the comparability of pre- and post-1996 data for accounts relating to these items.

Revenues:

- Data for fiscal years beginning in 1990 through 1996 are for current fund revenues.
- Figures for fiscal years beginning in 2001 and 2002 are estimates.

Expenditures:

- For fiscal years beginning in 1990 through 1996, figures for Net Grant Aid to Students and Independent Operations are estimates; figures for Other Expenses were extrapolated from the total.
- Data for Operation and Maintenance of Plant are included in Institutional Support.

For a description of accounts used in the NCES Integrated Post-Secondary Education (IPEDS) see https://surveys.nces.ed.gov/ipeds/downloads/forms/ipedsglossary.pdf (accessed August 1, 2021).

See notes to the relevant tables in the *Digest of Education Statistics*

Figure 0.2. Major emerging markets for U.S. higher education, based on the nominal value of contracts with American colleges and universities, 2014–2019.

Based on annual data presented in U.S. Department of Education, Office of Federal Student Aid, Data.Gov, *Foreign Gifts and Contracts Report, 2020*. The underlying data are based on the nominal value of contracts between U.S. colleges and universities and parties in Latin America and the Caribbean; East, Southeast, Central, South, and Western Asia; the Middle East; and Sub-Saharan Africa. To avoid double-counting, contracts in the same nominal amount concluded by the same parties on the same date were excluded from the calculation. See notes to *Foreign Gifts and Contracts Report, 2020*, https://studentaid.gov/data-center/school/foreign-gifts (accessed August 1, 2021).

Chapter 2

Figure 2.1. Technology transfer: gross license income received by U.S. universities, 1991–2020.

Based on annual data presented in Association of University Technology Managers, Technology Transfer Database, https://autm.net/surveys-and-tools/databases/statt/ (accessed October 1, 2021). Figures are in millions of current U.S. dollars.

"License income received" includes license issue fees, payments under options, annual minimums, running royalties, termination payments, the amount of equity received when cashed-in, and software and biological material end-user license fees equal to $1,000 or more, but not research funding, patent expense reimbursement, a valuation of equity not cashed in, software and biological material end-user license fees less than $1,000, or trademark licensing royalties from university insignia. In addition, license income does not include income received in support of the cost to make and transfer materials under material transfer agreements.

Chapter 3

Figure 3.1. U.S. post-secondary degree-granting institutions, 1990–2019.

Based on annual data presented in U.S. Department of Education, Institute of Education Sciences, NCES, Table 317.10 "Degree-granting postsecondary institutions, by control and level of institution," *Digest of Education Statistics* (annual issues, 1990–2020), https://nces.ed.gov/programs/digest/ (accessed August 1, 2021). Data through 1995–1996 are for institutions of higher education, while data for later years are for degree-granting institutions.

See notes to the relevant tables in the *Digest of Education Statistics*.

Figure 3.2. U.S. post-secondary degree-granting institutions, numbers by control and enrollments, fall 2019.

Based on annual data presented in U.S. Department of Education, Institute of Education Sciences, NCES, Table 317.40 "Number of degree-granting postsecondary institutions and enrollment in these institutions, by enrollment size, control, and classification of institution," *Digest of Education Statistics* (annual issues, 1990–2020), https://nces.ed.gov/programs/digest/ (accessed October 1, 2021).

See notes to the relevant tables in the *Digest of Education Statistics*.

Figure 3.3. U.S. post-secondary degree-granting institutions, enrollments by control and size, fall 2019.

Based on annual data presented in U.S. Department of Education, Institute of Education Sciences, NCES, Table 317.40 "Number of degree-granting postsecondary institutions and enrollment in these institutions, by enrollment size, control, and classification of institution," *Digest of Education Statistics* (annual issues, 1990–2020), https://nces.ed.gov/programs/digest/ (accessed October 1, 2021).

See notes to the relevant tables in the *Digest of Education Statistics*.

Figure 3.4. U.S. post-secondary degree-granting institutions, numbers by classification and size, fall 2019.

Based on annual data presented in U.S. Department of Education, Institute of Education Sciences, NCES, Table 317.40 "Number of degree-granting postsecondary institutions and enrollment in these institutions, by enrollment size, control, and classification of institution," *Digest of Education Statistics* (annual issues, 1990–2020), https://nces.ed.gov/programs/digest/ (accessed October 1, 2021).

See notes to the relevant tables in the *Digest of Education Statistics*.

Figure 3.5. Sources of revenue in thousands of current dollars, U.S. public post-secondary degree-granting institutions, 1990–2018.

Based on fiscal year data presented in U.S. Department of Education, Institute of Education Sciences, NCES, Table 333.10 "Total revenue of public degree-granting postsecondary institutions, by source of revenue and level of institution," *Digest of Education Statistics* (annual issues, 1990–2020), https://nces.ed.gov/programs/digest/ (accessed August 1, 2021).

The total amount includes operating and non-operating revenues, but excludes capital appropriations, grants, and gifts and additions to permanent endowment. Post-2002 data are based on GASB Statement No. 34. Figures for fiscal years beginning in 2001 and 2002 are estimates. For fiscal years beginning in 1990 through 2000, figures for "Other Operating Revenues" have been extrapolated.

For a description of accounts used in the NCES IPEDS see https://surveys.nces.ed.gov/ipeds/downloads/forms/ipedsglossary.pdf (accessed August 1, 2021).

See notes to the relevant tables in the *Digest of Education Statistics.*

Figure 3.6. Sources of revenue in thousands of current dollars, U.S. private post-secondary degree-granting institutions, 1990–2018.

Based on fiscal year data presented in U.S. Department of Education, Institute of Education Sciences, NCES, Table 333.40 "Total revenue of private non-profit degree-granting postsecondary institutions, by source of funds and level of institution," *Digest of Education Statistics* (annual issues, 1998–2020), https://nces.ed.gov/programs/digest/ (accessed August 1, 2021).

Data for the fiscal years beginning in 1990 through 1996 are for current fund revenues. Figures for fiscal years beginning in 2001 and 2002 are estimates.

Accounting standards are set by the FASB. FASB Statement No. 124 (issued in November 1995 to be effective after December 1995) changed the manner in which investments and unrealized gains and losses are reported. See FASB Statement No. 124 "Accounting for Certain Investments Held by Not-for-Profit Organizations," November 1995. This change impacts the comparability of pre- and post-1996 data in accounts relating to these items.

For a description of accounts used in the NCES IPEDS see https://surveys.nces.ed.gov/ipeds/downloads/forms/ipedsglossary.pdf, (accessed August 1, 2021).

See notes to the relevant tables in the *Digest of Education Statistics.*

Figure 3.7. Classes of expenditure in thousands of current dollars, U.S. public post-secondary degree-granting institutions, 1990–2018.

Based on fiscal year data presented in U.S. Department of Education, Institute of Education Sciences, NCES, Table 334.10 "Total expenditures of public degree-granting postsecondary institutions, by purpose and level of institution," *Digest of Education Statistics* (annual issues, 1998–2020), https://nces.ed.gov/programs/digest/ (accessed August 1, 2021).

Figures for fiscal years beginning in 2001 and 2002 are estimates. For fiscal years beginning in 2003 through 2008, figures for "Other Expenses" have been extrapolated.

GASB Statement No. 34 (issued in June 1999 to be effective for all public entities after June 2003) changed the manner in which capital assets are reported, as well as the content and format of financial statements. See GASB Statement No. 34 "Basic Financial Statements—And Management's Discussion and Analysis—For State and Local Governments," June 1999. This change impacts the comparability of pre- and post-2003 data in accounts relating to these items.

For a description of accounts used in the NCES IPEDS see https://surveys.nces.ed.gov/ipeds/downloads/forms/ipedsglossary.pdf (accessed August 1, 2021).

See notes to the relevant tables in the *Digest of Education Statistics.*

Figure 3.8. Classes of expenditure in thousands of current dollars, U.S. private post-secondary degree-granting institutions, 1990–2018.

Based on fiscal year data presented in U.S. Department of Education, Institute of Education Sciences, NCES, Table 334.30 "Total expenditures of private non-profit degree-granting postsecondary institutions, by purpose and level of institution," *Digest of Education Statistics* (annual issues, 2002–2020), https://nces.ed.gov/programs/digest/ (accessed August 1, 2021).

For fiscal years beginning in 1990 through 1996, figures for Net Grant Aid to Students and Independent Operations are estimates; figures for "Other Expenses" have been extrapolated. Data for Operation and Maintenance of Plant are included in Institutional Support.

For a description of accounts used in the NCES IPEDS see https://surveys.nces.ed.gov/ ipeds/downloads/forms/ipedsglossary.pdf (accessed August 1, 2021).

See notes to the relevant tables in the *Digest of Education Statistics*.

Figure 3.9. Aggregate revenues and aggregate expenditures in thousands of current dollars, U.S. public post-secondary degree-granting institutions, 1990–2018.

Based on fiscal year data presented in U.S. Department of Education, Institute of Education Sciences, NCES, Table 333.10 "Revenues of public degree-granting postsecondary institutions, by source of revenue and level of institution;" and Table 334.10 "Total expenditures of public degree-granting postsecondary institutions, by purpose and level of institution," *Digest of Education Statistics* (annual issues, 1998–2020), https://nces.ed.gov/programs/digest/ (accessed August 1, 2021). See notes to Figures 3.5 and 3.7 in this appendix.

Figure 3.10. Aggregate revenues and aggregate expenditures in thousands of current dollars, U.S. private non-profit post-secondary degree-granting institutions, 1990– 2018.

Based on fiscal year data presented in U.S. Department of Education, Institute of Education Sciences, NCES, Table 333.40 "Total revenue of private non-profit degree-granting postsecondary institutions, by source of funds and level of institution;" and Table 334.30 "Total expenditures of private non-profit degree-granting postsecondary institutions, by purpose and level of institution," *Digest of Education Statistics* (annual issues, 1998–2020), https:// nces.ed.gov/programs/digest/ (accessed August 1, 2021). See notes to Figures 3.6 and 3.8 in this appendix.

Figure 3.11. Aggregate revenues net of aggregate expenditures in thousands of current dollars, U.S. post-secondary degree-granting institutions, 1990–2018.

Based on fiscal year data presented in U.S. Department of Education, Institute of Education Sciences, NCES, Table 333.10 "Revenues of public degree-granting postsecondary institutions, by source of revenue and level of institution;" Table 333.40 "Total revenue of private non-profit degree-granting postsecondary institutions, by source of funds and level of institution;" Table 334.10 "Total expenditures of public degree-granting postsecondary institutions, by purpose and level of institution;" and Table 334.30 "Total expenditures of private non-profit degree-granting postsecondary institutions, by purpose and level of institution," *Digest of Education Statistics* (annual issues, 1998–2020), https://nces.ed.gov/ programs/digest/ (accessed August 1, 2021).

Because of differences in GASB and FASB accounting standards, which relate primarily to definitions and timing (see notes to Figure 0.1 in this appendix), the magnitude of values in the chart should be viewed as a "reasonable approximation."

See notes to the relevant tables in the *Digest of Education Statistics*.

Figure 3.12. Aggregate revenues net of aggregate expenditures in thousands of current dollars per institution, U.S. post-secondary degree-granting institutions, 1990-2018.

Based on fiscal year data presented in U.S. Department of Education, Institute of Education Sciences, NCES, Table 333.10 "Revenues of public degree-granting postsecondary institutions, by source of revenue and level of institution;" Table 333.40 "Total revenue of private non-profit degree-granting postsecondary institutions, by source of funds and level of institution;" Table 334.10 "Total expenditures of public degree-granting postsecondary institutions, by purpose and level of institution;" Table 334.30 "Total expenditures of private non-profit degree-granting postsecondary institutions, by purpose and level of institution;" and Table 317.10 "Degree-granting postsecondary institutions, by control and level of institution," *Digest of Education Statistics* (annual issues, 1990–2020), https://nces. ed.gov/programs/digest/ (accessed August 1, 2021).

Because of differences in GASB and FASB accounting standards, which relate primarily to definitions and timing (see notes to Figure 0.1 in this appendix), the magnitude of values in the chart should be viewed as a "reasonable approximation."

See notes to the relevant tables in the *Digest of Education Statistics*.

Figure 3.13. Closures of U.S. post-secondary degree granting institutions, 1990–2019.

Based on fiscal year data presented in U.S. Department of Education, Institute of Education Sciences, NCES, Table 317.50 "Degree-granting postsecondary institutions that have closed their doors, by control and level of institution," *Digest of Education Statistics* (annual issues, 2018–2020), https://nces.ed.gov/programs/digest/ (accessed August 1, 2021).

See notes to relevant tables in *Digest of Education Statistics*.

Figure 3.14. Total fall enrollments, U.S. Post-secondary degree-granting institutions, 2019.

Based on annual data presented in U.S. Department of Education, Institute of Education Sciences, NCES, Table 303.10 "Total fall enrollment in degree-granting postsecondary institutions, by attendance status, sex of student, and control of institution," *Digest of Education Statistics* (annual issues, 2010–2020), https://nces.ed.gov/programs/digest/ (accessed August 1, 2021).

See notes to relevant tables in *Digest of Education Statistics*.

Figure 3.15. Average fall enrollments per institution, U.S. post-secondary degree-granting institutions, 1990–2019.

Based on annual data presented in U.S. Department of Education, Institute of Education Sciences, NCES, Table 303.10 "Total fall enrollment in degree-granting postsecondary institutions, by attendance status, sex of student, and control of institution;" and Table 317.10 "Degree-granting postsecondary institutions, by control and level of institution," *Digest of Education Statistics* (annual issues, 2018–2020), https://nces.ed.gov/programs/ digest/ (accessed October 1, 2021).

See notes to relevant table in *Digest of Education Statistics*.

Figure 3.16. Cost of a U.S. college education relative to U.S. disposable income per capita, 1970–2019.

Based on academic year data presented in U.S. Department of Education, Institute of Education Sciences, NCES, Table 330.10 "Average undergraduate tuition and fees and room and board rates charged for full-time students in degree-granting postsecondary institutions, by level and control of institution: selected years," *Digest of Education Statistics* (annual issues, 1980–2020), https://nces.ed.gov/programs/digest/ (accessed August 1, 2021); and annual data presented in Federal Reserve Bank of St. Louis, Economic Research Division, Federal Reserve Economic Data, A229RC0, https://fred.stlouisfed.org/series/a229rc0 (accessed August 1, 2021).

See notes to relevant tables in *Digest of Education Statistics* and Federal Reserve Economic Data.

Figure 3.17. Cost of a U.S. college education as a percentage of U.S. disposable income per capita, 1970–2019.

Based on academic year data presented in U.S. Department of Education, Institute of Education Sciences, NCES, Table 330.10 "Average undergraduate tuition and fees and room and board rates charged for full-time students in degree-granting postsecondary institutions, by level and control of institution: selected years," *Digest of Education Statistics* (annual issues, 1980–2020), https://nces.ed.gov/programs/digest/ (accessed August 1, 2021); and annual data presented in Federal Reserve Bank of St. Louis, Economic Research Division, Federal Reserve Economic Data, A229RC0, https://fred.stlouisfed.org/series/a229rc0 (accessed August 1, 2021).

See notes to relevant tables in *Digest of Education Statistics* and Federal Reserve Economic Data.

Figure 3.18. Private gifts in thousands of current dollars to U.S. post-secondary degree-granting institutions, 1990–2018.

Based on fiscal year data presented in U.S. Department of Education, Institute of Education Sciences, NCES, Table 333.10 "Revenues of public degree-granting postsecondary institutions, by source of revenue and level of institution;" and Table 333.40. "Total revenue of private non-profit degree-granting postsecondary institutions, by source of funds and classification of institution," *Digest of Education Statistics* (annual issues, 1998–2020), https://nces.ed.gov/programs/digest/ (accessed August 1, 2021).

For private institutions, figures for the fiscal years beginning in 1990 through 1995 are estimates. For public institutions, figures for the fiscal years beginning in 2001 and 2002 are estimates.

See notes to the relevant tables in the *Digest of Education Statistics*.

Figure 3.19. Student aid and nonfederal loans in millions of current dollars, 1970–2019.

Based on academic year data presented in Table 2 "Student Aid and Nonfederal Loans in Current Dollars," The College Board, Trends in Student Aid 2020, https://research.collegeboard.org/trends/student-aid (accessed July 15, 2021). The figures for Academic Year 2019 are estimates.

See notes to the relevant table in Trends in Student Aid 2020.

Figure 3.20. Investment income in thousands of current dollars, U.S. post-secondary degree-granting institutions relative to annual movements in the Dow Jones Industrial Average, 1990–2018.

Income figures are based on fiscal year data presented in U.S. Department of Education, Institute of Education Sciences, NCES, Table 333.10 "Revenues of public degree-granting postsecondary institutions, by source of revenue and level of institution;" and Table 333.40 "Total revenue of private non-profit degree-granting postsecondary institutions, by source of funds and classification of institution," *Digest of Education Statistics* (annual issues, 1998–2020), https://nces.ed.gov/programs/digest/ (accessed July 15, 2021). Dow Jones figures are based on annual data provided by Macrotrends, www.macrotrends.net (accessed August 1, 2021).

Data for public institutions represent "investment returns," defined as "income from assets including dividends, interest earnings, royalties, rent, gains (losses) etc." Data for private institutions represent "investment income," defined as "revenues derived from the institution's investments, including investments of endowment funds. Such income may take the form of interest income, dividend income, rental income or royalty income and includes both realized and unrealized gains and losses." U.S. Department of Education, Institute for Education Services, NCES, IPEDS 2020–2021 Data Collection System, Glossary, https://surveys.nces.ed.gov/ipeds/public/glossary (accessed July 15, 2021).

For public institutions, figures for 2001–2002 are estimates. For private institutions, figures for post-1995 years are based on FASB Statement No. 124, which requires that investments in equity securities with readily determinable fair values and all investments in debt securities be reported at fair value. FASB Statement No. 124 "Accounting for Certain Investments Held by Not-for-Profit Organizations," issued November 1995.

See notes to the relevant tables in the *Digest of Education Statistics*.

Figure 3.21. Government funding in thousands of current dollars, U.S. post-secondary degree-granting institutions, 1990–2018.

Based on fiscal year data presented in U.S. Department of Education, Institute of Education Sciences, NCES, Table 333.10 "Revenues of public degree-granting postsecondary institutions, by source of revenue and level of institution;" and Table 333.40. "Total revenue of private non-profit degree-granting postsecondary institutions, by source of funds and classification of institution," *Digest of Education Statistics* (annual issues, 1998–2020), https://nces.ed.gov/programs/digest/ (accessed August 1, 2021).

The term "funding" includes operating contracts grants, government appropriations, and non-operating grants. Because of differences in GASB and FASB accounting standards, which relate primarily to definitions and timing, the magnitude of values in the chart should be viewed as a "reasonable approximation." For private institutions, figures for the fiscal years beginning in 1990 through 1995 are estimates.

See notes to the relevant tables in the *Digest of Education Statistics*.

Chapter 4

Figure 4.1. U.S. college-age population, 1970–2020.

Based on annual data presented in U.S. Department of Education, Institute of Education Sciences, NCES, Table 101.10 "Estimates of resident population, by age group," *Digest of Education Statistics* (annual issues, 1990–2020), https://nces.ed.gov/programs/digest/ (accessed August 1, 2021).

See notes to relevant table in *Digest of Education Statistics*.

Figure 4.2. Percentage of U.S. college-age population enrolled in college, 1970–2020.

Based on annual data presented in U.S. Department of Education, Institute of Education Sciences, NCES, Table 302.60 "Percentage of 18- to 24-year-olds enrolled in college, by level of institution and sex and race/ethnicity of student," *Digest of Education Statistics* (annual issues, 1980–2020), https://nces.ed.gov/programs/digest/ (accessed August 1, 2021).

See notes to relevant table in *Digest of Education Statistics*.

Figure 4.3. U.S. college-age population as a percentage of total U.S. population relative to college participation rate, 1970–2020.

Based on annual data presented in U.S. Department of Education, Institute of Education Sciences, NCES, Table 101.10 "Estimates of resident population, by age group;" and Table 302.60 "Percentage of 18- to 24-year-olds enrolled in college, by level of institution and sex and race/ethnicity of student," *Digest of Education Statistics* (annual issues, 1990–2020), https://nces.ed.gov/programs/digest/ (accessed August 1, 2021).

See notes to relevant tables in *Digest of Education Statistics*.

Figure 4.4. Foreign students enrolled in U.S. colleges and universities by global region, 1990–2020.

Based on academic year data presented in U.S. Department of Education, Institute of Education Sciences, NCES, Table 310.20 "Foreign students enrolled in institutions of higher education in the United States, by continent, region, and selected countries of origin," *Digest of Education Statistics* (annual issues, 1990–2020), https://nces.ed.gov/programs/digest/ (accessed August 1, 2021); and Institute of International Education, "International Students by Place of Origin," Open Doors 2021, https://opendoorsdata.org/data/international-students/all-places-of-origin/ (accessed January 20, 2022).

The regional classification of countries is based on the United Nations geo-scheme (see United Nations, Department of Economic and Social Affairs, Statistics Division, "Methodology for Geographic Regions," https://unstats.un.org/unsd/methodology/m49/ (accessed June 15, 2021)) with the following exception: "Arab World" consists of the member states of the Arab League. These states have been carved out of "Sub-Saharan Africa" and "Central and Western Asia" to form a separate regional category.

See notes to relevant tables in *Digest of Education Statistics* and Open Doors.

Figure 4.5. U.S. tertiary education, gross enrollment ratios, 1970–2019.

Data provider: The World Bank, DataBank, https://data.worldbank.org/indicator/se.ter.enrr (accessed November 1, 2021). Underlying source: UNESCO Institute for Statistics, "Gross enrolment ratio, tertiary, both sexes (%);" and "School enrollment, tertiary (% gross)", http://data.uis.unesco.org (accessed November 1, 2021).

"Tertiary education includes what is commonly understood as academic education but also includes advanced vocational or professional education." UNESCO Institute for Statistics Glossary, http://uis.unesco.org/en/glossary (accessed July 15, 2021).

Figures for the following years are estimates: 1997, 1999-2005, 2005-2013. They were calculated by taking the difference between the data value for the year immediately preceding the gap and the data value immediately following the gap, they accruing the difference over the gap years.

See notes to relevant World Bank and UNESCO table.

Figure 4.6. Fall enrollments in U.S. post-secondary degree-granting institutions, actual and projected, 1970–2029.

Based on academic year data presented in U.S. Department of Education, Institute of Education Sciences, NCES, Table 303.10 "Total fall enrollment in degree-granting postsecondary institutions, by attendance status, sex of student, and control of institution," *Digest of Education Statistics* (annual issues, 1990–2020), https://nces.ed.gov/programs/digest/ (accessed August 1, 2021).

See notes to relevant table in *Digest of Education Statistics*.

Figure 4.7. Annual growth rates in fall enrollments per post-secondary degree-granting institution, 1970–2019.

Based on annual data presented in U.S. Department of Education, Institute of Education Sciences, NCES, Table 303.10 "Total fall enrollment in degree-granting postsecondary institutions, by attendance status, sex of student, and control of institution," *Digest of Education Statistics* (annual issues, 1990–2020), https://nces.ed.gov/programs/digest/ (accessed October 1, 2021). See notes to relevant table in the *Digest of Education Statistics*.

Figure 4.8. Average institutional grants per full-time equivalent student, 1970–2019.

Based on annual data presented in U.S. Department of Education, Institute of Education Sciences, NCES, Table 307.10 "Full-time-equivalent fall enrollment in degree-granting postsecondary institutions, by control and level of institution," *Digest of Education Statistics* (annual issues, 1990–2020), https://nces.ed.gov/programs/digest/ (accessed

October 1, 2021); and academic year data presented in College Board, Table 2 "Student aid and nonfederal loans," Trends in Student Aid (annual reports, 2000–2020), https://research. collegeboard.org/trends/student-aid/resource-library (accessed August 1, 2021). All.

Institutional grants include scholarships and fellowships granted and funded by the institution and/or individual departments within the institution, (i.e., instruction, research, public service) that may contribute indirectly to the enhancement of their programs; also, scholarships targeted to certain individuals (based on state of residence, major field of study, athletic team participation, etc.), for which the institution designates the recipient. U.S. Department of Education, IPEDS Data Collection System, 2019–2020 Glossary, http://surveys. nces.ed.gov/ipeds/visglossaryall.aspx (accessed July 15, 2021).

See notes to relevant table in *Digest of Education Statistics* and in Trends in Student Aid.

Figure 4.9. Average institutional grants as a percentage of average higher education costs, 1970–2019.

Based on annual data presented in U.S. Department of Education, Institute of Education Sciences, NCES, Table 307.10 "Full-time-equivalent fall enrollment in degree-granting postsecondary institutions, by control and level of institution;" academic year data presented in Table 330.10 "Average undergraduate tuition and fees and room and board rates charged for full-time students in degree-granting postsecondary institutions, by level and control of institution;" in Table 330.50 "Average and percentiles of graduate tuition and required fees in degree-granting postsecondary institutions, by control of institution," *Digest of Education Statistics* (annual issues, 1990–2020), https://nces.ed.gov/programs/digest/ (accessed October 1, 2021); and in Table 2 "Student aid and nonfederal loans in current dollars (in millions)," Trends in Student Aid (annual reports, 2000–2020), https://research. collegeboard.org/trends/student-aid/resource-library (accessed October 1, 2021). All.

Because the underlying figures are based on full-time equivalent fall enrollments, without distinction as to actual undergraduate and graduate enrollments, they are approximate.

See notes to relevant tables in *Digest of Education Statistics* and in Trends in Student Aid.

Figure 4.10. Average financial responsibility composite scores of U.S. private post-secondary degree-granting institutions, 2007–2018.

Based on annual data provided by U.S. Department of Education, Office of Student Financial Aid, https://studentaid.gov/data-center/school/composite-scores (accessed August 1, 2021).

See website notes.

Figure 4.11. Aggregate revenues net of aggregate expenditures per employee, U.S. private post-secondary degree-granting institutions, 1996–2018.

Based on fiscal year data presented in U.S. Department of Education, Institute of Education Sciences, NCES, Table 333.40 "Total revenue of private non-profit degree-granting postsecondary institutions, by source of funds and level of institution;" Table 333.55. "Total revenue of private for-profit degree-granting postsecondary institutions, by source of funds and level of institution;" Table 334.30 "Total expenditures of private non-profit degree-granting postsecondary institutions, by purpose and level of institution;" Table 334.50 "Total expenditures of private for-profit degree-granting postsecondary institutions, by purpose and level of institution;" and academic year data presented in Table 314.20 "Employees in degree-granting postsecondary institutions, by sex, employment status, control and level of institution, and primary occupation," *Digest of Education Statistics* (annual issues, 1998–2020), https://nces.ed.gov/programs/digest/ (accessed August 1, 2021). Figures are in current U.S. dollars. Both private non-profit and private for-profit institutions are subject to Generally Accepted Accounting Principles.

See notes to the relevant tables in the *Digest of Education Statistics*.

Figure 4.12. Aggregate revenues net of aggregate expenditures per employee, U.S. public post-secondary degree-granting institutions, 2003–2018.

Based on fiscal year data presented in U.S. Department of Education, Institute of Education Sciences, NCES, Table 333.10 "Revenues of public degree-granting postsecondary institutions, by source of revenue and level of institution;" Table 334.10 "Total expenditures of public degree-granting postsecondary institutions, by purpose and level of institution;" and academic year data presented in Table 314.20 "Employees in degree-granting postsecondary institutions, by sex, employment status, control and level of institution, and primary occupation," *Digest of Education Statistics* (annual issues, 1998–2020), https://nces.ed.gov/programs/digest/ (accessed August 1, 2021). Figures are in current U.S. dollars.

See notes to the relevant tables in the *Digest of Education Statistics*.

Figure 4.13. Percent change in estimated annual enrollments from previous year, U.S. Post-secondary degree-granting institutions, fall 2019—fall 2021.

Based on academic year data presented in National Student Clearinghouse Research Center, Table 1 "Estimated National Enrollment by Institutional Sector: 2018 to 2021;" and Table 2 "Estimated First-Time Freshman Enrollment by Institutional Sector: 2015 to 2021," Current Term Enrollment Estimates Fall 2021, https://nscresearchcenter.org/current-term-enrollment-estimates/ (accessed January 20, 2022).

See notes to relevant tables in Current Term Enrollment Estimates.

Chapter 5

Figure 5.1. Foreign students enrolled in U.S. higher education institutions by global region, 1990–2020.

Based on academic year data presented in U.S. Department of Education, Institute of Education Sciences, NCES, Table 310.20 "Foreign students enrolled in institutions of higher education in the United States, by continent, region, and selected countries of origin," *Digest of Education Statistics* (annual issues, 1996–2020), https://nces.ed.gov/programs/digest/ (accessed August 1, 2021); and Institute of International Education, "International Students by Place of Origin," Open Doors 2021, https://opendoorsdata.org/data/international-students/all-places-of-origin/ (accessed January 20, 2022).

The regional classification of countries is based on the United Nations geo-scheme (see United Nations, Department of Economic and Social Affairs, Statistics Division, "Methodology for Geographic Regions," https://unstats.un.org/unsd/methodology/m49/ (accessed June 15, 2021)) with the following exception: "Arab World" consists of the member states of the Arab League. These states have been carved out of "Sub-Saharan Africa" and "Central and Western Asia" to form a separate regional category.

See notes to relevant tables in the *Digest of Education Statistics* and Open Doors.

Figure 5.2. Total internationally mobile tertiary education students enrolled in institutions in the United States, 2014–2019.

Based on annual data presented in UNESCO Institute for Statistics, "Inbound Internationally Mobile Students by Region of Origin," and "Inbound Internationally Mobile Students by Country of Origin," http://data.uis.unesco.org (accessed November 1, 2021).

Although the UNESCO database is well populated, significant gaps exist for some destination countries in specific years. To fill these gaps to derive total enrollment numbers for the region as a whole (i.e., the denominator in the market share calculation), the following methodology was used: (1) where annual data were reported before and after the gap year(s), the difference in data values was calculated, and then accrued over the gap period; (2) where no annual data were reported either before or after the gap year(s), the enrollment number(s) for the gap year(s) were estimated with reference to historical data for the destination country in question.

See notes to relevant UNESCO tables.

Figure 5.3. U.S. F-1 student visas issued to residents of various global regions, 1997–2020.

Based on annual F-1 visa data presented in U.S. Department of State, Bureau of Consular Affairs, Table XVI(B) "Nonimmigrant visas issued by classification," and Table XIX "Nonimmigrant visas issued by issuing office," Nonimmigrant Visa Statistics (annual reports, 2013–2020), https://travel.state.gov/content/travel/en/legal/visa-law0/visa-statistics/nonimmigrant-visa-statistics.html (accessed August 1, 2021).

The regional classification of countries is based on the United Nations geo-scheme (United Nations, Department of Economic and Social Affairs, Statistics Division, "Methodology for Geographic Regions," http://unstats.un.org/unsd/methodology/m49/ (accessed June 15, 2021)) with the following exception: "Arab World" consists of the member states of the Arab League. These states have been carved out of "Sub-Saharan Africa" and "Central and Western Asia" to form a separate regional category.

See notes to relevant tables in Nonimmigrant Visa Statistics.

Figure 5.4. World population in thousands by global region, historical and projected, 1950–2100.

Based on mid-year data presented in United Nations, Department of Economic and Social Affairs, Population Division, File POP/1-1 "Total population (both sexes combined) by region, subregion and country," and File POP/1-1 "Total population (both sexes combined) by region, subregion and country, annually for 1950–2100, medium fertility variant," World Population Prospects 2019, Online Edition, Rev. 1, http://population.un.org/wpp/ (accessed August 1, 2021).

The regional classification of countries is based on the United Nations geo-scheme (see United Nations, Department of Economic and Social Affairs, Statistics Division, "Methodology for Geographic Regions," https://unstats.un.org/unsd/methodology/m49/ (accessed June 15, 2021)) with the following exception: "Arab World" consists of the member states of the Arab League. These states have been carved out of "Sub-Saharan Africa" and "Central and Western Asia" to form a separate regional category.

See notes to relevant tables in World Population Prospects.

Figure 5.5. World college-age population in thousands by global region, historical and projected, 1950–2100.

Based on mid-year data presented in United Nations, Department of Economic and Social Affairs, Population Division, File SA5/POP/8-1 "Total population (both sexes combined) by broad age group, region, subregion and country, 1950–2100," World Population Prospects 2019, Online Edition, https://population.un.org/wpp/ (accessed August 1, 2021).

The regional classification of countries is based on the United Nations geo-scheme (see United Nations, Department of Economic and Social Affairs, Statistics Division,

"Methodology for Geographic Regions," http://unstats.un.org/unsd/methodology/m49/ (accessed June 15, 2021)) with the following exception: "Arab World" consists of the member states of the Arab League. These states have been carved out of "Sub-Saharan Africa" and "Central and Western Asia" to form a separate regional category.

See notes to relevant tables in World Population Prospects.

Figure 5.6. World college-age population as a percentage of total population by global region, historical and projected, 1950–2100.

Based on mid-year data presented in United Nations, Department of Economic and Social Affairs, Population Division, File SA5/POP/8-1 "Total population (both sexes combined) by broad age group, region, subregion and country, 1950–2100," World Population Prospects 2019, Online Edition, https://population.un.org/wpp/ (accessed August 1, 2021).

The regional classification of countries is based on the United Nations geo-scheme (see United Nations, Department of Economic and Social Affairs, Statistics Division, "Methodology for Geographic Regions," https://unstats.un.org/unsd/methodology/m49/ (accessed June 15, 2021)) with the following exception: "Arab World" consists of the member states of the Arab League. These states have been carved out of "Sub-Saharan Africa" and "Central and Western Asia" to form a separate regional category.

See notes to relevant tables in World Population Prospects.

Figure 5.7. Enrollment in higher education by global region, 1970–2019.

Data provider: The World Bank, DataBank; underlying source: UNESCO Institute for Statistics, File No. API_SE.TER.ENRL_DS12_en_excel_v2_2527377.xls "Enrolment in Tertiary Education, All Programmes, Both Sexes (number)," https://databank.worldbank.org/reports.aspx?source=1159&series=se.ter.enrl (accessed August 1, 2021).

"Tertiary education includes what is commonly understood as academic education but also includes advanced vocational or professional education." UNESCO Institute for Statistics Glossary, http://uis.unesco.org/en/glossary (accessed June 1, 2021).

The regional classification of countries is based on the United Nations geo-scheme (see United Nations, Department of Economic and Social Affairs, Statistics Division, "Methodology for Geographic Regions," https://unstats.un.org/unsd/methodology/m49/ (accessed June 15, 2021)) with the following exception: "Arab World" consists of the member states of the Arab League. These states have been carved out of "Sub-Saharan Africa" and "Central and Western Asia" to form a separate regional category.

The graph represents an imprecise "order of magnitude" based on a combination of statistical data and extrapolated values for the majority of countries within a particular global region. They reflect regional averages of country-specific data, unadjusted for variations in national population figures. In the UNESCO database, lapses in country reporting result in significant gaps in annual data, particularly for certain countries in Sub-Saharan Africa, Central and West Asia, and Oceania, for those countries that comprised Yugoslavia and the Soviet Union (1970–1977), and for the two Germanys (1970–1977). Accordingly, the following methodology was used to fill the gaps:

- Where available, estimates provided by national governments were incorporated in the underlying database.
- Statistical gaps were filled by taking the difference between the data value for the year immediately preceding the gap and the data value for the year immediately following the gap, then accruing the difference over the gap year(s).

Tertiary enrollment numbers for North Korea were estimated at 17.5% of the numbers for South Korea.

See notes to relevant UNESCO and World Bank tables.

Figure 5.8. Tertiary education gross enrollment ratios by global region, 1970–2019.

Data provider: The World Bank, DataBank; underlying source: UNESCO Institute for Statistics, "Gross enrolment ratio, tertiary, both sexes (%)," https://data.worldbank.org/indicator/se.ter.enrr (accessed August 1, 2021).

"Tertiary education includes what is commonly understood as academic education but also includes advanced vocational or professional education." UNESCO Institute for Statistics Glossary, http://uis.unesco.org/en/glossary (accessed June 1, 2021).

The regional classification of countries is based on the United Nations geo-scheme (see United Nations, Department of Economic and Social Affairs, Statistics Division, "Methodology for Geographic Regions," https://unstats.un.org/unsd/methodology/m49/ (accessed June 15, 2021)) with the following exception: "Arab World" consists of the member states of the Arab League. These states have been carved out of "Sub-Saharan Africa" and "Central and Western Asia" to form a separate regional category.

The graph represents an imprecise "order of magnitude" based on a combination of statistical data and extrapolated values for the majority of countries within a particular global region. They reflect regional averages of country-specific data, unadjusted for variations in national population figures. In the UNESCO database, lapses in country reporting result in significant gaps in annual data, particularly for certain countries in Sub-Saharan Africa, Central and Western Asia, and Oceania, for those countries that comprised Yugoslavia and the Soviet Union (1970–1977), and for the two Germanys (1970–1977). Accordingly, the following methodology was used to fill the gaps:

- Where available, estimates provided by national governments were incorporated in the underlying database.
- Data for countries that reported less than 50% of their expected annual values for the entire period and which accounted for less than 5% of the regional total were excluded from the calculation. Otherwise, being based on the number of countries in the region, annual averages and historical trends would have been significantly distorted.
- For all other countries, statistical gaps were filled by taking the difference between the data value for the year immediately preceding the gap and the data value for the year immediately following the gap, then pro-rating the difference over the gap year(s).

The gross enrollment ratio for Japan was estimated at 75% in 2019.

See notes to relevant UNESCO and World Bank tables.

Figure 5.9. Tertiary education gross enrollment potential by global region relative to world norm, 1970–2019.

Data provider: The World Bank, DataBank; underlying source: UNESCO Institute for Statistics, "Gross enrolment ratio, tertiary, both sexes (%)," https://data.worldbank.org/indicator/se.ter.enrr (accessed August 1, 2021).

"Tertiary education includes what is commonly understood as academic education but also includes advanced vocational or professional education." UNESCO Institute for Statistics Glossary, http://uis.unesco.org/en/glossary (accessed June 1, 2021).

The regional classification of countries is based on the United Nations geo-scheme (see United Nations, Department of Economic and Social Affairs, Statistics Division, "Methodology for Geographic Regions," https://unstats.un.org/unsd/methodology/m49/ (accessed June 15, 2021)) with the following exception: "Arab World" consists of the member states of the Arab League. These states have been carved out of "Sub-Saharan Africa" and "Central and Western Asia" to form a separate regional category.

The graph represents an imprecise "order of magnitude" based on a combination of statistical data and extrapolated values for the majority of countries within a particular global region. They reflect regional averages of country-specific data, unadjusted for variations in national population figures. In the UNESCO and World Bank databases, lapses in country reporting result in significant gaps in annual data, particularly for certain countries in Sub-Saharan Africa, Central and Western Asia, and Oceania, for those countries that comprised Yugoslavia and the Soviet Union (1970–1977), and for the two Germanys (1970–1977). Accordingly, the following methodology was used to fill the gaps:

- Where available, estimates provided by national governments were incorporated in the underlying database.
- Data for countries that reported less than 50% of their expected annual values for the entire period and which accounted for less than 5% of the regional total were excluded from the calculation. Otherwise, being based on the number of countries in the region, annual averages and historical trends would have been significantly distorted.
- For all other countries, statistical gaps were filled by taking the difference between the data value for the year immediately preceding the gap and the data value for the year immediately following the gap, then pro-rating the difference over the gap year(s).

The gross enrollment ratio for Japan was estimated at 75% in 2019.

See notes to relevant UNESCO and World Bank tables.

Figure 5.10. GDP per capita in current U.S. dollars by global region, historical and projected, 1980–2026.

Based on annual data presented in International Monetary Fund (IMF), World Economic Outlook Database, April 2021, "GDP per capita, current prices (U.S. dollars per capita)," https://www.imf.org/external/pubs/ft/weo/2020/01/weodata/index.aspx (accessed August 1, 2021).

The regional classification of countries is based on the United Nations geo-scheme (see United Nations, Department of Economic and Social Affairs, Statistics Division, "Methodology for Geographic Regions," https://unstats.un.org/unsd/methodology/m49/ (accessed June 15, 2021)) with the following exception: "Arab World" consists of the member states of the Arab League. These states have been carved out of "Sub-Saharan Africa" and "Central and Western Asia" to form a separate regional category.

For each region, annual averages in GDP per capita were calculated on the basis of country-specific empirical data and extrapolated values, adjusted to take into account differences in national population numbers. Although the IMF database for GDP per capita is fairly well populated with statistics, gaps exist for certain countries in Sub-Saharan Africa and Central and Western Asia for the 1980–1995 timeframe. These gaps were filled by taking the difference between the data value for the year immediately preceding the gap and the data value for the year immediately following the gap, then accruing the difference over the gap years.

See notes to relevant IMF table.

Figure 5.11. Net national income per capita in current U.S. dollars by global region, 1980–2019.

Based on annual data presented in the World Bank, DataBank, "Adjusted net national income per capita in current U.S. dollars," https://data.worldbank.org/indicator/ny.adj.nnty. pc.cd (accessed October 1, 2021).

"Adjusted net national income is calculated by subtracting from [Gross National Income] GNI a charge for the consumption of fixed capital (a calculation that yields net national income) and for the depletion of natural resources." The World Bank,

DataBank, Metadata Glossary, https://databank.worldbank.org/metadataglossary/world-development-indicators/series/ny.adj.nnty.cd (accessed October 1, 2021).

The regional classification of countries is based on the United Nations geo-scheme (see United Nations, Department of Economic and Social Affairs, Statistics Division, "Methodology for Geographic Regions," https://unstats.un.org/unsd/methodology/m49/ (accessed June 15, 2021)) with the following exception: "Arab World" consists of the member states of the Arab League. These states have been carved out of "Sub-Saharan Africa" and "Central and Western Asia" to form a separate regional category.

The graph represents an imprecise "order of magnitude" based on a combination of statistical data and extrapolated values for the majority of countries within a particular global region. They reflect regional averages of country-specific data, adjusted to take into account differences in national population numbers. In the World Bank database, lapses in country reporting result in significant gaps in annual data, particularly for certain countries in Sub-Saharan Africa, Central and Western Asia. Accordingly, the following methodology was used to fill the gaps:

- Where available, estimates provided by national governments were incorporated in the underlying database.
- Data for countries that reported less than 50% of their expected annual values for the entire period and which accounted for less than 5% of the regional total were excluded from the calculation. Otherwise, being based on the number of countries in the region, annual averages and historical trends would have been significantly distorted.
- For Armenia, Kazakhstan, Tajikistan, Vietnam, Mongolia, Turkmenistan, Estonia, Côte d'Ivoire, Ethiopia, Guinea, Namibia, Seychelles, and Tanzania, statistical gaps were filled by taking the difference between the data value for the year immediately preceding the gap and the data value for the year immediately following the gap, then accruing the difference over the gap year(s).

See notes to relevant World Bank table.

Figure 5.12. Government expenditure on education as a percentage of GDP by global region, 1999–2018.

Based on annual data presented in the World Bank DataBank, "Government expenditure on education as a percentage of GDP," https://data.worldbank.org/indicator/se.xpd.totl.gd.zs (November 15, 2021).

The regional classification of countries is based on the United Nations geo-scheme (see United Nations, Department of Economic and Social Affairs, Statistics Division, "Methodology for Geographic Regions," https://unstats.un.org/unsd/methodology/m49/ (accessed June 15, 2021)) with the following exception: "Arab World" consists of the member states of the Arab League. These states have been carved out of "Sub-Saharan Africa" and "Central and Western Asia" to form a separate regional category.

The graph represents an imprecise "order of magnitude" based on a combination of statistical data and extrapolated values for the majority of countries within a particular global region. They reflect regional averages of country-specific data, unadjusted for differences in in national population numbers. In the World Bank database, lapses in country reporting result in significant gaps in annual data, particularly for certain countries in Sub-Saharan Africa, Central and Western Asia. Accordingly, the following methodology was used to fill the gaps:

- Where available, estimates provided by national governments were incorporated in the underlying database.

- Data for countries that reported less than 50% of their expected annual values for the period and which accounted for less than 5% of the regional total were excluded from the calculation. Otherwise, being based on the number of countries in the region, annual averages and historical trends would have been significantly distorted.
- For all other countries, statistical gaps were filled by taking the difference between the data value for the year immediately preceding the gap and the data value for the year immediately following the gap, then pro-rating the difference over the gap year(s).

See notes to relevant World Bank table.

Figure 5.13. Gross enrollment potential relative and GDP per capita by global region, 2019.

Based on annual data presented in the World Bank, DataBank, https://data.worldbank.org/indicator/se.ter.enrr, and The World Bank, DataBank, "GDP per capita in current U.S. dollars," https://data.worldbank.org/indicator/ny.gdp.pcap.cd (accessed August 1, 2021); and UNESCO Institute for Statistics, "Gross enrolment ratio, tertiary, both sexes (%);" and "School enrollment, tertiary (% gross)," http://data.uis.unesco.org (accessed July 15, 2021).

"Tertiary education includes what is commonly understood as academic education but also includes advanced vocational or professional education." UNESCO Institute for Statistics Glossary, http://uis.unesco.org/en/glossary (accessed July 15, 2021).

"GDP is the sum of gross value added by all resident producers in the economy plus any product taxes and minus any subsidies not included in the value of the products. It is calculated without making deductions for depreciation of fabricated assets or for depletion and degradation of natural resources. GDP per capita is gross domestic product divided by midyear population." The World Bank, DataBank, Metadata Glossary, https://databank.worldbank.org/metadataglossary/all/series?search=gdp%20per%20capita (accessed July 15, 2021).

Gross Enrollment Potential = (1—the Gross Enrollment Ratio for a particular country or region). See notes to Figure 5.9 for an explanation of how the world norm was calculated.

The regional classification of countries is based on the United Nations geo-scheme (see United Nations, Department of Economic and Social Affairs, Statistics Division, "Methodology for Geographic Regions," https://unstats.un.org/unsd/methodology/m49/ (accessed June 15, 2021)) with the following exception: "Arab World" consists of the member states of the Arab League. These states have been carved out of "Sub-Saharan Africa" and "Central and Western Asia" to form a separate regional category.

The graph represents an imprecise "order of magnitude" based on a combination of statistical data and extrapolated values for the majority of countries within a particular global region. They reflect regional averages of country-specific data, unadjusted for variations in national population figures. In the UNESCO and World Bank databases, lapses in country reporting result in significant gaps in annual data, particularly for certain countries in Sub-Saharan Africa, Central and Western Asia. Accordingly, the following methodology was used to fill the gaps:

- Where available, estimates provided by national governments were incorporated in the underlying database.
- Data for countries that reported less than 50% of their expected annual values for the entire period and which accounted for less than 5% of the regional total were excluded from the calculation. Otherwise, being based on the number of countries in the region, annual averages and historical trends would have been significantly distorted.

- For all other countries, statistical gaps were filled by taking the difference between the data value for the year immediately preceding the gap and the data value for the year immediately following the gap, then pro-rating the difference over the gap year(s).
- The gross enrollment ratio for Japan was estimated at 75% in 2019.

See notes to relevant UNESCO and World Bank tables.

Figure 5.14. Gross enrollment potential relative to NNI per capita by global region, 2019.

Based on annual data presented in the World Bank, DataBank, https://data.worldbank.org/indicator/se.ter.enrr, and the World Bank, DataBank, "Adjusted net national income per capita in current U.S. dollars," https://data.worldbank.org/indicator/ny.adj.nnty.cd (accessed August 1, 2021); and UNESCO Institute for Statistics, "Gross enrolment ratio, tertiary, both sexes (%);" and "School enrollment, tertiary (% gross)," http://data.uis.unesco.org (accessed July 15, 2021).

"Tertiary education includes what is commonly understood as academic education but also includes advanced vocational or professional education." UNESCO Institute for Statistics Glossary, http://uis.unesco.org/en/glossary (accessed July 15, 2021).

"Adjusted net national income is calculated by subtracting from [Gross National Income] GNI a charge for the consumption of fixed capital (a calculation that yields net national income) and for the depletion of natural resources." The World Bank, DataBank, Metadata Glossary, https://databank.worldbank.org/metadataglossary/world-development-indicators/series/ny.adj.nnty.cd (accessed July 15, 2021).

Gross Enrollment Potential = (1—the Gross Enrollment Ratio for a particular country or region). See notes to Figure 5.9 for an explanation of how the world norm was calculated.

The regional classification of countries is based on the United Nations geo-scheme (see United Nations, Department of Economic and Social Affairs, Statistics Division, "Methodology for Geographic Regions," https://unstats.un.org/unsd/methodology/m49/ (accessed June 15, 2021)) with the following exception: "Arab World" consists of the member states of the Arab League. These states have been carved out of "Sub-Saharan Africa" and "Central and Western Asia" to form a separate regional category.

The graph represents an imprecise "order of magnitude" based on a combination of statistical data and extrapolated values for the majority of countries within a particular global region. They reflect regional averages of country-specific data, unadjusted for variations in national population figures. In the UNESCO and World Bank databases, lapses in country reporting result in significant gaps in annual data, particularly for certain countries in Sub-Saharan Africa, Central and Western Asia. Accordingly, the following methodology was used to fill the gaps:

- Where available, estimates provided by national governments were incorporated in the underlying database.
- Data for countries that reported less than 50% of their expected annual values for the entire period and which accounted for less than 5% of the regional total were excluded from the calculation. Otherwise, being based on the number of countries in the region, annual averages and historical trends would have been significantly distorted.
- For all other countries, statistical gaps were filled by taking the difference between the data value for the year immediately preceding the gap and the data value for the year immediately following the gap, then pro-rating the difference over the gap year(s).

The gross enrollment ratio for Japan was estimated at 75% in 2019.
See notes to relevant UNESCO and World Bank tables.

Chapter 6

Figure 6.1. International branch campuses by home country of sponsoring institution, 2020.

Based on data presented in Cross-Border Education Research Team (November 20, 2020), C-BERT International Campus Listing [data originally collected by Kevin Kinser and Jason E. Lane], http://cbert.org/resources-data/intl-campus/ (accessed August 1, 2021).

Data for China exclude two branch campuses of sponsoring institutions based in Hong Kong S.A.R.

See notes to C-BERT Campus Listing.

Figure 6.2. Regional branch campuses by home country of sponsoring institution, 2020.

Based on data presented in Cross-Border Education Research Team (November 20, 2020), C-BERT International Campus Listing [data originally collected by Kevin Kinser and Jason E. Lane], http://cbert.org/resources-data/intl-campus/ (accessed July 15, 2021).

Data for China exclude two branch campuses of sponsoring institutions based in Hong Kong S.A.R.

See notes to C-BERT Campus Listing.

Figure 6.3. Major U.S. service providers in global emerging markets for higher education, by nominal value of service contracts, 2014–2019.

Based on data presented in U.S. Department of Education, Office of Federal Student Aid, Data.Gov, *Foreign Gifts and Contracts Report, 2020*. The underlying data are based on the nominal value of contracts between U.S. colleges and universities and parties in Latin America and the Caribbean; East, Southeast, Central, South, and Western Asia; the Middle East; and Sub-Saharan Africa. To avoid double-counting, contracts in the same nominal amount concluded by the same parties on the same date were excluded from the calculation. See notes to *Foreign Gifts and Contracts Reports, 2020*, https://studentaid.gov/data-center/school/foreign-gifts (accessed August 1, 2021).

Figure 6.4. U.S. exports of educational services, by global region, 2006–2020.

Based on annual data presented in U.S. Department of Commerce, Bureau of Economic Analysis, International Data: International Transactions, International Services, and International Investment Position, Table 2.2 "U.S. Trade in Services, by Type of Service and by Country or Affiliation," https://apps.bea.gov/itable/itable.cfm?reqid=62&step=7&isuri=1&tablelist=30568&thetableflexibleareas=1&product=4&filter_—5=&tablelistsecondary=30573&filter_—4=0&filter_—3=112&filter_—2=0&filter_—1=0 (accessed October 1, 2021).

"Educational services" include instruction and training provided by schools, colleges, and universities, as well as other specialized establishments, such as training centers. These institutions may be public, private non-profit, or private for-profit. Such services include food and accommodation provided to students. U.S. Department of Commerce, Bureau of Economic Analysis, "Regional Economic Accounts," https://apps.bea.gov/itable/definitions.cfm?did=2113&reqid=70 (accessed October 1, 2021).

The regional classification of countries is based on the U.S. Department of Commerce geo-scheme. Because ten Arab states are included in the broad category "Africa," the figures for Africa are significantly greater than those for the subcategory "Sub-Saharan Africa." Furthermore, because African states, data for which are reported under the heading "Other," cannot be identified with specificity, segregating figures for African countries that are part of the "Arab World" has not been feasible.

The graph represents an imprecise "order of magnitude" based on a combination of statistical data and extrapolated values for the majority of countries within a particular global region. Statistics for the following regions and years are unavailable: Latin America: 2015–2017, 2019; Middle East: 2013, 2015–2017, 2019; Asia and Pacific: 2013, 2017. These omissions resulted in significant gaps in the overall report. The gaps were filled by taking the difference between the data value for the year immediately preceding the gap and the data value for the year immediately following the gap, then accruing the difference over the gap year(s).

The surge in the value of exports in 2020 reflects a massive increase in the number of non-U.S. residents who took online courses offered by U.S. educational institutions during the Global Pandemic.

See notes to Bureau of Economic Analysis data.

Figure 6.5. Principal countries of destination for internationally mobile tertiary education students from East and Southeast Asia, 2014–2019.

Based on annual data presented in UNESCO Institute for Statistics, "Inbound Internationally Mobile Students by Region of Origin," and "Inbound Internationally Mobile Students by Country of Origin," http://data.uis.unesco.org (accessed November 1, 2021). In the relevant UNESCO database, the region is listed under the heading "East Asia and Pacific."

The underlying figures were derived by subtracting (1) enrollment numbers by country of destination for countries of origin in Oceania from (2) corresponding figures for the broader East Asia and Pacific region. Otherwise, the results for East and Southeast Asia would have been skewed in favor of two major destination countries: Australia and New Zealand. The latter two countries are the principal destinations for internationally mobile students from countries of origin in Oceania. Methodologically, the purpose of this calculation was to create a regional category for East and Southeast Asia that is consistent with other such categories used in this book.

The following destination country enrollment numbers are estimates: France in 2014 and Malaysia in 2018.

See notes to relevant UNESCO tables.

Figure 6.6. Estimated market shares of principal countries of destination for internationally mobile tertiary education students from East and Southeast Asia, 2014–2019.

Based on annual data presented in UNESCO Institute for Statistics, "Inbound Internationally Mobile Students by Region of Origin," and "Inbound Internationally Mobile Students by Country of Origin," http://data.uis.unesco.org (accessed November 1, 2021). In the relevant UNESCO database, the region is listed under the heading "East Asia and Pacific."

Although this database is fairly well populated, significant gaps exist for some destination countries in specific years. To fill these gaps to derive total enrollment numbers for the region as a whole (i.e., the denominator in the market share calculation), the following methodology was used: (1) where annual data were reported before and after the gap year(s), the difference in data values was calculated, then accrued over the gap period; and (2) where no annual data were reported either before or after the gap year(s), the enrollment number(s) for the gap year(s) were estimated with reference to historical data for the destination country in question.

Total enrollment numbers for the region exclude figures for Japan as a destination country. These figures were reported as negative numbers in the UNESCO database.

See also notes to Figure 6.5.

Figure 6.7. Principal countries of destination for internationally mobile tertiary education students from South Asia, 2014–2019.

Based on annual data presented in UNESCO Institute for Statistics, "Inbound Internationally Mobile Students by Country of Origin," http://data.uis.unesco.org (accessed November 1, 2021). In the relevant UNESCO database, the region is listed under the heading "South Asia."

Because the relevant UNESCO database contains no listing for the South Asian region as a whole, the figures were derived by aggregating destination country enrollments for individual South Asian countries of origin. Methodologically, the purpose of the calculation was to create a regional category for South Asia that is consistent with other such categories used in this book.

The following destination country enrollment numbers are estimates: Malaysia in 2018 and 2019.

See notes to relevant UNESCO tables.

Figure 6.8. Estimated market shares of principal countries of destination for internationally mobile tertiary education students from South Asia, 2014–2019.

Based on annual data presented in UNESCO Institute for Statistics, "Inbound Internationally Mobile Students by Region of Origin," and "Inbound Internationally Mobile Students by Country of Origin," http://data.uis.unesco.org (accessed November 1, 2021). In the relevant UNESCO database, the region is listed under the heading "South Asia."

Although the UNESCO database is fairly well populated, significant gaps exist for some destination countries in specific years. To fill these gaps to derive total enrollment numbers for the region as a whole (i.e., the denominator in the market share calculation), the following methodology was used: (1) where annual data were reported before and after the gap year(s), the difference in data values was calculated, then accrued over the gap period; and (2) where no annual data were reported either before or after the gap year(s), the enrollment number(s) for the gap year(s) were estimated with reference to historical data for the destination country in question.

See also notes to Figure 6.7.

Figure 6.9. Principal countries of destination for internationally mobile tertiary education students from the Arab World, 2014–2019.

Based on annual data presented in UNESCO Institute for Statistics, "Inbound Internationally Mobile Students by Region of Origin," http://data.uis.unesco.org (accessed November 1, 2021). In the relevant UNESCO database, the region is listed under the heading "Arab States."

The following destination country enrollment numbers are estimates: Jordan in 2014, Malaysia in 2018, and United Arab Emirates in 2017 and 2018.

See notes to relevant UNESCO tables.

Figure 6.10. Estimated market shares of principal countries of destination for internationally mobile tertiary education students from the Arab World, 2014–2019.

Based on annual data presented in UNESCO Institute for Statistics, "Inbound Internationally Mobile Students by Region of Origin," and "Inbound Internationally Mobile Students by Country of Origin," http://data.uis.unesco.org (accessed November 1, 2021). In the relevant UNESCO database, the region is listed under the heading "Arab States."

Although the UNESCO database is fairly well populated, significant gaps exist for some destination countries in specific years. To fill these gaps to derive total enrollment numbers for the region as a whole (i.e., the denominator in the market share calculation), the following methodology was used: (1) where annual data were reported before and after the gap year(s), the difference in data values was calculated, then accrued over the gap period; and (2) where no annual data were reported either before or after the gap year(s), the enrollment number(s) for the gap year(s) were estimated with reference to historical data for the destination country in question.

See also notes to Figure 6.9.

Figure 6.11. Principal countries of destination for internationally mobile tertiary education students from Latin America and the Caribbean, 2014–2019.

Based on annual data presented in UNESCO Institute for Statistics, "Inbound Internationally Mobile Students by Region of Origin," http://data.uis.unesco.org (accessed November 1, 2021). In the relevant UNESCO database, the region is listed under the heading "Latin America and the Caribbean."

The following destination country enrollment numbers are estimates: Spain and Argentina in 2014 and 2015.

See notes to relevant UNESCO tables.

Figure 6.12. Estimated market shares of principal countries of destination for internationally mobile tertiary education students from Latin America and the Caribbean, 2014–2019.

Based on annual data presented in UNESCO Institute for Statistics, "Inbound Internationally Mobile Students by Region of Origin," http://data.uis.unesco.org (accessed November 1, 2021). In the relevant UNESCO database, the region is listed under the heading "Latin America and the Caribbean."

Although the UNESCO database is fairly well populated, significant gaps exist for some destination countries in specific years. To fill these gaps to derive total enrollment numbers for the region as a whole (i.e., the denominator in the market share calculation), the following methodology was used: (1) where annual data were reported before and after the gap year(s), the difference in data values was calculated, then accrued over the gap period; and (2) where no annual data were reported either before or after the gap year(s), the enrollment number(s) for the gap year(s) were estimated with reference to historical data for the destination country in question.

See also notes to Figure 6.11.

Figure 6.13. Principal countries of destination for internationally mobile tertiary education students from Sub-Saharan Africa, 2014–2019.

Based on annual data presented in UNESCO Institute for Statistics, "Inbound Internationally Mobile Students by Region of Origin," http://data.uis.unesco.org (accessed November 1, 2021). In the relevant UNESCO database, the region is listed under the heading "Sub-Saharan Africa."

The destination country enrollment number for Malaysia in 2018 is an estimate.

See notes to relevant UNESCO tables.

Figure 6.14. Estimated market shares of principal countries of destination for internationally mobile tertiary education students from Sub-Saharan Africa, 2014–2019.

Based on annual data presented in UNESCO Institute for Statistics, "Inbound Internationally Mobile Students by Region of Origin," and "Inbound Internationally Mobile Students by Country of Origin," http://data.uis.unesco.org (accessed November 1, 2021). In the relevant UNESCO database, the region is listed under the heading "Sub-Saharan Africa."

Although the UNESCO database is fairly well populated, significant gaps exist for some destination countries in specific years. To fill these gaps to derive total enrollment numbers for the region as a whole (i.e., the denominator in the market share calculation), the following methodology was used: (1) where annual data were reported before and after the gap year(s), the difference in data values was calculated, then accrued over the gap period; and (2) where no annual data were reported either before or after the gap year(s), the enrollment number(s) for the gap year(s) were estimated with reference to historical data for the destination country in question.

See also notes to Figure 6.13.

Figure 6.15. Principal countries of destination for internationally mobile tertiary education students from Central and Western Asia, 2014–2019.

Based on annual data presented in UNESCO Institute for Statistics, "Inbound Internationally Mobile Students by Region of Origin," and "Inbound Internationally Mobile Students by Country of Origin," http://data.uis.unesco.org (accessed November 1, 2021). In the relevant UNESCO database, the central part of the region is listed under the heading "Central Asia."

Because the relevant UNESCO database does not contain a regional listing for the western part of the continent, the figures were derived by adding enrollment numbers for Central Asia to corresponding figures for individual non-Arab countries of origin in Western Asia. Methodologically, the purpose of this calculation was two-fold: (1) to avoid double counting the Arab states of Western Asia, which are included in the "Arab World" regional category; and (2) to form a separate category for Central and Western Asia that is consistent with other such categories used in this book.

The following destination country enrollment numbers are estimates: Russia in 2018, and Greece in 2017 and 2018.

See notes to relevant UNESCO tables.

Figure 6.16. Estimated market shares of principal countries of destination for internationally mobile tertiary education students from Central and Western Asia, 2014–2019.

Based on annual data presented in UNESCO Institute for Statistics, "Inbound Internationally Mobile Students by Region of Origin," and "Inbound Internationally Mobile Students by Country of Origin," http://data.uis.unesco.org (accessed November 1, 2021). In the relevant UNESCO database, the central part of the region is listed under the heading "Central Asia."

Although this database is fairly well populated, significant gaps exist for some destination countries in specific years. To fill these gaps to derive total enrollment numbers for the region as a whole (i.e., the denominator in the market share calculation), the following methodology was used: (1) where annual data were reported before and after the gap year(s), the difference in data values was calculated, then accrued over the gap period; and (2) where no annual data were reported either before or after the gap year(s), the enrollment number(s) for the gap year(s) were estimated with reference to historical data for the destination country in question.

See also notes to Figure 6.15.

Figure 6.17. Internationally mobile tertiary education students enrolled in institutions in the United States, by global region, 2014–2019.

Based on annual data presented in UNESCO Institute for Statistics, "Inbound Internationally Mobile Students by Region of Origin," and "Inbound Internationally Mobile Students by Country of Origin," http://data.uis.unesco.org (accessed November 1, 2021).

See notes to Figures 6.6–6.15.

Figure 6.18. U.S. market share of internationally mobile tertiary education students by global region, 2014–2019.

Based on annual data presented in UNESCO Institute for Statistics, "Inbound Internationally Mobile Students by Region of Origin," and "Inbound Internationally Mobile Students by Country of Origin," http://data.uis.unesco.org (accessed November 1, 2021).

See notes to Figures 6.6–6.15.

References

Agarwal, V.B., and D.R. Winkler, "Foreign Demand for United States Higher Education: A Study of Developing Countries in the Eastern Hemisphere." *Economic Development and Cultural Change*, vol. 33, no. 3 (1985): 623.

AllahMorad, S., and S. Zreik, "Education in Saudi Arabia." *World Education News and Reviews*, April 9, 2020, https://wenr.wes.org/2020/04/education-in-saudi-arabia (accessed August 25, 2021).

Altbach, P.G., "Globalisation and the University: Myths and Realities in an Unequal World." *Tertiary Education and Management*, vol. 10, no. 1 (2004): 3.

Altbach, P.G., "The Complexities of Global Engagement." In *Global Opportunities and Challenges for Higher Education Leaders*, edited by L.E. Rumbley, R. Matross Helms, P. McGill Peterson, and P.G. Altbach (2014).

Altbach, P.G., *Global Perspectives on Higher Education* (2016).

Altbach, P.G., and H. de Wit, "Are We Facing a Fundamental Challenge to Higher Education Internationalization?" *International Higher Education*, no. 93 (2018): 2–4.

Altbach, P.G., L. Reisberg, and L.E. Rumbley, *Trends in Global Higher Education: Tracking an Academic Revolution* (2009).

American Association of State Colleges and Universities, *Making Partnerships Work: Principles, Guidelines, and Advice for Public University Leaders* (2017).

Arnove, R., and B. L. Bull, "Education as an Ethical Concern in the Global Era." *FIRE: Forum for International Research in Education*, vol. 2, no. 2 (2015): 76–87, http://preserve.lehigh.edu/fire/vol2/iss2/6 (accessed July 15, 2021).

Association of American University Professors, *Defending the Freedom to Innovate: Faculty Intellectual Property Rights after Stanford v. Roche* (June 2014).

Bailey, T.M., "Projections of Education Statistics to 2028." (U.S. Department of Education, Institute of Education Sciences, National Center for Education Statistics, May 2020).

Barnett, B., and S.L. Jacobson, "Higher Education Partnerships for Studying and Improving Leadership Preparation and Development Around the World." In *Globalization and Internationalization in Higher Education*, edited by F. Maringe and N. Foskett (2010).

Bassett, R.M., "International Organizations and the Tertiary Education Sector: Understanding UNESCO, the OECD, and the World Bank Linking-Pin Organizations." In *Globalization and Internationalization in Higher Education*, edited by F. Maringe and N. Foskett (2010).

Baum, S., "College Education: Who Can Afford It?" In *The Finance of Higher Education: Theory, Research, Policy, and Practice*, edited by M.B. Paulsen and J.B. Smart (2001).

Baumol, W.J., and W.G. Bowen, *Performing Arts, the Economic Dilemma: A Study of Problems Common to Theater, Opera, Music, and Dance* (1966).

Bennetot Pruvot, E., T. Estermann, and H. Stoyanova, *Public Funding Observatory Report 2020/2021*, Part 1, (October 2020), and Part 2, (April 2021); *Public Funding Observatory Report 2019/2020* (February 2020).

Berger, J.B., and J. Milem, "Organizational Behavior in Higher Education and Student Outcomes." *Higher Education: Handbook of Theory and Research, Vol. XV*, edited by John C. Smart (2000).

Berman, J. "Connecting with Industry: Bridging the Divide." *Journal of Higher Education Policy & Management*, vol. 30, no. 2 (2008): 165.

Bird, K., and S. Turner, "College in the States: Foreign Student Demand and Higher Education Supply in the U.S." *EdPolicyWorks Working Paper Series*, no. 23 (2014).

Bloom, D., D. Canning, and K. Chan, *Higher Education and Economic Development in Africa* (2006).

Bok, D., *Universities in the Marketplace: The Commercialization of Higher Education* (2003).

Bowen, H.R., *The Costs of Higher Education: How Much Do Colleges and Universities Spend Per Student and How Much Should They Spend?* (1980).

Bowen, W.G., *Higher Education in the Digital Age* (2013).

Bransberger, P., C. Falkenstern, and P. Lane, *Knocking at the College Door*, 10th ed (Boulder, Western Interstate Commission for Higher Education, 2020).

Breneman, D.W., Liberal Arts Colleges: Thriving, Surviving, or Endangered? (1994).

Breneman, D.W., J.L. Doti, and L. Lapovsky, "Financing Private Colleges and Universities: The Role of Tuition Discounting." In *The Finance of Higher Education: Theory, Research, Policy, and Practice*, edited by M.B. Paulsen and J.B. Smart (2001).

Breznitz, S.M., and H. Etzkowitz, eds, *University Technology Transfer: The Globalization of Academic Innovation* (2016).

British Council, *Understanding India: The Future of Higher Education and Opportunities for International Cooperation* (2014).

Brown, R., *Higher Education and the Market* (2011).

Burke, J.C., and A.M. Serban, *Current Status and Future Prospects of Performance Funding and Performance Budgeting for Public Higher Education: The Second Survey* (1998).

Carroll, L., A. Reyes, and S. Trines, "Education in Colombia." *World Education News and Reviews*, June 23, 2020, https://wenr.wes.org/2020/06/education-in-colombia-2 (accessed August 25, 2021).

China Education Center, "Project 211 and 985." https://www.chinaeducenter.com/en/cedu/ceduproject211.php (accessed June 1, 2021).

Clark, B., *Academic Culture* (1980).

Clark, N., "Education in Singapore." *World Education News and Reviews*, June 1, 2009, https://wenr.wes.org/2009/06/wenr-june-2009-feature (accessed August 25, 2021).

Clark, N., "Education in Vietnam." *World Education News and Reviews*, May 5, 2014, https://wenr.wes.org/2017/11/education-in-vietnam (accessed August 25, 2021).

Clark, N., "Education in Malaysia." *World Education News and Reviews*, December 2, 2014, https://wenr.wes.org/2014/12/education-in-malaysia (accessed August 25, 2021).

Clotfelter, C.T., ed., *American Universities in a Global Market* (2010).

The College Board, *Trends in Student Financial Aid* (2020).

DeGeorge, R., *Competing with Integrity in International Business* (1993).

Denneen, J., and T. Dretler, "The Financially Sustainable University" (Bain & Company, 2012), https://www.bain.com/insights/financially-sustainable-university/ (accessed June 1, 2021).

Dilas, D.B., C. Mackie, Y. Huang, and S. Trines, "Education in Indonesia." *World Education News and Reviews*, March 21, 2019, https://wenr.wes.org/2019/03/education-in-indonesia-2 (accessed August 25, 2021).

Donaldson, T., *Ethics of International Business* (1989).

Etzkowitz, H., and D. Göktepe-Hultén, "De-reifying Technology Transfer Metrics to Address the Stages and Phases of TTO Development." In *University Technology Transfer: The Globalization of Academic Innovation*, edited by S.M. Breznitz and H. Etzkowitz (2016).

Feldman, M., and P. Clayton, "The American Experience in University Technology Transfer." In *University Technology Transfer: The Globalization of Academic Innovation*, edited by S.M. Breznitz and H. Etzkowitz (2016).

Feng, E., "China Closes a Fifth of University Partnerships." *Financial Times*, July 17, 2018.

Ferreyra, M.M., C. Avitabile, J.B. Álvarez, F.H. Paz, and S. Urzúa, *At a Crossroads: Higher Education in Latin America and the Caribbean* (The World Bank Group, 2017).

Financial Accounting Standards Board, "Standards." https://www.fasb.org (accessed June 1, 2021).

Fischer, K., "Do Colleges Need a Foreign Policy?" *The Chronicle of Higher Education*, June 22, 2021.

Flexner, A., Universities: American, English, German (1930).

Freeland, R.M., "Yes, Higher Ed Is a Business—But It's Also a Calling." *The Chronicle of Higher Education*, March 18, 2018.

Freeman, R.B., "What Does Global Expansion of Higher Education Mean for the United States?" In *American Universities in a Global Market*, edited by C.T. Clotfelter (2010).

Friga, P.N., "How Much Has Covid Cost Colleges? $183 billion." *The Chronicle of Higher Education*, February 5, 2021.

Gallup, "Immigration." https://news.gallup.com/poll/1660/immigration.aspx (accessed June 1, 2021).

Gardner, L., "Moody's Forecasts Widespread Drop in Tuition Revenue. Here's Why That Matters." *The Chronicle of Higher Education*, October 29, 2020.

Garrett, R., K. Kinser, J.E. Lane, and R. Merola (The Observatory for Borderless Higher Education and Cross Border Education Research Team), *International Branch Campuses: Trends and Developments, 2016* (2016).

Garrett, R., K. Kinser, J.E. Lane, and R. Merola (The Observatory on Borderless Higher Education with SUNY Albany and Pennsylvania State University), *International Branch Campuses—Trends and Developments* (2016).

Gieger, R.L., *To Advance Knowledge: The Growth of American Research Universities, 1900–1940* (1986).

Geiger, R.L., *Knowledge and Money: Research Universities and the Paradox of the Marketplace* (2004).

Gibbs, P. "Marketers and Educationalists—Two Communities Divided by Time?" *International Journal of Educational Management*, vol. 22, no. 3 (2008): 269.

Goodwin, L., "The Academic World and the Business World: A Comparison of Occupational Goals." *Sociology of Education*, vol. 42, no. 2 (1969): 170.

Government Accounting Standards Board, "Standards and Guidance." https://www.gasb.org (accessed June 1, 2021).

Government of India, Ministry of Human Resource Development, Department of Higher Education, *All India Survey on Higher Education 2018–19* (2019).

Grawe, N., *Demographics and the Demand for Higher Education* (2018).

Greenberg, M., "A University Is Not a Business (and Other Fantasies)." *EDUCAUSE Review*, vol. 39, no. 2 (2004): 10.

Gu, M., R. Michael, C. Zheng, and S. Trines, "Education in China." *World Education News and Reviews*, December 17, 2019, https://wenr.wes.org/2019/12/education-in-china-3 (accessed August 25, 2021).

Gulf News Journal Reports, "Roots of American Universities Grow Deeper in Qatar, Drawing Criticism." *Gulf News Journal*, June 8, 2015, https://gulfnewsjournal.com/stories/510548507-roots-of-american-universities-grow-deeper-in-qatar-drawing-criticism (accessed June 1, 2021).

Guri-Rosenblit, S., *Digitral Technologies in Higher Education: Sweeping Expectations and Actual Effects* (2009).

Hamilton, B.E., J.A. Martin, M.P.H. Osterman, and M.J.K. Osterman, "Births: Provisional Data for 2019." *NVSS Vital Statistics Rapid Release*, U.S. Department of Health and Human Services, Centers for Disease Control and Prevention, National Center for Health Statistics, National Vital Statistics System (May 2020), https://www.cdc.gov/nchs/data/vsrr/vsrr-8-508.pdf (accessed June 1, 2021).

Han Kim, E., and Min Zhu, "Universities as Firms: The Case of US Overseas Programs." In *American Universities in a Global Market*, edited by C.T. Clotfelter (2010).

Haskins, C.H., *The Rise of Universities* (2002).

Hawawini, G., *The Internationalization of Higher Education and Business Schools* (2016).

Hearn, J.C., "The Paradox of Growth in Financial Aid for College Students, 1965–1990." In *Higher Education Handbook of Theory and Research*: Volume IX, edited by J.C. Smart (1993).

Hearn, J.C., "Access to Post-Secondary Education: Financing Equity in an Evolving Context." In *The Finance of Higher Education: Theory, Research, Policy, and Practice*, edited by M.B. Paulsen and J.C. Smart (2001).

Higher Education Compliance Alliance, "Compliance Matrix." https://www.highered compliance.org/compliance-matrix (accessed June 1, 2021).

Higher Education Law of the People's Republic of China, adopted August 29, 1998 at the Fourth Session of the Standing Committee of the Ninth National People's Congress, China Education Center. https://www.chinaeducenter.com/en/cedu/hel.php (accessed June 1, 2021).

Hussar, W.J., and T.M. Bailey, *Projections of Education Statistics to 2028* (U.S. Department of Education, Institute for Education Sciences, National Center for Education Statistics, May 2020).

Institute of International Education, *What International Students Think About U.S. Higher Education; Attitudes and Perceptions of Prospective Students from Around the World* (2015).

Institute of International Education, *Open Doors* (2020).

International Association of Universities, *International Handbook of Universities* (2019).

Joseph, R.J., "Globalisation Can Threaten Liberal Traditions." *Financial Times*, March 27, 2014.

Judson, K.M., and S.A. Taylor, "Moving from Marketization to Marketing of Higher Education: The Co-Creation of Value in Higher Education." *Higher Education Studies*, vol. 4, no. 1 (2014): 51.

Keller, G., *Academic Strategy: The Management Revolution in American Higher Education* (1983).

Keppel, F., "The Higher Education Acts Contrasted, 1965–86: Has Federal Policy Come of Age?" *Harvard Educational Review*, vol. 57, no. 1 (1987): 49.

Kerr, C., *The Uses of the University* (1963).

Kingdom of Saudi Arabia, "Vision 2030." https://www.vision2030.gov.sa (accessed June 1, 2021).

Kinser, K., and J.E. Lane (The Observatory on Borderless Higher Education and Cross-Border Research Team), "International Branch Campuses: Evolution of a Phenomenon." *International Higher Education*, no. 85 (2016): 3.

Knapp, J.C. and D.J. Siegel, eds, *The Business of Higher Education* (2009).

Labi, A., "European Universities Consider How to Adapt to the New Economic Climate." *The Chronicle of Higher Education*, June 12, 2012.

Lane, J.E., and K. Kinser (Cross-Border Education Research Team and State University of New York, Albany), *A Snapshot of a Global Phenomenon: The Results of the First Global Survey of IBCs* (2011).

Lasher, W.F., and D.L. Greene, "College and University Budgeting: What Do We Know? What Do We Need to Know?" In *The Finance of Higher Education: Theory, Research, Policy, and Practice*, edited by M.B. Paulsen and J.B. Smart (2001).

Lay-Hwa Bowden, J., "Engaging the Student as a Customer: A Relationship Marketing Approach." *Marketing Education Review*, vol. 21, no.3 (2011): 211.

Li, H., "Higher Education in China, Complement or Competition to U.S. Universities." In *American Universities in a Global Market*, edited by C.T. Clotfelter (2010).

Long, B., "The Financial Crisis and College Enrollment: How Have Students and Their Families Responded?" In *How the Financial Crisis and Great Recession Affected Higher Education*, edited by J. Brown and C. Hoxby (2015).

Lovett, C.M., "The Global Contexts of Higher Education." *Change: The Magazine of Higher Learning*, vol. 45, no. 1 (2013): 73.

Maassen, P.A.M., "The Concept of Culture and Higher Education." *Tertiary Education and Management*, vol. 2, no. 2 (1996): 153.

Magaziner, J., "Education in Taiwan." *World Education News and Reviews*, June 7, 2016, https://wenr.wes.org/2016/06/education-in-taiwan (accessed August 25, 2021).

Mani, D., and S. Trines, "Education in South Korea." *World Education News and Reviews*, October 16, 2018, https://wenr.wes.org/2018/10/education-in-south-korea (accessed August 25, 2021).

Manning, K., *Organizational Theory in Higher Education* (2017).

Marginson, S., "Dynamics of National and Global Competition in Higher Education." *Higher Education*, vol. 52, no. 1 (2006): 1.

Marginson, S., and M. van der Wende, "The New Global Landscape of Nations and Institutions." *Higher Education to 2030, Volume 2, Globalisation* (Organization for Economic Cooperation and Development, 2009): 17.

Maringe, F., "The Meanings of Globalization and Internationalization in HE: Findings from a World Survey." In *Globalization and Internationalization in Higher Education*, edited by F. Maringe and N. Foskett (2010).

Masland, A.T., "Organizational Culture in the Study of Higher Education." *The Review of Higher Education*, vol. 8 no. 2, 1985: 157.

Massy, W.F., "A New Look at the Academic Department." *Pew Policy Perspectives*, June 2, 1990.

Massy, W.F., and A. Wilger, "Productivity in Postsecondary Education: A New Approach." *Educational Evaluation and Policy Analysis*, vol. 14 (1992).

Mazzarol, T., and G.N. Soutar, *The Global Market for Higher Education* (2001).

Mazzarol, T., and G.N. Soutar, "Revisiting the Global Market for Higher Education." *Asia Pacific Journal of Marketing and Logistics*, vol. 24, no. 5 (2012): 717.

McGee, J., *Breakpoint: The Changing Marketplace for Higher Education* (2015).

McIntosh, C., and Z. Varoglu, *Perspectives on Distance Education. Lifelong Learning & Distance Higher Education* (2005).

McKie, A., "Vision or Mirage in Saudi Arabia?" *Inside Higher Ed*, July 5, 2018.

McMahon, M.E., "Higher Education in a World Market. An Historical Look at the Global Context of International Study." *Higher Education*, vol. 24, no. 4 (1992): 465.

McPherson, M.S., and M.O. Schapiro, *Keeping Colleges Affordable, Government and Educational Opportunity* (1991).

McPherson, M.S., and M.O. Schapiro, *The Student Aid Game: Meeting Need and Rewarding Talent in Higher Education* (1998).

Molesworth, M., E. Nixon, and R. Scullion, "Having, Being and Higher Education: the Marketisation of the University and the Transformation of the Student into Consumer." *Teaching in Higher Education*, vol. 14, no. 3 (2009): 277.

Molesworth, M., R. Scullion, and E. Nixon, *The Marketisation of Higher Education and the Student as Consumer* (2010).

Monroy, C., and S. Trines, "Education in Mexico." *World Education News and Reviews*, May 23, 2019, https://wenr.wes.org/2019/05/education-in-mexico-2 (accessed August 25, 2021).

Moody's Investor Service, "Outlook for US Higher Education Sector Remains Negative in 2021 as Pandemic Effects Curtail Revenue." December 8, 2020, https://www.moodys.com/research/moodys-outlook-for-us-higher-education-sector-remains-negative-in—pbm_1255981 (accessed June 1, 2021).

Mumper, M., "The Transformation of Federal Aid to College Students: Dynamics of Growth and Retrenchment." *Journal of Education Finance*, vol. 16 (1991): 315.

Mumper, M., "State Efforts to Keep Public Colleges Affordable in the Face of Fiscal Stress." In *The Finance of Higher Education: Theory, Research, Policy, and Practice*, edited by M.B. Paulsen and J.B. Smart (2001).

Naidoo, R., Avi Shankar, and Ekant Veer, "The Consumerist Turn in Higher Education: Policy Aspirations and Outcomes." *Journal of Marketing Management*, vol. 27, no. 11, (2011): 1142.

Natale, S.M., and C. Doran, "Marketization of Education: An Ethical Dilemma." *Journal of Business Ethics*, vol. 105, no. 2 (2012): 187.

National Association of Independent Colleges and Universities, "Survey: The Financial Impact of Covid 19 on Private Nonprofit Colleges." http://naicu.imediainc.com/naicu/media/pdf/covid-19/covid-survey-summary-release.pdf (accessed June 1, 2021).

National Clearinghouse Center, *Term Enrollment Estimates Fall 2020*, National Student Clearinghouse Research Center (2021).

Newman, S., and K. Jahdi, "Marketisation of Education: Marketing, Rhetoric and Reality." *Journal of Further and Higher Education*, vol. 33, no. 1 (2009): 1.

Ohorodnik, M., "Was It Worth It? International Student Views on the Value of Their U.S. Education." *World Education News and Reviews*, October 8, 2019, https://wenr.wes.org/2019/10/was-it-worth-it-international-student-views-on-the-value-of-their-u-s-education (accessed June 1, 2021).

Organization for Economic Co-operation and Development, *Quality and Internationalisation in Higher Education* (1999).

Organization for Economic Co-operation and Development, *Higher Education to 2030 (Vol.1): Demography* (2008).

Organization for Economic Co-operation and Development, *Higher Education to 2030 (Vol.2): Globalisation* (2009).

Organization for Economic Co-operation and Development, *Education in China, a Snapshot* (2016).

Organization for Economic Co-operation and Development, *Education at a Glance 2019: India* (2019).

Organization for Economic Co-operation and Development, *Education at a Glance (annual reports, 1998–2020)*. https://www.oecd.org/education/education-at-a-glance/ (accessed June 1, 2021).

Organization for Economic Cooperation and Development, *OECDiLibrary*. https://www. oecd-ilibrary.org (accessed June 1, 2021).

Palmer, L.B., and E. Urban, "International Students' Perceptions of the Value of U.S. Higher Education." *Journal of International Students*, vol. 6, no. 1 (2016): 153.

People's Daily (China), http://en.people.cn (accessed June 1, 2021).

Peterson, M.W., and M.G. Spencer, "Understanding Academic Culture and Climate." *New Directions for Institutional Research*, no. 68 (1990): 3.

Pressman, L., M. Planting, J. Bond, R. Yuskavage, and C. Moylan, *The Economic Contribution of University/Non-Profit Inventions in the United States, 1996–2017* (Biotechnology Innovation Organization and AUTM, 2019).

Qiang, Z., "Internationalization of Higher Education: Towards a Conceptual Framework." *Policy Futures in Education*, vol. 1, no. 2 (2003): 248.

Qingquan, L., "China's Double First Class Programme Should Open to Regional Universities." *Times Higher Education*, July 21, 2020.

Redden, E., "Global Development and Profits." *Inside Higher Ed*, January 24, 2013.

Rudolph, F., *The American College and University: A History* (1990).

Ruth, J., and Y. Xiao, "Academic Freedom and China." American Association of University Professors (Fall 2019), https://www.aaup.org/article/academic-freedom-and-china#.x9vtgi2cars (accessed June 1, 2021).

Santiago, P., K. Tremblay, E. Basri, and E. Arnal (Organization for Economic Cooperation and Development), *Tertiary Education for the Knowledge Society, Volume 1, Special Features: Governance, Funding, Quality* (2008).

Scholars at Risk, *Obstacles to Excellence: Academic Freedom and China's Quest for World-Class Universities* (2019).

Scott, J.D., "The Mission of the University: Medieval to Postmodern Transformations." *Journal of Higher Education*, vol. 77, no. 1 (2006): 1.

Shanghai Jiao Tong Academic Ranking of World Universities, Shanghai Ranking Consultancy, August 2020. http://www.shanghairanking.com (accessed June 1, 2021).

Slaughter, S., and L.L. Leslie, *Academic Capitalism: Politics, Policies, and the Entrepreneurial University* (1997).

Slowey, M., and H.G. Shuetze, eds, *Global Perspectives on Higher Education and Lifelong Learners* (2012).

Spring, J., *Globalization of Education*, 2nd ed. (New York, Routledge, 2015).

St. John, E.P., and M.B. Paulsen, "The Finance of Higher Education: Implications for Theory, Research, Policy, and Practice." In *The Finance of Higher Education: Theory, Research, Policy, and Practice*, edited by M.B. Paulsen and J.B. Smart (2001).

Stein, S., "Rethinking the Ethics of Internationalization: Five Challenges for Higher Education." *InterActions: UCLA Journal of Education and Information Studies*, vol. 12, no. 2 (2016) (unpaginated), https://escholarship.org/content/qt2nb2b9b4/qt2nb2b9b4.pdf?t=obfpwa&v=lg (accessed July 15, 2021).

Stoller, E., "The Business of Higher Education." *Inside Higher Ed*, June 5, 2014.

Straumsheim, C., "2U Ends Semester Online." *Inside Higher Ed*, April 3, 2014, https://www.insidehighered.com/news/2014/04/03/online-education-provider-2u-disband-semester-online-consortium (accessed August 15, 2021).

Taylor, S.A., and K.M. Judson, "A Service Perspective on the Marketization of Undergraduate Education." *Service Science*, vol. 3, no. 2 (2011): 110.

Tierney, W.G., "Organizational Culture in Higher Education: Defining the Essentials." *The Journal of Higher Education*, vol. 59, no. 1 (1988): 2.

The Times Higher Education, "Times Higher Education World University Rankings 2020." August 2020, https://www.timeshighereducation.com (accessed June 1, 2021).

Toutkoushian, R.K., "Trends in Revenues and Expenditures for Public and Private Higher Education." In *The Finance of Higher Education: Theory, Research, Policy, and Practice*, edited by M.B. Paulsen and J.B. Smart (2001).

Toutkoushian, R.K., and M.B. Paulsen, *Economics of Higher Education: Background, Concepts, and Applications* (2016).

Trines, S., "Education in India." *World Education News and Reviews*, September 13, 2018, https://wenr.wes.org/2018/09/education-in-india (accessed August 25, 2021).

U.S. Department of Commerce, Bureau of Economic Analysis, "Regional Economic Accounts." https://apps.bea.gov/itable/definitions.cfm?did=2113&reqid=70 (accessed June 1, 2021).

U.S. Department of Education, "Department of Education Establishes New Student Aid Rules to Protect Borrowers and Taxpayers." October 8, 2010, https://www.ed.gov/news/press-releases/department-education-establishes-new-student-aid-rules-protect-borrowers-and-taxpayers (accessed June 1, 2021).

U.S. Department of Education, Bureau of Educational and Cultural Affairs, Bridge USA, "Other U.S. Student Visas." https://j1visa.state.gov/basics/other-u-s-visas (accessed June 1, 2021).

U.S. Department of Education, Institute for Education Sciences, National Center for Education Statistics, "Digest of Education Statistics" (annual issues, 1990–2020), https://nces.ed.gov (accessed August 1, 2021).

U.S. Department of Education, Office of Federal Student Aid, "Foreign Gift and Contract Report" (annual reports for 2018–2020), https://studentaid.gov/data-center/school/foreign-gifts (accessed August 1, 2021).

U.S. Department of Education, Office of Student Aid, "Financial Responsibility Composite Scores." https://studentaid.gov/data-center/school/composite-scores (accessed July 1, 2021).

U.S. Department of Homeland Security, U.S. Citizenship and Immigration Services, "Students and Employment." https://www.uscis.gov/working-in-the-united-states/students-and-exchange-visitors/students-and-employment (accessed June 1, 2021).

U.S. Department of State, Bureau of Consular Affairs, "Nonimmigrant Visa Statistics" (annual reports, 2013–2020), https://travel.state.gov/content/travel/en/legal/visa-law0/visa-statistics/nonimmigrant-visa-statistics.html (accessed June 1, 2021).

U.S. Department of the Treasury and U.S. Department of Education, *The Economics of Higher Education* (2012).

UNESCO Institute for Statistics, "Glossary." http://uis.unesco.org/en/glossary (accessed July 1, 2021).

UNESCO Institute for Statistics, "UIS.Stat." http://data.uis.unesco.org (accessed June 1, 2021).

United Nations, Department of Economic and Social Affairs, Population Division, "World Population Prospects 2019." https://population.un.org/wpp (accessed June 1, 2021).

United Nations, Department of Economic and Social Affairs, Population Division, "World Population Prospects 2020: Highlights, and Volume 1: Comprehensive Tables."

United Nations, Department of Economic and Social Affairs, Population Division, "International Migration 2020 Highlights." https://www.un.org/development/desa/pd/sites/www.un.org.development.desa.pd/files/undesa_pd_2020_international_migration_highlights.pdf (accessed June 1, 2021).

United Nations, Department of Economic and Social Affairs, Statistics Division, "Methodology, Geographic Regions." https://unstats.un.org/unsd/methodology/m49 (accessed June 1, 2021).

University Grants Commission (India), https://www.ugc.ac.in (accessed June 1, 2021).

Vasquez, M., "A Professor's Year Teaching in Saudi Arabia Was a Nightmare. Should an American College Have Stepped In?" *The Chronicle of Higher Education*, November, 6, 2019, https://www.chronicle.com/article/a-professors-year-teaching-in-saudi-arabia-was-a-nightmare-should-an-american-college-have-stepped-in/ (accessed July 15, 2021).

Veblen, T, *The Higher Learning in America: A Memorandum on the Conduct of Universities by Business Men* (1918).

Veysey, L., *The Emergence of the American University* (1965).

Ward, J., "Understanding the Business of Higher Education." *College and University*, vol. 84, no. 1 (2008): 53.

Weber, M., "'Objectivity' in Social Sciences and Social Policy." In *The Methodology of the Social Sciences*, edited by E.A. Shils and H.A. Finch (1949).

Weber, M., "Bureaucracy." In *From Max Weber*, edited by H.H. Gerth and C. Wright Mills (1958).

Weisbrod, B.A., J.P. Ballou, and E.D. Asch, *Mission and Money, Understanding the University* (2008).

Wilkins, S., "Ethical Issues in Transnational Higher Education: The Case of International Branch Campuses." *Studies in Higher Education*, vol. 42, no. 8 (2017): 1385–1400.

Williams, J., *Consuming Higher Education: Why Learning Can't Be Bought* (2012).

World Bank, "DataBank." https://databank.worldbank.org/home.aspx (accessed June 1, 2021).

World Bank, "Higher Education." https://www.worldbank.org/en/topic/tertiaryeducation#what_why (accessed June 1, 2021).

Zemsky, R., "The Lattice and the Ratchet: Toward More Efficient Higher Education Systems." Presentation at the Annual Conference of the Education Commission of the States, Seattle, WA, July 13, 1990.

Zemsky, R., S. Shaman, and S.C. Baldridge, *The College Stress Test* (2020).

Zumeta, W., "State Policy and Private Higher Education: Past, Present, and Future." In *The Finance of Higher Education: Theory, Research, Policy, and Practice*, edited by M.B. Paulsen and J.B. Smart (2001).

Zumeta, W., D.W. Breneman, P.M. Callan, and J.E. Finney, *Financing American Higher Education in the Era of Globalization* (2021).

Index